CW00850478

We're West Ham United - We Play On The Floor

the 2011-12 promotion season and other world events

First published in paperback 2012 by *mardibooks*
This edition published 2012 by *mardibooks*
www.mardibooks.com

ISBN 978-1-909227-11-8

Copyright © Martin Godleman 2012

Typeset by flamin ape ltd
Printed and bound by CPI Group (UK) Ltd, Croydon, CR0 4YY

Visit **www.mardibooks.com** to read more about all our writers,
and our books. You will find features and interviews and can
get up to date with the latest information about us on our blog.

AUTHOR'S NOTE

I am very grateful to Steve Blowers, Nick London and David Powter for their invaluable assistance and advice during the making of this book.

We're West Ham United.
We play on the floor.

ALSO BY MARTIN GODLEMAN

WEST HAM UNITED

Our Days Are Few

Hammers through the Looking Glass

The DVD Book of West Ham United

West Ham United – 101 Beautiful Games

NOVELS

1909

Mercy

www.mardibooks.com

MARTIN GODLEMAN

WE'RE WEST HAM UNITED -

WE PLAY ON THE FLOOR

CONTENTS

Chapter 1

Renegade

June 2011

May you live in interesting times.

Does it get more interesting than the biggest Royal Wedding for thirty years? Than the first UK coalition government for nearly a century? Than the British Queen on a state visit to Ireland? Than me going on strike for the first time in twenty-two years?

If you'd told me on 31st May 2005 that West Ham United would stay in the Premiership until the CIA found Osama Bin Laden – and killed him - I'd have taken that. But then that's the other interesting thing that's just happened... Hammers getting relegated, that is.

So without the benefit of hindsight, what interesting times and events lie ahead?

Today, 1st June 2011, 'Big Sam' Allardyce was finally appointed the manager of West Ham United. He might not want to reflect upon the fact that he's the seventh manager in eight years at the Boleyn since Glenn Roeder, Trevor Brooking (he had two goes), Alan Pardew (a man who stayed long enough to acquire the genial nickname 'Pards'), Alan Curbishley, Gianfranco Zola and Avram 'Hugh' Grant (whom David Gold said he appointed, 'for experience, ability and his great sense of humour'). West Ham have only had eight other managers in their ninety years prior to that of course, those being the legendary Charlie Paynter, Syd King, Ted Fenton, 'Sir' Ron Greenwood, John Lyall, Lou Macari, and the twins, Billy and Harry, separated over an alleged act of treason. I'm certain Einstein once had something to say about the ratio effect of volume over longevity, but it's all speculation for the moment.

'Big Sam' (I wonder if he hates that sobriquet) has made the cut over the usual list of would be's and deadbeats, though this time nobody is declaring their interest in the job. There have been few sudden and unexpected resignations from the handful of celebrity managers who tend to step off the appointment merry-go-round of failure with all the restraint of a Premiership striker on a viagra drip. It's not even worth listing them, other than to say they all managed at least a season playing for Manchester United in the nineties.

Looking back to the last occasion West Ham dropped out of the Premier League after a run of ten successive *Redknapp* seasons, the manager who took them down on that occasion and the man now charged with taking them back up have several unexpected connections. Sam Allardyce and Glenn Roeder were ten years ago selected as two (then) Premier League managers to be filmed undertaking parallel day-by-day health monitoring tests, presumably to calculate the two extremes of physical fitness in the Premiership. Ironically it was Sam who was shown to have the more successful health profile. This was demonstrated for any stats doubters several months later when Roeder suffered an allegedly stress-related brain tumour after a game against Middlesbrough.

The image of both men walking towards you across the Upton Park pitch offers two complementary pictures. Allardyce offering his hand to deliver a cordial and bone-crushing handshake, then a wincing expression followed by a smile as he relays a few hints about the team news. Roeder more guarded, looks for a 'laughing at rather than laughing with' response from the person greeting him, and once he doesn't get it, offering up something of a searching look.

What does it mean in the bigger scheme of things? Roeder with what might slightly unkindly be called 'Harry Redknapp's team', managed a creditable seventh position in his first season in the Hammers' hot seat. In his second, with one of the potentially greatest squads ever gathered at Upton Park, some of whom he had personally signed or nurtured, he took them down. Down, down, deeper and down. The majority left. A whole squadload, cultivating the most effective deployment of that young collective noun. Lou Macari had been a panic gamble managerial appointment in 1989 to replace the great but tired John Lyall. The glamour of Macari soon fizzled out and he disappeared under a cloud of betting allegations without even a full season under his Sporran. Bonds and Redknapp returned the 'home grown' style and achieved some quality, but not a single positive top flight goal difference despite ten seasons spent amongst football's elite. Even in the 1998-99 season when they finished

5th under Harry Redknapp, they conceded four or more goals on eight separate occasions.

Trevor Brooking, unwilling to take the job on permanently, restored some pride. He looked to have made a wise decision to return to the quiet certainty of an FA appointment, after his last West Ham team scrambled a late draw at home to Burnley. Still, flashes of hope. Pardew was the bright new kid on the block with Reading, but his seeming indifference to manage his move away from the Berkshire club with humility hinted at difficult times ahead with the press. Who can manage those strange and unreliable bedfellows? Those nest featherers whose disingenuous praise often echoes with a bitter hollowness barely months after manufacture. And so it proved for Pardew, whose efforts over three seasons included West Ham's first FA Cup Final appearance for a quarter of a century and some memorable victories over Arsene Wenger's Arsenal. The new Icelandic boardroom team, in for just a few months, wanted their own appointment. Pardew was on his way, his leaving slightly less embarrassing than Roeder's 'Reverse at Rotherham', though it was still after a 4-0 thrashing at the hands of emerging nemesis Bolton Wanderers. This, after three years as the Hammers' manager, and just seven months after leading them out to face Liverpool in the FA Cup Final of 2006. Then Curbishley, an exciting appointment, but one where financial and team-running promises were made and broken in less than two years, and 'Curbs' walked out The snipping of his contract earning him £3m from the cashless Icelandic Directors. Next up Gianfranco Zola, this time for an even shorter tenure and, finally, Avram Grant, lasting just one season, and leading West Ham United to the most ignominious relegation season since 1988-89 with a team that, with the exception of Scott Parker, few will remember let alone mourn. Reading all that back, what would you conclude? That Sam Allardyce will be gone by Christmas?

The 2007-08 News of the World Football Annual, a real dodo for two reasons, has West Ham United listed under the heading 'fewest managers', listing 'just eleven' in their 106 year history. Three years later and we're already onto number fourteen.

Back to the subject of health and fitness, Gerard Houllier and Aston Villa have unexpectedly parted company today. A fact possibly not unconnected to the size of Houllier's private health bills after another season spent under the heart consultant's even beadier eye at Birmingham General. So who would be a manager?

Over the first few days of Big Sam settling his buttocks into the managerial chair, Kevin Nolan arrives from Newcastle and is appointed captain. Demba Ba goes in the other direction, taking with him a stunning achievement. This is a striker who scored 7 goals in just 12 appearances - a goal per game ratio that was even better than Geoff Hurst's. Not only that, but the Sengalese striker managed to finish top scorer for the club over the whole season with just seven goals. Not bad for a player with just two letters in his surname. He was also the first West Ham striker to top the goalscoring season charts with single figures for eleven years. The last to achieve that distinction was Ian Wright, who signed off with nine from 25 appearances in 1998-99. In Ba's season, West Ham finished bottom of the league and were relegated. In Wright's season, West Ham came fifth, their best ever Premier League finish.

The only concern left for West Ham fans pre-season now is will Scott Parker stay?

The main difference between 2003 and 2011 as relegation seasons go is who Hammers will lose. Let's, for fickle fancy's sake, imagine a game where the departing players from Relegation Irons 2003 play the Loser Leavers from 2011.

West Ham's starting eleven for their final game of the 2002-03 season was:

RELEGATION IRONS

David James, Tomas Repka, Christian Dailly, Rufus Brevett, Glen Johnson, Trevor Sinclair, Steve Lomas, Joe Cole, Jermain Defoe, Les Ferdinand, Frederick Kanoute.
Subs On: Paolo Di Canio, Don Hutchison
Caretaker Manager: Trevor Brooking
And for their final game of the 2010-11 season, it was:

LOSER LEAVERS

Robert Green, Jordan Spence, Wayne Bridge, Danny Gabbidon, James Tomkins, Luis Boa Morte, Thomas Hitzlsperger, Jack Collison, Freddie Sears, Zavon Hines, Frederic Piquionne.
Subs On: Scott Parker, Victor Obinna, Lars Jacobsen
Caretaker Manager: Kevin Keen

1) David James v Rob Green

James is still slumming it in the Championship even in 2011 with Bristol City. He doesn't know when he's beaten, even though it's pretty much any time someone sends over a high cross out of the sky towards his greasy palms.

Green is one of the best keepers West Ham have been lucky enough to have. True, he always has a nightmare against Bolton Wanderers, but he has a great record saving penalties and getting across his goal to keep out long shots.

Verdict: Rob Green

2) Tomas Repka v Jordan Spence

Repka had a touch of the headless chicken about him, particularly in the 2003-04 season in the Championship, but he was a rarity - a foreign import who stayed at the club and won over the fans. Check out footage of his last game at Upton Park v Fulham; there wasn't a dry eye in the house.

Spence made his first full team debut start in the penultimate game of 2010-11 against Wigan. Is currently at Bristol City on loan, ironically playing in front of the 'old man' David James.

Verdict: Tomas Repka

3) Christian Dailly v Wayne Bridge

Dailly will always be remembered by anyone who's ever copped a fierce one in the gonads for his play-off semi-final goal at Upton Park against Ipswich Town that took us to the play-off final at Cardiff in May 2004. All I can say against him was that he's Scottish, but then he is Scotland's most best-capped player with 67. He also never bothered with an agent and negotiated all his deals himself, as well as featuring in the classic West Ham fans' song, *Oh Christian Dailly, you are the love of my life, oh Christian Dailly, I'd let you shag my wife...* My only worry is that he finished his career with 666 league and cup appearances. G-d help him if he has that number tattooed on his neck.

Bridge will be remembered for refusing to shake John Terry's hand. But then again, he knew exactly where it had been, and that he probably hadn't washed it since. Had his only halfway decent game for West Ham in the memorable 0-0 draw at White Hart Lane on March 19th 2011, but £90,000 per week?

Verdict: Christian Dailly

4) Rufus Brevett v Danny Gabbidon

Brevett was injury prone and played few games for West Ham after joining from Fulham towards the end of the 2002-03 season. He did score a stonking goal at Crewe on the half hour in a 3-2 win in August 2004, but he didn't stop Dean Ashton scoring two for Crewe that afternoon.

Gabbidon was a great signing by Alan Pardew, and West Ham had some good years playing him alongside fellow Welsh International James Collins. After a long injury he came back in later years, but was never quite the same player, as was to be proved by disappointing performances for QPR in the Premier League.

Verdict: Danny Gabbidon

5) Glen Johnson v James Tomkins

Johnson only ever played sixteen games for West Ham. Remember Glen Johnson, that brilliant West Ham and England defender? You're remembering his appearances for Chelsea and Portsmouth, that is the sad fact. But a thoroughbred, nevertheless.

Tomkins, if I could only forget his nightmare performance in March 2010 against Wolves when Hammers went down 1-3 and started to look like relegation certainties. It also gave rise to the 'we won't go down' versus 'it's looking pretty bad' banter. He does look a class act in the Championship, however.

Verdict: Glen Johnson

6) Trevor Sinclair v Luis Boa Morte

Sinclair came to West Ham in January 1998 with fans' eyes full of his QPR dreadlocks and that famous FA Cup overhead kick goal against Barnsley. By the time he left in May 2003 he had made 206 appearances and scored 38 goals. My personal favourite was the dipping volley against Charlton in a 5-0 thrashing on Boxing Day 2001. He even managed a late flourish in his England career with four appearances in the 2002 World Cup. He now lives in Dubai with his wife and kids and hosts some 'soccer' talk show over there. Wild.

Luis Boa Morte was at West Ham forever. Or to be more precise, four seasons and eighty-eight appearances, scoring just two goals. Like Brevett, he came from Fulham, but unlike Brevett, he couldn't blame a lack of opportunities on injuries. He did, however, enjoy some memorable achievements, including his 2006 World Cup appearances for Portugal. Then there was his rant against the

West Ham Board on Match of the Day before subsequently being awarded a new contract! He managed the 'Knees Up Mother Brown' fanzine awards of 'worst player' (2007/08) and 'most improved player' (2008/09, runner-up).
Verdict: Trevor Sinclair

7) Steve Lomas v Thomas Hitzlsperger
Lomas, along with Sinclair, was another inspired Harry Redknapp signing in April 1997. An Irishman who was born in Germany and captained the side for much of his West Ham career, managing 227 appearances. This was a phenomenal achievement for a modern player. Lomas was one of the unsung heroes of the modern Upton Park generation.

Hitzlsperger got injured at the beginning of the 2010-11 relegation season, a few hours after getting signed on a three year deal. He may well have got injured as he was being signed. We certainly didn't get three years out of him, though he scored a couple of decent goals. Once he was released by West Ham he was caught speeding in the UK at 107 mph but escaped a ban because he said he was unemployed and needed his car to drive round the country looking for another club. With alleged savings of £1m, he was fined £750 and received six penalty points on his licence. He subsequently buggered off back to Germany in his car, without a new contract. Thanks, Thomas.
Verdict: Steve Lomas

8) Joe Cole v Jack Collison
Cole was Harry Redknapp's hope for the modern world, certain that 'this boy is magic' but not wanting to 'ruin' him by too much early exposure. Hopeless optimism was drowned by Roeder throwing Cole to the journalism junkies and making him captain of the side before he was old enough to own a licensed gun. Hammers had to get shot of him after they went down and we have spent years watching him wax and wane ever since. Last seen enjoying himself in France.

Collison is a sublime graduate of the West Ham Youth Academy, also precocious, but with a wise head on young shoulders. Many fans believe the timing of the Welsh international's various injury lay-offs have contributed to the club's recent relegation. No matter, he will mature more effectively in the Championship.
Verdict: Joe Cole

9) Jermain Defoe v Freddie Sears

Defoe showed his predilection for poor advice when he originally joined West Ham's Academy, allowing himself to be poached from Charlton Athletic's youth team. The Charlton fans were calling him 'Judas' even before he'd made his West Ham debut. This is a player who scored 41 goals in 105 appearances, and who has managed to miss key penalties against West Ham on more than one occasion. For all the mystique that surrounds the name 'Jermain Defoe', however, fans should remember that his middle name is 'Colin'.

Sears has been forced to live in the shadow of scoring on his debut for West Ham against Blackburn Rovers in March 2008. He scored a 'goal' for Crystal Palace where he was on loan, which referee Rob Shoebridge disallowed after it had 'come back into play' after hitting the stanchion. Other than that, it's all been a triumph of experience over hope for Sears. His two goals last season suggested the spark may yet ignite, particularly in the less demanding corners of the Championship.

Verdict: Jermain Defoe

10) Les Ferdinand v Zavon Hines

Ferdinand may well have been enjoying his last legs for West Ham in 2002-03, but his twelve league goals in twenty-nine appearances for Leicester City the following season showed he still knew where the goal was (unlike Rob Shoebridge). 'Sir Les' Ferdinand is still is the joint fifth highest scorer in the Premier League with 149 goals.

Hines has yet to demonstrate the fifty-seven varieties of his footballing talents, having scored just once for West Ham. He is clearly a promising player. However, he'll be spending it in the claret and blue of Burnley since signing for the club for £250,000 in August 2011.

Verdict: Les Ferdinand

11) Frederic Kanouté v Frederic Piquionne

Kanoute proved a superb signing for West Ham; it was Glen Roeder's bad luck to lose him for the greater part of the 2002-03 season. His goals would almost certainly have kept them up, and it could have been a very different East London story to the one we are telling now. In ninety-two appearances for the club, Kanouté scored 33 goals. He later won the African Player of the Year in 2007 when he was playing in Spain for Sevilla. His most curious achievements are being booked in 2009 for a 'political statement': he raised his shirt after scoring to reveal a black shirt with the word 'Palestine' on it. In 2007 he refused to wear the Sevilla shirt emblazoned with the sponsors' name '888.com' because of his Muslim anti-gambling beliefs.

Piquionne joined West Ham at the beginning of the 2010-11 relegation season on a three year contract but, unlike Thomas Hitzlsperger, he stayed. 41 appearances and 9 goals from a poor season is still a reasonable return.
Verdict: Frederick Kanouté

12) Paolo Di Canio v Scott Parker

Di Canio is a legend. Bought for a relative pittance, a famous Redknapp gamble that came off (unlike Futre, Raducioiu, Margas...). Someone who over a few seasons helped to take West Ham back to European competition and helped make them a team that generated memories and heroes. Since then there's been very little to cheer apart from an FA Cup final appearance and wins at Highbury and the Emirates.

Parker is the first Hammer to win Hammer of the Year three times in succession since Trevor Brooking did it back in 1976-78. A brilliant achievement, yes, but made easier for him by the ever-changing teams of wankers the club have had on their books over the last year. Parker is old-style West Ham, so much so that we built a team around him. Unfortunately whenever he didn't play, we lost. Di Canio had Cole, Lampard, Ferdinand, Sinclair, Lomas, Hislop, Moncur and some. Parker was a brilliant bloke playing on his own in the park who, in the end, took his ball and went off to play for Spurs. Only Martin Peters and, possibly, Michael Carrick, have ever been forgiven for making that move. Spurs weren't as loathed in Peters' time, and he won the bloody World Cup, for g-d's sake.
Verdict: Paolo Di Canio

13) Don Hutchison v Victor Obinna

Hutchison had two spells at Upton Park, impressing and breaking the club transfer fee in both. He returned an older and wiser man after being signed by Glenn Roeder in 2005, he mustered sixty-three league appearances and five goals. His greatest football claim to fame remains scoring the only goal of an international fixture for Scotland against Germany, away in Bremen, in April 1999. And there was that Budweiser label incident, come to think of it.

Obinna joined West Ham in August 2010 on loan from Internazionale and in his seven appearances, he managed three goals, two yellow cards and a stack of somersaults.

Verdict: Victor Obinna

Manager - Trevor Brooking v Kevin Keen

Two ex-Hammers, players and caretaker managers in more than one spell, but only one did both jobs well. I prefer to remember Kevin Keen on the wing, setting up chances for Trevor Morley, Jimmy Quinn and Clive Allen. Trevor Brooking almost saved the 2002-03 team from a relegation they should never have had to endure. Kevin Keen, through no fault of his own it has to be admitted, merely shepherded the side over the edge of football's Beachy Head.

Verdict: Trevor Brooking

Final Team: Robert Green, Tomas Repka, Christian Dailly, Danny Gabbidon, Glen Johnson, Trevor Sinclair, Steve Lomas, Joe Cole, Jermain Defoe, Les Ferdinand, Frederick Kanoute. Subs: Paolo Di Canio, Victor Obinna

Final Score: Relegation Irons 10 Loser Leavers 4

THOSE WHO STAYED BEYOND RELEGATION

2003: David James, Tomas Repka, Christian Dailly, Rufus Brevett, Jermain Defoe, Don Hutchison (6/13)
2011: Robert Green, Jordan Spence, James Tomkins, Jack Collison, Freddie Sears, Frederic Piquionne (6/14)

Relegation affects different fans in different ways. I should imagine most Manchester United fans would regard it with the same wizened eye as most might regard the Second World War. If you are a West Bromwich Albion follower, however, it's as familiar as lying and choking on a Saturday evening across the threshold of your local public house. Those poor buggers have seen their side promoted four times and relegated three times just this century. The giant steel girder clamped across the fold of club chairman Jeremy Peace's wallet may offer some explanation as to why this phenomenon could have occurred so frequently. The club's good fortune at grabbing Roy Hodgson on the rebound from his Liverpool departure might prove the moment where the black country yo-yo finally comes to a halt.

I have had the misfortune to experience five relegations as a follower of West Ham United in my 54 years on this planet. The first was 1977-78, as a 20 year old, then eleven years later in 1988-89 and for a third time just three years later from the position of my first year as club commentator in 1991-92. There were to be just two more seasons to forget. In 2002-03, strangely my final year as full time club commentator, I felt the drop at age 44. Now, eight years on at the end of 2010-11, I have had to endure my fifth such experience.

Cliff Richard enjoyed number one hits at least once every decade for sixty years from 1958 to 2000. I have managed a similar repetitive experience as a follower of the Irons, and twice in my thirties. This is why I always find the first season after any West Ham United relegation worth documenting. This next year will, I am sure, be no different.

Ron Sexsmith might sound to you like an Ann Summers' stocking filler, but to a few of us lurking on the periphery of what is left of the 'music scene' this is a Canadian songwriter of immense talent and yet quite breathtaking obscurity. There aren't many singers who can release twelve albums and still remain largely unknown beyond their own country of origin. Fewer still can manage the feat and be feted by singers as diverse and successful as Elvis Costello, Emmylou Harris and Bob Dylan. Another famous singer songwriter who enjoys Sexsmith's work is the Kinks' Ray Davies, who has given Ron a headliner slot on his 2011 Meltdown Festival at the South Bank on Thursday 16th June 2011.

Sexsmith's latest album *Long Player, Late Bloomer* has been lovingly curated by Metallica and Aerosmith producer Bob Rock, and the results are spectacular. A very unusual album in 2011, one without a bad track. Charles Shaar Murray said something about music no longer being sacred because of its ubiquity. This is one of those rare moments of delight when someone has managed to transcend that all too often poignant definition and created something holy. The BBC's decision to show Douglas Arrowsmith's 2010 film about Ron, *Love Shines*, last month on BBC4, along with a live set with fellow songwriters' Fran Healy and Graham Gouldman, is perhaps indicative that this will finally be Ron's year.

More reminders that I'm not getting any younger. Another fine and not that well-known American singer-songwriter Andrew Gold (no relation to David), who wrote and performed with Graham Gouldman in Wax in the late 1980s has died of a heart attack in Los Angeles at the age of just 59. Though I never got to see him live, I bought his first three albums which still sound as good as the day they were released. My favourite tracks are *Lonely Boy*, *Never Let Her Slip Away* and *That's Why I Love You*. Perhaps the most interestingly obscure fact about his talent is that he plays all instruments on Art Garfunkel's 1975 chart-topping version of *I Only Have Eyes For You*, He will be missed.

A little later in the month, the 29th June 2011 to be precise, is when I finally meet a legend. For all the abuse that term has taken, there can be no doubt of its worth this evening, and my Art Garfunkel reference ensures a smooth segué to this moment. I am at the Hammersmith Apollo to witness Paul Simon and his crew. They are fresh from performing at Glastonbury, and tonight are playing a few Greatest Hits and some tracks from the new album that has a song on it with 'Christmas' in the title.

I am wondering if he'll play *America* or *Save The Life of my Child*. I am also wondering at my accomplishment of securing a place just two rows and six seats from the coveted spot furthest from the stage, Block 1 Row Z Seat 85. This is a breathtaking achievement for someone who bought his seat barely a minute after tickets went on sale on the HMV Apollo website sometime back in 2005. Clicking 'best available', I had no idea there were just 25 seats left in the auditorium. Or maybe they start selling them from the back. And I have a seven foot man in front of me who must have bought his ticket in 1970.

This gig should have taken place yesterday, but because Simon has a sore throat, his management instructs 'Tickettwats' to e-mail the entire 3,632 audience (takings for the night equivalent to around £272,400) to tell them the concert has been moved forward a day. If you've mortgaged your house for a ticket, you'll move heaven, earth and your number one pressing engagement to ensure you don't let this very late adjustment force you to miss it. It is another example of the modern world's ability to manage the intricate subtleties of mass communication. Paul Simon gig, take two.

He opens the concert with *Crazy Love* from Graceland, and although his Hobson's Choice is a bit knackered, the audience are soon forced to admit that they are fortunate to have had the financial muscle to witness this special musical outing.

The band are as sound as you'd expect but as the concert settles I find I am replacing Simon's croaking with memories of his performances on the originals. This only becomes a problem with the material from his new album, which I don't know. That's when I start focusing on the misery of my shit seat, and the fact that the overall sound is a bit pants.

There are some magical moments to keep my temper at bay, these being *50 Ways to Leave your Lover, Mother and Child Reunion, Slip Sliding Away*, an almost sacred acoustic *Sound of Silence, Boy in the Bubble, Still Crazy After All These Years* and, of course, *You Can Call Me Al*. But that's only seven songs out of 26, a quarter of the gig. Nothing from my favourite PS album *Bookends* and, in the final analysis, a sum total of eleven quid a song.

For every relegated team there's a side with promotion in their sights, often against all the odds. One such side attempting the mighty struggle in 2010-11 for the second successive season were AFC Wimbledon. Formed and financed by frustrated fans in 2002 to deal with the seeming theft of their club by a collection of newtownies in Milton Keynes, AFC Wimbledon bought their ground from Kingstonian FC, and set about on a 'return to the League' mission.

AFC Wimbledon's first ever goal was scored in 2002 by Glenn Mulcaire, the 'private investigator' or 'spineless criminal mercenary' from News of the World who was sent to prison for six months for hacking the phones of royalty. The goal was a stupendous left foot volley from outside the area that hit the back of the net before the goalkeeper had even moved. Mulcaire did very little moving himself after being sent down five years later.

Nine years after Mulcaire's goal and several promotions, the dream was almost complete. While last season they found themselves dwarfed, even at semi-pro level, by the heavily financed Crawley Town FC, the back door access was still open to them through the play offs. They reached them with six wins and a draw from their last seven league matches. They then beat fellow promotion-climbing newbies Fleetwood 8-1 on aggregate in the play-off semis to earn a place in the final against Luton Town at the City of Manchester Stadium on Saturday 21st May.

The Wimbledon v Luton Town fixture has some history. Twenty-three years earlier it was an FA Cup semi-final, won 2-1 on the day by Wimbledon on their way to beating Liverpool 1-0 in the final. Two weeks later Luton Town beat Arsenal 3-2 at Wembley to win the League Cup. Subsequent Irons' legend Tim Breacker played a part in both those Luton games. Today the winner of this fixture will gain full league status. The game could lay claim to being the most important football game in the year, switching your status from semi-pro to professional in just one afternoon.

Six days before this memorable occasion I had witnessed West Ham's predictably spineless exit from the Premier League after a 0-3 home caning at the hands of Sunderland. I had planned something more inspiring to round off a generally miserable season. I had got myself a ticket for the Blue Square Bet Premier play off final. It wouldn't be the last time I'd use my ingenuity to get a ticket to watch an AFC Wimbledon match. This time I used my press links as a football journalist and writer to put in an accreditation request.

Joining me for the journey up to Manchester was Clive Leatherdale, managing director of Desert Island Books, that bastion of sports literature and Transylvanian tales. They published two of my books, 'Hammers Through The Looking Glass' and 'West Ham: 101 Beautiful Games'. He has written books about the original Wimbledon FC, but his greatest achievement is the publication of 'West Ham United: The Elite Era', club historian John Helliar's bible of West Ham United statistics. It's not a cheap hardback, but no serious fan of the club should be without one.

Clive is, by his own admission, not an easy publisher to work for. He warned me that if I took up his offer to publish my second Hammers' book, his exacting style of management and demanding deadlines should not be taken personally. I of course didn't warn him that I was one of the collected 'Authors from Hell' he subsequently sent me an article about, having worked with me for just four months. We should have realised that there might be a problem finding a country big enough for our respective personalities, but the books got published, and Clive ended up giving me some very handy information about my health once he learned I had been diagnosed with atrial fibrillation in 2008.

We had an enjoyable journey up to the new Manchester City ground, a venue neither of us had hitherto visited, and sat through the game's ninety minutes with a concentrated nervousness. There were few chances in the game, such was the clear desire of each team to gain promotion to the Football League. AFC Wimbledon had thought of little else in the previous nine years, and Luton Town, out of the league for twenty-four months, clearly regarded their Blue Square Premier status as temporary. In the end, after a further thirty minutes of extra time, it came down to penalties. Though Luton looked the more talented side, it seemed that AFC Wimbledon's industry and belief might give them the edge in a battle of spot kick neurosis. And so it proves, with Danny Kedwell holding his nerve to hit home the penalty that takes them up to the Football League for the first time in their reincarnated lives. The Crazy Gang. And that's what the whole of this fan-owned club's nine year nothing to something success is, crazy.

From 22nd February 2003 to 4th December 2004, AFC Wimbledon remained unbeaten for a total of 78 games, a run that remains a record for league games at any senior level of football in the UK. Now they have achieved full football league status, it seems unlikely that they will be in danger of breaking their own record for some time. They do, however, have a challenging but achievable short term goal of securing a couple of league fixtures against the rebranded MK Dons, which at the time of writing is just a promotion (or relegation) away.

After a furious morning of disbelief spent surfing the net, I have established the breathtaking revelation that West Ham are *not making an end of season DVD for 2010-11*. There have already been slabs of trolling from fans who, despite being put through the misery of probably West Ham's worst performance-related relegation season since 1988-89, are furious about being denied the chance of owning the shocker on DVD to watch again and again.

I have more than a vested interest in this non-event, having produced the end of season DVD for the club for ten seasons right up to 2007-08. It had always been a labour of love for me and, apart from 2002-03 when I was told for the first time not to include highlights from every league game, I had generally been left to my own devices. This was until 2007-08 when, in my opening review of new players joining the club, I inexplicably referred to Craig Bellamy as Lee Bellamy. Despite the company having two people employed to check for errors (I'll resist naming them - they know who they are), they both missed it, and when I asked them later *how?* they both said they knew I never made mistakes, so hadn't bothered checking.

Great.

The second problem on that DVD was a goal celebration later on in the season which culminated in Carlton Cole declaring in carved brutal language exactly how he was feeling about scoring. I'd missed this as well, so I have to hold my hands up. Nobody wants their five year old child viewing (and then possibly repeating) their goalscoring hero's goalscoring rant in the garden every time they manage to beat the dog with a close range shot.

The production company didn't tell me they were doing the 2008-09 season DVD without me. They simply allowed a slow leak of the feedback about the mistakes to find its way back to me over the first few months of 2008-09. Can you blame them? Who wants an argument when there are easier ways to organise change? And they had appointed me as match announcer at the club for the first four months that season, so I wasn't exactly out of pocket..

Once I realised they would be covering West Ham's end of season ninth placed finish in house, I shrugged my shoulders. They are based in the North West of England, and I don't feel they quite understand what it means to be a West Ham fan. That was originally why they had given me the job. And you can see how well they managed. If you've forgotten, take out your copy and have a watch. I think you'll see the problem. Then check out your 2009-10 season DVD, done by the same people, considerably shorter in length and quality. Then take out your 2010-11 copy and... *oh yeah... there isn't going to be one.*

Chapter 2

The Allah Dice Man

July 2011

It was when Andy Murray qualified his British credentials by insisting he was 'Scottish' (not quite sure why I've put that in parenthesis) that I lost interest in him. It was also the result of my irrational fear that he might actually win Wimbledon one day, thereby disturbing the neat symmetrical list of last hurdle failures that the Brits always seem to produce in tennis, and most other sports. I needn't have worried. Murray has proved that he may well be English. He had us fooled with all that Sean Connery backed devolution pose. This year, with Roger Federer safely dispatched to his next Grand Slam tournament courtesy of the twenty-four year old French serve and volleyer Jean De Hoh Hee Hoh, Murray has just managed to abandon competitive membership of his semi-final with the impossible Rafa Nadal, despite being a set and a game up, and has withered away into oblivion for another year.

Women's football, now I could be a fan of that. However, despite quietly getting on with occasionally winning, even the England women's team, competing in Germany in the 2011 World Cup, has managed only a lame draw against Mexico. They will be out of the tournament if they fail to beat New Zealand this evening. Is there *anything* that any team or player I might choose to follow the fortunes of could actually win?

Lee Bowyer must feel a bit like that at times. This is the player who left a very poor Leeds United team in January 2003 to join Glenn Roeder at West Ham, the club he supported as a boy. West Ham had the option to let him go at the end of the season if they were relegated; his salary would be too much for a champo side. Ten appearances later, West Ham were relegated. If he'd gone back to Leeds, it would've been to join a team that had the words 'relegation candidates' running through them like a stick of Blackpool rock, so he decided to go to Newcastle on a free transfer. Two years and nearly a hundred appearances later, he got himself involved in a brawl on the pitch with a player from his own side, Kieron Dyer, and he was red carded, heavily fined and universally vilified. Analysis on Sky Sports'

Goals on Sunday programme highlighted teammates clearly choosing not to pass to Loveable Lee when he was clearly well placed. This time he managed to leave Newcastle before they too were relegated, joining West Ham again in June 2006. He played in both European defeats against Palermo and sixteen other games that season, including a 3-4 reverse against Spurs, in which he gave away a penalty with West Ham 2-0 up and about to win their first game in eleven. The following season he managed four goals, but in only twelve games. The season after, he made just four appearances by the end of January, when he went on loan to Birmingham, a move he finally made permanent at the end of the season, having helped them gain promotion to the Premier League. Then he featured in the club's first League Cup triumph since 1963, but gets relegated with them and decides to leave for fellow championship side Ipswich Town. He will most likely be appearing at Upton Park again in the midweek home fixture on Tuesday 27th September.

Relegation is never a barrel of giraffes, but the Class of 2011 may well have been the worst West Ham side I have ever seen in all my time as a fan. Whose fault is it? Wrong question. Blame is like people who want to help you moan about your luck. No help at all, and no road back to previous successes.

But, what the hell? Let's dig up the misery of last season and remember.

For a start, *how* can a side whose captain is the Football Writers' Association's Footballer of the Year for 2011, a side who turn Manchester United over 4-0 in the League Cup, a side who finally beat Tottenham Hotspur at Upton Park after a five year wait, a side who beat a brilliant and resurgent Liverpool outfit 3-1, a side who get to the semi-final of the League Cup, a side who get to the quarter final of the FA Cup... *How can that side get relegated?* Above all, how can any side in the Premier League win more games in the two domestic cup competitions (eight) than they do in the league (seven)? I mean, has that ever been done before? This team also manages to lose six of their last seven league games, when two wins and two draws would have kept them up.

Okay, vitriol dispensed. I can see that there is a great pile of overpaid lazy players on big-assed contracts that West Ham finally have the chance to dispense with. I am sad to see Demba Ba leave. As I will be if Carlton Cole goes. These are two hard-working players who both produced moments of quality last season. Scott Parker might have stayed if West Ham had not been relegated, but only the hardest of hearts will blame him for leaving. How good a player is he if he can be Player of the Year in this SOS (shower of shite – with apologies) team. Not just once, but for three successive years?

It's never been done at West Ham before. Not by anyone – even the World Cup Winners triumvirate. I know the first award was more by default than anything else and with only 17 appearances out of a possible 44, but he's certainly earned the last two. One thing I will guarantee and that is whoever he ends up joining, and they say it looks like it'll be Tottenham (ouch!), I'll bet he will be very close to being their Player of the Year by the end of 2011-12.

So I suppose that just leaves Avram Grant. The manager who took Jose Mourinho's Chelsea team to within a penalty kick of winning the UEFA Champions League for the first time in their rouble-studded history. And still got sacked. West Ham were one off the bottom of the League by Christmas 2010, and he kept his job. So he looked like a frog. So did Kermit, but I've never heard anyone offer anything barbed about him. I think what I particularly found a problem, though, was the fact that he rarely showed emotion throughout what was a very emotional season. And I'm talking *majorly* emotional. Very little. It was, I think, emotional impotence. Keeping cool in times of stress is to be commended, sure, but putting someone in a coma in charge of a Premier League club makes very little sense to me.

So what of 2011-12? I can see it looming in the distance like a limping angry man with a shotgun, and wonder just what the next season has in store. Journeys to Peterborough and the red and white hooped livery of Doncaster Rovers. Not to mention more sleeping giants than a sixteen week run of Jack and the Beanstalk. And it's as if the referees in the Premier League aren't below par. The 'npower' Championship features men in black or lime out to prove themselves by scoring the highest red card count, or oldies who have been booted out of the Premier League for the kind of refereeing that you wouldn't want to see down the park on a Sunday. Then there is the word I hate more than any other championship team word. *Expectation*. We all know how brilliant West Ham fans are, how patient, how dedicated. Yes, they all expect to go straight back up, with a better manager and a better team. And they all *expect* not to have it rammed down their throats that this is *The Academy* and playing football *The West Ham Way* is more important than winning. Says who? I'll be happy with three points if the opposition score own goals, miss penalties and have their back four all sent off in the first ten minutes. Every match. I'll be happy if West Ham score goals from debatable decisions and come bottom of the Opta index ratings and Fair Play league, week in, week out. Let's worry about playing *The West*

Ham Way once we're back in the Premier League, and safe with three games to go....

Then, before the football season has even begun to rear its ugly head, the weird twenty-first century world has fashioned two shattering events on the same day. First, a lunatic has set off a bomb in Oslo and then run amok on an island off the mainland killing eighty-five people in total. No-one has a clue yet why he has done it. This is the only kind of crazed incident that could possibly keep the other big story off the top of the news programme tonight. Amy Winehouse is dead, at 27.

On Monday November 26th 2007 I had the good fortune to be at the Brighton Conference Centre to see one of the last scheduled gigs on Amy Winehouse's *Back to Black* UK Tour. Her second album had been selling well and it was generally understood that she had made it to the top, musically, for inevitable critical acclaim, music awards, the lot. I had missed going to see her live after her first album, but this time had managed to grab a ticket for a midweek concert at Brighton when they had gone on sale six months earlier, the typical waiting time between purchasing time and the actual gig. Her gathering notoriety for drink, drugs and great music meant these tickets were now hot property, though which Amy would turn up at each gig was anyone's guess. Her planned September 2007 America and Canada Tour had been cancelled, but a handful of UK gigs at the tail end of November survived, this being one of them.

I asked one of the venue's bouncers what time she might be on as I passed the door on the way to drop my gear off at the hotel, and he declared, '9.30,' barely concealing a spontaneous fit of sniggering. I smiled at the observation, and some five or so hours later, with the time approaching eleven o'clock, smiled again as Ms Winehouse and her brilliant backing band the Dap-Kings finally took to the stage. Rough, perhaps, for the day trippers from London who would have just enough time to catch the first eight or nine minutes of the gig before they had to run to the station to make the last train back. My booked hotel room excused me from such a predictable enterprise. For those who stayed, she played for over two hours, sober, and I still think it was one of the best gigs I've ever seen. I did get another ticket to see her Island Records 50th anniversary concert headliner at the Shepherd's Bush Empire at the end of May 2009, but she cancelled that one.

I must have been the only person in the UK never to have seen her live before, and I dutifully pushed my way to the front that night to catch the magic. I can't see any point in comparing her to Sarah Vaughan, Billie Holiday or any other singing great. She was simply Amy, and that night put in a sublime performance. It was to be the last date of that tour and, indeed, her last scheduled UK tour date, other than a handful of festival appearances and private party shows. A few weeks later her label said she was cancelling all future gigs and public appearances for the rest of the year after her doctor had advised her to take a complete rest.

Nearly four years on, a text appears on my phone, ironically from the friend who I met at the gig that night. *Amy Winehouse is dead. Check the Net.* It's no surprise that it's no surprise. No more handouts of her genius, is my first selfish thought. Then I begin to reflect on the fact that she died alone.

The last Saturday in July is our first chance to take a look at what Mr Allardyce is preparing for us over the next ten months. The usual Mediterranean opponents have been shipped in to feign European competition, and to moreover guarantee the appearance of more than ten thousand fans to make the whole enterprise financially viable. In the event they fail to meet the target by about 1300, but it still turns out to be a match well worth attending.

Friendly, Upton Park
Saturday 30th July 2011 (8,769)
Referee: Peter Walton (Northants)

West Ham United 2   **Real Zaragoza 0**
Taylor 24
Sears 90

The ground is three-quarters empty, as is the Press Box Media Area. Nolan receives a rapturous welcome when his name is called out - 'West Ham's new captain, Kevin *Nolan!*' With Scott Parker and Mark Noble still on the books, that transfer window will be gaping open like a hangman's trap door next month ready for Harry Redknapp to swoop for maybe both of them as cover for Modric, who he may well then reluctantly sell.

Zaragoza play some neat one touch football in the opening few minutes, but no-one is breaking a sweat. Faubert's early right-sided cross is chested down by Nolan at the edge of the area, but Paredes sweeps in and clears.

Contini, the midfield dynamo in waiting, looks the part early on. Parker feeds Faubert on eight minutes, and his low shot is gathered clumsily at the second grab by Leo Franco. Faubert's shaven head makes him look not unlike Trevor Sinclair from behind, especially as he hovers on the right wing. Nolan, who seems hungry to score, pokes Matt Taylor's corner wide. Proof of his goal hunger is in the fact that he has already managed to get into an offside position three times in the first fifteen. Joey O'Brien, an overlapping full back, sits ten yards behind Faubert as the game develops. Have they been working on this in training? I hope not, because it's not working.

Maybe Zaragoza fancied a weekend in London. They aren't too bothered about this practice match it would seem. O'Brien throws adventurously forward, but possession is clumsily lost by Piquionne. Freddie Sears and Jordan Spence are warming up to a tickle of touchline applause. Zaragoza's number 11, Juan Carlos, playing on the left of midfield, shows a couple of neat touches, but Parker and Nolan are the ones dominating this game.

It's sometimes difficult to know whether it's the wind or indifference that has sucked all the energy and importance out of this game. As I write this, the game crackles into life. Parker threads a run through the Zaragoza defence, beating three players, and squares it neatly for a 24th minute tap-in from Matt Taylor. The crowd and Zaragoza wake simultaneously as from a deep sleep. Parades crosses well but Adam Pinter - not a very foreign sounding name, cannot control the ball in the area and Hammers clear. Green finally has something to do, catching a deflected left wing cross from the industrious Carlos. Pinter's 28th minute curler misses by a foot with Green a spectator. A delicate flicked header at the other end on the half hour by Faubert has Franco stretching to tip the ball over. The game is gathering pace. Suddenly Juan Carlos is free on the right but hammers his shot across the goal with the net hanging like Christmas tinsel before him.

West Ham have a free kick just outside the D for a foul on Parker. Taylor curls it left footed round the wall and hits the inside of the post. The offside Piquionne nets to no avail. Less than a minute later, Taylor is shepherding the ball out to safety after a Zaragoza counter attack; he looks useful. Parker crosses from the right, but Taylor fails to control and is forced to chase the ball out to the touchline, where he swivels to put in a superb cross, Faubert has snatched off his eager head by the crimson-kitted Franco. Nolan then breaks through the middle and sets up Noble who hammers in a 39th minute shot that Franco fingertips past the post. Pablo Barrera (wearing number 21) comes on for Faubert to take the ensuing corner which Reid heads wide.

Referee Peter Walton gives Zaragoza a free kick which Carlos lays off to the captain Ponzio to drive left-footed past the wall and Green goes down low to save. In the last minute of what has become a rather satisfying first half, Carlos speculatively chips Green from nearly forty yards but the ball gathers speed and distance to sail comically high and wide into the sky like an abandoned child's balloon. 1-0 is a half-time score that Allardyce would clearly have settled for, but like many of these pre-season Saturday Upton Park matches (this one doesn't even carry the 'Bobby Moore Cup' title), it seems like a pre-wedding run through for the season.

Jeremy Nicholas spends much of the half-time break advertising season tickets; this isn't even really a rehearsal for anything real. By this time next week Hammers will most likely have sold several of these players. There is Matthew Upson, clearly the main candidate for the 'non-playing' West Ham captain of the century. A footballer who faced with ninety minutes of Bolton's Kevin Davies or Chelsea's Drogba, would unaccountably collapse with terminal influenza or a temporary death in the family. Now he's just a free agent - and chances are he probably doesn't even have an agent and may struggle to find a club.

Zaragoza's 20 and 4 are replaced by 17 and 21. Lafita (17), sounding like a misspelt country, is immediately on the ball and bursts through wide on the right to hammer in a powerful shot that skids inches wide. Forty seconds later, the red booted one hits a shot from twenty-five yards that has Green fumbling for his contacts in the grass.

Rob Pritchard, the editor of the club programme, has lost interest and is trading tweets with his romantic interest. Maurizio Lanzaro foreheads in a diving header from Mateos' low right wing cross, but Green beats it out. Uche's effort gets a deflection and bounces wide for a corner. Eventually O'Brien smacks a fifty yard clearance and the succession of opposition attacks is broken. A great tackle from Reid concedes another RZ corner, but Green rises above the others supremely to snatch the ball off the heads. Now O'Brien goes off to generous applause, to be replaced by Jordan Spence, wearing 14. Jeremy Nicholas has already stressed that West Ham will be wearing 1-11 on their shirts with all but the keeper continuing down to 21. (yes, that's *ten* substitutes) The keeper (Ruud Boffin, surely a made up name) will wear 31. Matt Taylor takes off his shirt for some reason, revealing four figures worth of painstaking elite tattoo work on his arms and upper chest. A 56th minute flicked header by Piquionne then beats the keeper but is cleared off the line by the industrious but anonymously-named Juan Carlos. Piquionne chases back positively to win a midfield tackle. Noble and Parker are linking up well. The number 10 shirt seems to suit Noble - will he step up to the plate or will he step off it to follow a career with a minor Premiership club...

Parker, Taylor and Noble look like a formidable Championship midfield line-up, now if only... Media head Greg Demetriou has let me know that he is looking for a team to film WHU games from the gantry so Sam Allardyce can have his own DVD at the end of every game. I'm already wondering whether I could put a team together for a figure competitive enough to be offered the gig. The media company my brother and I had formed in February 2006 had begun filming the U-18 games live on Saturday mornings at the youth academy's Chadwell Heath ground from the 2006-07 season, editing commentary-less highlights for placement on the club website on Saturday evening or first thing on the Sunday. It was a professional but basic package then, but rewarding to be involved with the club at the vital end of Tony Carr's talent factory. The skill was to consider who looked good enough to make it at the top level from watching those games. We also filmed some of the reserve games that were played at Upton Park, particularly if they featured a named player coming back to first team action. A reserve team hat-trick by a returning Bobby Zamora, filmed by us, had been deemed significant enough to put on the club's end of season DVD.

Even in the limited time we had been involved with filming live games for the club, we had already seen several decent players who looked a good bet for a professional future in the game. Unfortunately, the necessary belt-tightening slashed outside expenses (and some inside ones, too), and the job went back to being a lower spec in house operation to save money. Could that be about to change?

Scott Parker is replaced in the 63rd minute by Carlton Cole to as much rapturous applause as the small crowd are able to generate. Will either of them or the crowd be here next week?

West Ham's infuriating broadband connection (for which I tried in vain over the last year to secure the password) has been dispensed with, only to be replaced by 'The Cloud', that bottom wipe attention-grabber which, like a licentious short-sighted girlfriend in high heels, disappears down a flight of stairs in reception terms before you can even find a conversation topic to massage with her. 9 goes off for 26 for Zaragoza on 69 minutes.

We approach the legendary 76th minute, which is actually two minutes. Matt Taylor on 71 minutes has done enough to get loud, grateful applause as he is replaced by Freddie Sears. Piquionne is also off for the now accent-less Frank Nouble. Noble is playing deep in the midfield and is clearly working on the role of creator that he threatened to develop last season, and back in his early Championship days under Alan Pardew.

Cole, wearing 18, is making a nuisance of himself, and has earned a corner which the keeper beats away lazily as if playing volleyball on the beach. As the game draws to a close, Pinter departs for Kevin Lacuise, and Carlos is off for Joel Valencia - fancy having a holiday destination named after you? Rob Green manages a long distance tip round the post; Lafita's corner just finds Cole who comes away with the ball, and that's all we're getting from the 76th minute of this match. So what do I know? Barrera breaks away down the left and fires in a shot-come-cross that misses everyone and the far post. Another sub – as Jlloyd Samuel slinks off for Cristian Montano in the 79th minute. Still a goal to the good, Hammers are ten minutes away from another friendly victory to round off the start of their 2011-12 pre-season escapades.

Forthcoming fixtures against Cardiff and Aldershot sound like an Eddie Stobart round trip rather than the first two home games of West Ham's season. Cole volleys way over from the eighteen yard distance he wears a number for on his shirt. James Tomkins, who has had a quiet match, manages a couple of blocks and hits a seventy yard free kick out to Barrera; then Nouble runs half the length of the pitch before hitting a long swerving wide shot, all power and no precision.

Hammers last three friendlies have ended up 1-0, 0-0 and 1-0. Binary football. No goals conceded - this will make it four wins and a sterling defensive showing. Will this be the Allardyce way?

They haven't announced the attendance yet... In the 89th minute, just like against FC Copenhagen, the Danish Champions, Freddie Sears finds the back of the net - slapping the ball home on the right after a shimmy, from just inside the area. Noble leaves the field right at the end to give a minute's run around for Junior Stanislas. Two minutes' injury time. Barrera looks nimble; shame I can't remember him from last season. In the end, the ref plays only ninety seconds of injury time.

How typical will this starting XI be in terms of what's put out for the rest of the season? I'm guessing it's a long enough road ahead to ensure that perhaps only four or five of these boys will be putting on the West Ham first team shirt come the end of April 2012.

West Ham: 1 Robert Green, 2 Joey O'Brien, 3 Jlloyd Samuel, 4 Kevin Nolan (capt.), 5 James Tomkins, 6 Winston Reid, 7 Julien Faubert, 8 Scott Parker, 9 Freddie Piquionne, 10 Mark Noble, 11 Matt Taylor

Having worked with the club as in house commentator for twelve years from 1991-2003, I had improved my knowledge of the game behind the scenes, and had also started to produce West Ham's DVDs from the 1998-99 season. Although the commentary opportunities lessened with the advent of regular Sky coverage, I found myself working with other London clubs and with Leeds United, Ipswich Town, Everton and Wolverhampton Wanderers projects. Recognising my London brogue, I would always get asked who my team was and then would closely scrutinise anything in their programmes where West Ham appeared. I usually farmed commentaries and overdubs for those parts of the programme out to other journalists. I had undertaken live commentaries for Everton throughout the 2000-01 season, when West Ham were on the road, and had once found myself professionally compromised during an Everton v West Ham fixture where Paolo Di Canio caught the ball in the penalty area rather than score after the Everton keeper Paul Gerrard had been injured. Thankfully all applauded his sportsmanship, while UEFA went one better, awarding him a special 'Fair Play' award. All that, and he probably would have missed.

My experience working with different clubs had taught me that they all love an anniversary. Clubs enjoy celebrating twenty years of this, ten years since they'd won the cup, five years since they last beat their local rivals or served Alsatian burgers in the club canteen. QPR, after the ignominy of losing to a car showroom (Vauxhall Motors) in the FA Cup in 2002, had risen eight years later from near administration days to be in with a chance of promotion to the Premier League. They also had new 'financially embarrassed' owners, so were looking a good bet for top league status in the years to come. My maths told me that 2010-11 represented a 35 year gap since they had finished second in the old 1975-76 First Division Championship, losing out to Liverpool at the very last hurdle. Why had no one ever put a DVD together of all the available action from that season? Well, plenty of reasons, perhaps, but it was worth considering as a project, and I duly wandered down with good friend, fellow Londoner, football enthusiast and FIFA commentator Nick London to see what the West London club's media and club shop people thought of the idea. Nick is a savvy soul who spent his formative years in Advertising, almost as if it were a place, and retired at 30 to follow, along with other pursuits, a career in football journalism. He and I were both of the opinion that providing a footballing community with what it has been for thirty-five years, to coincide with its team gaining promotion to the Barclays Premier League for the first time in fifteen years, just might carve you a place in that club's history yourself. You might be giants.

Our idea got a positive reaction and, most importantly, an order number. We arranged interviews with captain Gerry Francis, goalkeeper (and West Ham legend) Phil Parkes, 'old hand' and Arsenal double winner Frank McLintock and the true genius, the sublime and enigmatic Stan Bowles. Subsequently all of the reactions have been favourable (apart from the usual brainless Net trolls who'd complain about a Lottery Win for coming at the wrong time) and it looked like one of the better things the company had been a part of in the five years of our existence. In the end there was an issue with the footage. Some was from BBC, some was from ITV, some was shot on 35mm. We could revoice commentary on a newly prepared audio track (and did for a test run), but cold feet kept the finished project from going on sale for more than a week or two, even though a lot of the club's heritage season footage is still freely available to watch on You Tube. It's not unlike the Allies and Russians inability to trust each other to withdraw from Berlin after the War in 1945. Sixty-five years it's the BBC (Russia) and ITV (Allies) jealously guarding their TV footage rather than pool it collectively with those willing to knit it together for the benefit of the football fan world. Hence we now have a cold war football footage situation. Those copyright lawyers have a lot to answer for.

As 2011-12 was about to begin, QPR and West Ham had travelled in different directions, but it didn't look like I was going to be able to set the QPR DVD project in motion, despite delivering the DVDs to the club shop in May 2011. At least we were able to gain access to and enjoy the experience of filming interviews with the four players from that period. Stan Bowles, in particular, was a scream. His shock of silver hair, perennial cigarette and self-deprecating delivery made great copy, especially the revelation that he sought out (and collected) his win bonus from club secretary Ron Phillips before the last match of the season against Leeds United. QPR won the game, 2-0, before you ask, so his confidence was justified. His stories were a mixture of hardened Apocrypha and show-stopping admissions, as you will realise if you get the chance to lay your hands on one of the few copies that leaked out before the legal door on the project was pushed shut. I was able, throughout all of this, to reflect on the fact that West Ham were the only club not to be beaten by QPR in that great 1975-76 season, drawing at Loftus Road and winning 1-0 at Upton Park in the return.

The sparkle and joy Harry Redknapp put into West Ham United's football in his seven years in charge at the club, with its top ten placings, European football fixtures, great cup runs, Paolo Di Canio and victories over the top clubs in English football, all subsided after Glenn Roeder's 'Redknapp honeymoon' season of 2001-02.

Strangely enough, the direct speaking, slightly nervous and occasionally paranoid Alan Pardew soon grew into his position at the club, and suddenly began to demonstrate the potential he had often shown as the manager of Reading, back in 2002-03. Unlucky not to get West Ham back into the Premiership in their first season in the Championship, he was then fortunate to secure passage back through the backdoor against Preston North End in the play-off final the following year. It was the 2005-06 season, his third, that raised the bar for the club. Pardew got Peter Grant in as assistant manager to put his coaching ideas into practice at Chadwell Heath, and several of his signings, Paul Konchesky, Hammer of the Year Danny Gabbidon, James Collins, Nigel Reo-Coker and Yossi Benayoun proved him sound in the transfer market. Three of Pardew's strikers that season, Dean Ashton, with his brilliant FA Cup Final finish, ten goal Bobby Zamora and Marlon Harewood, with a 2005-06 season tally of sixteen, secured at the highest level, also struck gold.

The team was unrecognisable from the stable of stars Roeder inexplicably took down just three years earlier. Pardew had taken them to ninth position in the league with 55 points, two less than Roeder's 53 which had been enough in 2001-02 to finish seventh.

So how could it be with such success in the short term and having missed out on Hammers' first silverware in over a quarter of a century by just a couple of injury time minutes, that within just six months Pardew would be sacked? How could he, after all of that supreme success, manage just four wins in the first 20 games of the following season?

If you were a Hammers' fan in the 2006-07 season, you would have to conclude that it was a season of turmoil even more inexplicable than that of 2002-03. A similarity was the fact that both seasons saw Lee Bowyer join the club. The difference was that, whereas the foundations of the 2002-03 season were laid with the cheap bricks of the Roeder appointment, the failings of the 2006-07 season were ignited with the sparks of greed and fed by the ruthless doctrine of Mammon. Or put simply, neither poverty nor riches did the club any good at all.

A third successive appearance at the Millennium stadium, the first as a Premier League club, playing in an FA Cup final that BBC veteran commentator John Motson declared to be the most exciting he had ever seen, got things a tad out of kilter. The close season saw movements behind the scenes at Upton Park that suggested the concept of pride and a fall lurking in the shadows.

The trusty and reliable Head of Media Peter Stewart was pensioned off for the younger figure of Miranda Nagalingam, and Danny Francis stepped in to take on the new role of Website Manager. I didn't know much about Miranda, but Danny was an established journalist who had worked at the club for most of the time I had been there. It was certainly a backhanded compliment to Peter that, though they were both younger, it had taken two people to replace him!

Other faces became regularly seen at the training ground, like the ex-editor of Hello! and News of the World, Phil Hall, whose shiny black slip on shoes, leather document holders and striped suits were as comfortable and welcome at the club as a dose of syphilis. Hall had, for some reason, been appointed 'media consultant' for the club programme, which had experienced a shape shift for the first time since August 1983 from its familiar 240 x 165cm format to the virtually square 240 x 210cm dimensions. Hall had thrown out established contributions from regular writers including my own column 'My Story', a regular feature for three seasons, focusing on how fans had come to support their beloved West Ham United. When I asked him why he'd dropped it, the oleaginous one declared that 'they' had found it a bit 'old-fashioned'. No-one, in the new world of PR and multimedia, would be taking on the rather 'old-fashioned' idea of 'editing' the programme. Glossing it up and changing its shape would surely be enough, wouldn't it?

In his defence, during his time at the News of the World, Phil Hall could claim success with his November 1999 issue which bore the headline,

'Archer quits as News of the World exposes false alibi'. It was a sensational story, exposing the former Tory MP as a liar and perjurer, culminating in 'Lord Archer' going to jail. A rare example of the paper seemingly justified in its subterfuge and covert taping approach to news stories. It was a piece of public interest journalism, and should have been viewed as a triumph for the editor at the time, who was Phil Hall. In fact, it led to his dismissal in May 2000 because Rupert Murdoch didn't want the Archer scoop published. Hall had chosen to defy him. Hall's departure was naturally dressed up as a resignation, but it illustrated how, when it came to the News of the World, the News Corporation boss always liked to have his own way. Appearing together again, those inseparable twins pride and fall, who would have their day with Rupert Murdoch too, several years later.

West Ham Chairman Terence Brown by the edition of the first programme of the 2006-07 season was also a man who could claim success. He had now become 'Terence Brown FCIS ATTI FCCA', and for that first edition wrote a giant two page spread, puffing up the season ahead, with the Hammers back in Europe thanks to FA Cup Winners Liverpool qualifying for the Champions League. It was unclear, however, just what these three new sets of letters after his name stood for. 'FCIS' was probably 'Fellow of the Chartered Institute of Secretaries' (glorified PA), though it could just as easily have been 'Funeral Consumers Information Society'. ATTI apparently stands for 'Acoustic Test Target Insertion' and FCCA for 'Fellow of the Chartered Certified Accountants', not really anything to be boasting about. From the staff list in that first programme of 2006-07, there was now someone with two positions at the club. Scott Duxbury was both company secretary and, more ominously, commercial and legal director. West Ham had always had a commercial director, but I'd never seen 'legal director' anywhere before. Turned out they'd be needing one by the end of the season… but that was still a way away for the time being.

Having led West Ham to the FA Cup Final in just his third season at the club as well as a place in Europe, Alan Pardew must have felt his feet were firmly under the table and his position safe from directors and the meddling boardroom staff all managers fear. If only they had let him hold the reins just a little longer. Pardew had, amongst other close season purchases, bought Rob Green from Norwich City, the new 'England international' goalkeeper in waiting, and had secured Carlton Cole, a squad player striker, from Chelsea. Cole scored his first goal on debut within seconds of arriving as a late substitute on the opening day of the season 3-1 victory over Charlton Athletic. Hammers then went top of the Premiership three days later after an away draw at Watford. They were subsequently narrowly defeated at Liverpool 2-1 after Bobby Zamora had put them ahead, a lead they had held for most of the first half, and were still a creditable sixth in the mathematical table by the end of the day. Zamora was the Premier League's form striker, having struck four goals in three games, and was already being closely watched by England manager Steve McClaren.

Then it happened. Thursday August 31st 2006, Transfer Deadline Day. The story goes that sometime around 6.30 Alan Pardew got a phone call from the new PR and Media department to give him some wonderful news. A company called MSI (Media Sports Investments) had set up a deal with the club, involving two Argentinian international players, Carlos Tevez and Javier Mascherano, who were joining West Ham from Brazilian club Corinthians on 'permanent deals' for 'undisclosed fees'. The two players, who had just starred for Argentina at the 2006 World Cup, had been linked with Manchester United, Chelea and Arsenal, but had chosen to come to West Ham. Kia Joorabchian, who had left MSI some months earlier but had retained an 'investment' in the two players, was fronting the deal, whose exact details were to remain 'confidential and undisclosed'.

Quite how something 'confidential' could be anything other than 'undisclosed' also remained undisclosed. And though I love the club more than life itself, why would these two brilliant World Cup players decide to come to West Ham?

Pardew subsequently chaired the press conference for the club on the signing of the two players. The press might have wondered why the 'presser' was taking place at Upton Park and not the more informal portakabins of Chadwell Heath. They might also have wondered why it should have been set up midweek, when the next home game wasn't until Sunday, a live Sky 'Super Sunday' fixture against Aston Villa.

If you had been at the press conference, you would not have found the answer in the eyes of the manager. Alan Pardew looked like a man who had found two full sized international footballers deep down in his pants, where his testicles should have been. If he had been involved in the deal, he looked that morning as if he was already having second thoughts. The price tag on Tevez had been thought to be around £30 million, and the previous May Joorabchian had even declared Tevez's release clause from

Corinthians to have a price tag of between £69 and £83 million. So, West Ham's establishment of regular journalists were all wondering, where had the Acoustic Test Target Insertion got £30 million pounds from?

Now Tevez is at Manchester City, via Manchester United, earning the kind of money that can make a person lose their marbles. Welcome to Mad-chester! It is like the next part of a book you were reading that is moving inexorably toward a grand finale, but lacks the excitement of the early chapters. That said, Tevez will always be worshipped by grateful West Ham fans for his part in rescuing the club from relegation at the end of the 2006-07 season, but I still believe that had the whole 'rebranding' and 'new broom'ing of West Ham not happened at the beginning of that crazy season, the Tevez 'rescue performances' would not have been necessary. If West Ham's 'Belgrano' moment hadn't happened, what might things be like at the club now? We'll return to that a bit later on.

So what of the Allah Dyce man? This is a man from the Midlands, a footballer with a career spanning over 400 games with nine clubs. He even played the game in America. As a manager he had major Premier League success with Bolton, kept them in the top tier and took them into Europe. He seems to have been unfairly removed from his posts at Blackburn and Newcastle because of 'differences' with the newly arrived chairmen, but at least Gold, Sullivan and Brady have chosen him. All recent history would have me conclude is that so long as they stay at the club, things should be okay if he is able to get them back into the Premier league, hopefully at the first time of asking. It was a task beyond the likes of Alan Pardew, but the Dyce Man may prove different, especially with a purported £1m promotion bonus offer to additionally motivate him.

I think there was enough in that game to suggest it could turn out to be a good appointment from the big three. It can't be any worse than their last one, anyway.

Chapter 3

The Season Starts Here

August 2011

There are many moments in the West Ham part of my life when unforgettable things have happened. The first of these was seeing them live for the first time at the age of twelve in August 1970 in a 2-2 draw against Chelsea. Then there was my first commentary for the club, in August 1991 in a 0-0 draw against Luton Town. In August 2008 I was to experience a third such moment, in the first home game of the season, against Wigan Athletic, which West Ham won 2-1.

One week earlier the club had retired the number 6 shirt. This was to recognise a new partnership with the Bobby Moore Fund for Cancer Research, and to acknowledge that there would never be another Bobby Moore. To commemorate the occasion, suitably challenging opponents were sought and found in the form of Spanish giants Villareal. They were runners-up in La Liga from the previous season, and therefore qualifiers for the Champions League tournament that season.

Legendary stadium announcer Jeremy Nicholas took up his position at the edge of the pitch and welcomed the sides as they came out, a little late after all the pre-match formalities. Matthew Upson was the captain, and he wore the number 6 shirt as he had done the previous season. He would be 'retiring it' at half time, when he would resume with number 15 on his back. It's poignant to look at the ten last seasons of West Ham players who wore the number six shirt before it was retired.

Season	No.	Player	League apps	Cup apps	Goals
2007-08	6	Matthew Upson	29 league apps	4 cup apps	1 goal
2006-07	6	George McCartney	22 league apps	3 cup apps	0 goals
2005-06	6	Carl Fletcher	12 league apps	5 cup apps	1 goal
2004-05	6	Carl Fletcher	32 league apps	3 cup apps	2 goals
2003-04	6	Michael Carrick	35 league apps	5 cup apps	1 goal
2002-03	6	Michael Carrick	30 league apps	4 cup apps	1 goal
2001-02	6	Hayden Foxe	6 league apps	1 cup app	0 goals
2000-01	6	No Number 6			
1999-00	6	Neil Ruddock	15 league apps	10 cup apps	1 goal

Apart from Carrick, there isn't anyone worthy. Carrick was in fact the only Number 6 since Bobby Moore left the club to be recognised by the fans when he was voted Hammer of The Year Runner-Up (in 2003-04). This was as much for the fact that he was the only international in the side who'd stayed at Upton Park after that terrible relegation season as anything else.

West Ham weren't the first sporting club to 'retire' a number. In 1934 the Totonto Maple Leafs Ice Hockey team retired their number 6, in tribute to Ace Bailey. Closer to home in both senses, Manchester City, Lens and Lyon all retired numbers in honour of Marc Vivien-Foé, who died in 2003 whilst playing in the Confederations Cup. Cameroon also wanted to retire his international number, but FIFA in their legendary wisdom, refused.

Foé played for West Ham in the 1998-99 and 1999-2000 seasons, under Harry Redknapp, wearing shirt number 13. That number was not worn again by an outfield player until 2007, though Stephen Bywater wore it in 2005-06 for one substitute appearance. Luis Boa Morte, is the only outfield player to wear it since. He took it when he joined the club in January 2007, but then wore 34 throughout the following season. From 2008-09 he went back to wearing it for three years until his departure at the end of 2010-11.

Prior to Foé, the other West Ham players who have worn the number 13 make for an interesting and obscure bunch: David Terrier wore it in 1997-98 for just one substitute appearance against Barnsley in the opening game of the season. He never played for the club again. In 1996-97, Hugo Porfirio wore the number with four goals in twenty-seven mercurial appearances. You then have to go back three seasons earlier for the first recorded use of it, with Gerry Peyton, West Ham's reserve goalkeeper, in 1993-94. Despite a career totalling 608 appearances, Peyton didn't ever take to the field for the Hammers.

Is it an unlucky number? Roy Carroll lost a substantial five figure sum to Teddy 'Devil Fish' Sheringham, playing poker in the Upton Park 'Academy' Card School. I don't really have an opinion either way. All I know is that Marc-Vivien Foe is the most talented player to have worn it for West Ham United since the club first took squad numbers.

Jeremy Nicholas is now welcoming both sides onto the pitch for this historic friendly, the winners to be given the Bobby Moore Cup. As I look down the list of names, I look nervously at the stadium announcer. Just how would he pronounce the following?

Joan Capdevila, Santi Cazorla, Guillermo Franco, Javi Venta, Sebastian Eguren, Ariel Ibagaza... and the list went on. As if that wasn't tough enough, the company operating the big screens had decided to pioneer a new approach to presenting the West Ham Team, with giant sized football card pictures of the players to synchronise with their names being read out. It all went horribly wrong as the person cuing up the photos was unable for some reason to show them at the right time. It looked terrible, but that wasn't all. Unfortunately for Jeremy the referee Rob Styles seemed uninterested in the fact that the opposition names were still to be read out, and blew the whistle for kick-off as they came up on he screen. Rather than continue reading them as the sides played, Jeremy said, resignedly, 'You can work the rest out for yourselves.' Fans could indeed have then turned to page 37 of the lavish A4 programme to acquaint themselves with the remaining Villareal names should they have wished to hurl abuse at them individually, or indeed to practise their Spanish pronunciation.

It was a good decision as, with the first move of the match, West Ham attacked, and before you could say Andoni Zubizarreta Urreta, Carlton Cole had tucked the ball in the back of the Villareal goal. Cazorla (stress on the second syllable 'zor') equalised half an hour later, and that was how it stayed until full time. In keeping with the sporting atmosphere of the day, both sides shared the trophy, presented by Bobby Moore's widow, Stephanie.

What was to become known as the 'sacking season' then claimed its first victims when West Ham's (since himself departed) club CEO Scott Duxbury went into the PA Room at half time and sacked everyone in his eyeline, This included the advertising board team, the big screen operators, the replay and sound operators and last of all, incredibly, *he sacked Jeremy Nicholas*. He had not been happy about the sloppy PA image the club had seemingly presented on such a sensitive afternoon, and he left behind him a suitably stunned room of unemployed people.

On my way home from the game, I was blissfully ignorant of all of this, and remained so until a telephone call on the Monday of the following week. I had not undertaken any official match day duties for the club since they had decided not to continue with me as match commentator after relegation at the end of the 2002-03 season. Belt tightening, austerity measures, general meanness, however you want to see it, any club about to lose its Premiership funds has to dispense with some of its costs. Six seasons later, however, the CEO's dismissal of the entire PA department had left a gaping hole which the club had a matter of days to fill. An eleventh hour offer from the company who had run the PA operation and big screens at the club restored everyone's terms of employment for the first game of the season the following Saturday against Wigan Athletic. Everyone that was, except the stadium announcer.

'*Do you think you could do it?*' the voice at the other end of the line asked.

'*Of course,*' a voice from inside of me spoke. '*But what's happening to Jeremy?*'

The company that ran the operation at the club had told Duxbury that things would work better if they employed their own man to do the announcing. And now, it was becoming clear, I was their man. I had worked with them as commentator for five years, and had produced the club videos and DVDs for a decade. *But what would happen to Jeremy?*

My boss at the club was a tall imposing woman, probably half my age but with several times the business stature, who went under a name that demanded deference. Nicola Lord. She was well-briefed and well-organised, she knew what she wanted, and it was clear that she was going to get it. Her professionalism was infectious, and she had the whole team focused within the first minute of her arrival in the PA room. I knew what my job was; I had discussed its demands and responsibilities many times with Jeremy. The only difference was that I would be in the PA Room, and would not be inhabiting his spot in the dugout with the team. This place would be filled by our new floor manager, who was to liaise with me on the talkback, West Ham footage and stats legend Jason Stone.

Before the ground was opened, I made a few announcements to ensure the volume was right on my voice, and heard the results. There is something untoward about hearing your voice booming round the stadium from speakers beyond the glass in front of you. It is almost as if they're being spoken by another person doing a passable imitation. But I was not fazed by the challenge, and was thrilled to be the man on the mike for the afternoon. It seemed obvious to me that Jeremy Nicholas would return once the CEO had calmed down. In the meantime I would enjoy my new-found position, and it wasn't long before I had announced two West Ham goals, scored in the third and tenth minute by Dean Ashton. As his name left my lips, the cheers rang round the ground. What was particularly strange was getting a text from my mate Mike in New York, who had heard my voice announce the goals, from the bar where he was watching the football live in the East Village over breakfast. (NYC time is five hours behind ours) We won the game 2-1 after a tough second half and I sent the crowd home to *Twist and Shout*. As far as the coverage went, I decided that my approach would be, 'if it ain't broke, don't fix it.'

Game One: npower Championship 2011-12, Upton Park
Sunday 7th August 2011 (25,680)
Referee: Howard Webb (Yorks)

West Ham United 0   **Cardiff City 1**
                                          Phillips 90

(West Ham: 22nd in the table, 0 points from 3)

Arguably the most significant West Ham v Cardiff City fixture came in April 1962, at Ninian Park. It was the first time Bobby Moore, Geoff Hurst and Martin Peters had ever played for the first team together. Hammers had beaten Cardiff 4-1 at home three days earlier, with Peters making his debut, but this time Peters found himself having to go in goal in just his third game for the club. This was for the last half hour after the stand-in keeper and debutant Brian Rhodes had dislocated his shoulder. It was already 2-0 by then, but Peters conceded one more to make the final score 3-0. Cardiff were still relegated at the end of their second season in the top division, and they haven't been back since.

50 years later and Malky MacKay, manager of Cardiff and ex-Championship Hammer, gets a big hand. That's nothing compared with the deafening roar of applause for Sam Allardyce. Big man, big accolade. Perhaps for the time being, we'll call him Sam Accolade.

The referee is World Cup Final whistler Howard Webb, moonlighting on his only Premiership-free weekend for some time. That's either a great compliment or a man desperate for cash.

Earnshaw volleys over from the right from an acute angle on seventy seconds, as Hammers spend the first few minutes on a very sunny Sunday in a kind of 'we're a relegated team – oh, shit' haze. Irons force a corner after three minutes, which is wasted.

Cardiff seem like a team happy to be where they are. Piquionne picks up a loose ball on the right and hares down on goal, his flat shot deflected for a corner by Cardiff's David Marshall. Another wasted corner. Has Sam got an approach where corners are concerned? If he did, that would make him the first West Ham manager ever to do so. Classic West Ham for corners: send the big men up.

Now Parker breaks through the middle, beating the Cardiff offside trap

- will the soon-to-be-leaving score the first in a promotion season? Nope. Number 6 Anthony Gerrard, a typical Championship defender slides in with a perfectly timed Championship tackle to take the ball of the 2011 Hammer of the Year's toes.

James Tomkins looks powerful and strong in defence, though the memory of his nightmare against Wolves in 2009-10 still hovers across the frontal lobe.

Matt Taylor's free kick curls over the wall, the ball dipping late to force a fingertip save from Marshall. Now it's Parker running to the line to flick a cross in that Taylor heads over. Next Sears blasts over from the edge of the six-yard box when it would have been easier to write a five act restoration comedy.

The Sir Trevor Brooking Stand is occupied by about three hundred Cardiff fans. A policeman on the tube told me they had been forced to hire a fleet of coaches from Cardiff to Southend from where they had been told to pick up their tickets for the game. There are about twenty people in the upper tier - strange.

Cardiff muster their first attack for ten minutes with a throw-in towards the near post by Aron Gunnarsson. This catches the wind and loops out for a free-kick untouched by human foot, head or hand - unlike the far post header from Cowie that deflects off Ilunga's shoulder and is tipped round the post by Green.

Nolan picks out Taylor on the left with a spectacular forty yard pass... Hammers have a free-kick wide on the right - which Taylor takes left-footed - Reid's header looks good but is fortuitously blocked by a defender. Kenny Miller is in trouble for a poorly-timed tackle on Reid, but Webb is in World Cup Final no send off mood.

Half an hour gone and Hammers still goalless in 2011-12. West Ham's right back is Reid, a New Zealander, and recent World Cup performer. Hammers' captain Nolan hits the ball just over right-footed from the edge of the area. Taylor picks out Piquionne wide on the right, but he has neither the ideas nor the pace to turn the pass into anything. Piquionne's Samsonite shorn dreadlocks seem to have taken away his insight, vision and trickery. All there is left now is a guy with a businessman's haircut going to an interview for a job he won't get.

Now Cardiff have a free-kick in a dangerous position; Rob Earnshaw shapes as if he knows something... Green waits... Shot goes into the wall from Earnshaw... Webb says take it again... Parker ran out too soon... Whittingham beats the wall with a low shot, but not Green, who turns it away for a corner.

It is pissing down. Having another look at that Green save on the giant screens - excellent. Taylor tries a long range shot that is deflected up and into the keeper's arms. Three minutes until half-time. Suddenly a gloom descends from grey clouds, and the game starts to have a tired mid-season look about it. Really, it's a win at any cost, isn't it? Hammers have looked as enterprising as you'd expect the home side in such a fixture to look, but not much more than that. And this is Cardiff City, remember. Webb blasts a shrill lungful to send the fans off to the loos and the booze. Jeremy Nicholas - remember him? - plays Hard-Fi's *Hard To Beat* - does he mean Cardiff? It's still raining.

Football is my religion. Upton Park is my church. So say the new tee-shirts on the block. They should perhaps add I am a Championship relegation atheist. Otherwise all it is going to promote is sympathy or, worse, ridicule.

The strains of that 1975 classic by the FA Cup Winners bounce round the empty Walls of the Sir Trevor Brooking stand and back into play. Cardiff haven't turned up for the second half yet. when they do arrive - a full ninety seconds later, they are booed.

First action of the second half sees Nolan forcing his way into the area as the ball follows him, a defender tackles. Wasted. Peter Whittingham wins a free-kick for Cardiff at the other end. Green is beaten but it's wide - he looks to have touched it on the replay, but a goal kick is given. The long ball game that Accolade's critics have feared is in full flow. Green bowls one out this time, just to be different. McNaughton finds Earnshaw, but even Cardiff are already looking tired.

Piquionne and Hudson get in a tussle fighting for the ball out on the right; it's no surprise when Howard Webb blows in favour of the defender. I am starting to feel a tremendous sadness for the Cardiff fans, up at sunrise, Southend bound to collect their tickets with the promise of a sunny day... and now this. Looking across at them (they've gone awfully quiet) you could probably cram them all into an overnighter from Calais. It wouldn't be much of a detour from Southend. The bottom corner of the Chicken Run have decided that there night be something to gain from entering into a barney-baiter with the 200 Cardiff fans. At least West Ham have reduced their season ticket costs by 10%. Not a bad deal, as there will be more games and they've got a better manager. Or at least a horse manager for the course that is the nPower Championship, who's managed in the Premier League for years!

Parker breaks down the right and slips the ball back to Taylor who fires in a low left-footed shot that Marshall sees late and claws away. Piquionne's shot is painfully blocked by Hudson... this is more like it. Parker down the right again, cross blocked. Watching Parker's antics is like watching your favourite uncle tell his best stories at a family gathering before he emigrates. And you know he'll have to go, as Jim Reeves might have said. There is a country music song in this somewhere. Let's commission Rufus Wainwright VI to write it.

On the hour Sears fires in a cross which Piquionne meets powerfully only to see his shot come back off the angle of post and crossbar. Closest yet.

Enger-land, Enger-land, Enger-land! the Hammers' fans suddenly start singing. It's been that kind of a game. Cardiff sub Rudy Gestede replaces Earnshaw and almost immediately has an excellent chance to head in from a low right-wing cross. He fluffs it. Glad we're in the Championship, otherwise it really was Welsh curtains.

20 minutes to go and we have a corner. Taylor will take. Ilunga to loft back in... Great header in the scramble by Tomkins... Another corner. Noble tries to beat one too many defenders in the area and the ball goes loose again. Joey O'Brien pushes it forward to Sears, but Marshall is alert to the danger. Hammers are almost caught on the break, but this isn't the Premiership, remember.

Triple substitution: Noble off for Collison, Piquonne off for Cole and Conway off for Joe Mason. Carlton Cole might have thought if no-one stepped in for him that he was pretty much guaranteed that front striker's place. If he scores in the last 14 minutes... 'Waltzer Fuckin Poynt?' yells Mud Mouth from behind. His first contribution of the afternoon. Mud Mouth and his twin have season ticket seats just behind the upper section of the Media section, and only yell their torn-throat inanities when the team are playing badly. If the team play well, they are silent. Fuck, but they're going to irritate me this season.

Great cross by Taylor gets a corner and, from it, Tomkins header is steered towards the goal-line by Nolan, but cleared off it by McNaughton. Parker hammers in the ricochet but over the bar. Now the third sub and Pablo Barrera is on for Sears. Taylor's ball in finds Cole just offside. The Cardiff fans are singing now- an away point at Upton Park looks like a good catch, especially with so many draws in the championship yesterday. Six minutes to go - is there some magic ending still to come?

Cardiff's a shithole, Cardiff's a shithole... The Hammers fans sing. Two headed opportunities open up, first for Cardiff (Gestede again) and then frustration for Taylor at the far post. Crazy rain. Peter Whittingham hits a left foot shot that misses by not very much. Now Cardiff do score, two minutes into injury time, and it's new signing Kenny Miller. Gestede robs Ilunga down the right and hits the ball back behind the six yard line where Miller scoops it onto his better foot, brings it under control and fires past Green, whose hands become momentarily virtual.

One-nil to the sheep shaggers! the Cardiff fans sing. And well they might. In the last minute of injury time Barrera hits in a low cross, but Marshall is in control and grabs it comfortably. Nightmare start. But then no-ones under any illusions about what this season might be offering.

Are they?

West Ham: 1 Green, 2 Reid, 4 Nolan, 5 Tomkins, 8 Parker, 14 Taylor, 16 Noble (10 Collison 74), 17 O'Brien, 19 Sears (12 Barrera 82), 23 Ilunga, 30 Piquionne (9 Cole 75)

A Riot Of My Own. And where better to start than in Tottenham. It's Monday night and the family of the young man who was shot last week by police have been waiting outside the police station for five hours for an explanation of what happened. They haven't been given one, and so the local yokels have an excuse for smashing up a few shops, burning cars and looting.

My media company, formed five years ago, has covered games for West Ham over the last few years, and now has been offered the chance to cover the games that the BBC and Sky are not bothered about sending more than one cameraman to. Big Sam wants complete DVDs of each game to pore over after the match as he fine tunes his promotion. We got the good news that we're in the frame for the job earlier today.

I have a small fleet of camera operators to draw on; most are currently on holiday but I have scraped together a crew for Wednesday night's first round Carling Cup game against Aldershot. I needn't have bothered. First sporting casualty of the developing riots is the cup game the following night, spelt out on a BBC News crawler under the orange blur of a blazing furniture warehouse in Croydon.

There haven't been any riots like this for thirty years, so the news crews on every channel have gone into overdrive about the potential causes. Social, political, racial... all are agreed, disputed and invariably rejected. Social networking supposedly has a part to play, but the gormless ecstasy of trainer and mobile phone looting seems an impossible conclusion to a carefully planned operation of protest. Most of the hooded children on the rampage already own the very items that they are stealing, a fact evidenced by the discarded detritus on the streets.

I think, further to that comment about anniversaries, that this may be connected to the Brixton Riots, thirty years ago, also occurring two years into a new political administration's term, though in April, a little earlier in the year. The 1981 riots were then described as the worst example of civil unrest in a century, and attributed to 'social and economic problems', not exactly a radical conclusion. Then we had Lord Scarman, but for this century's worst example of civil unrest, we'll have the 'Riots, Communities and Victims panel' chaired by Darra Singh, and with its very own tweeting address for communal involvement, @riotspanel. (spoiler alert: Easy to read that as Riot Spaniel). Fantastic. I guess they'll reach the same kind of conclusion, though, with a walk on part for the 'Global Financial Crisis' somewhere in the summary.

Game Two: npower Championship, 2011-12, Keepmoat Stadium
Saturday 13th August 2011 (11,344)
Referee: Scott Mathieson (Cheshire)

Doncaster Rovers 0   West Ham United 1
                             Nolan 5

(West Ham: 14th in the table, 3 points from 6)

This might unimaginatively be referred to as a potential banana skin for Sam, but the Big Man is already getting up after last week's injury time mugging, so the floor isn't too far to fall. His choice signing Kevin Nolan, who was a little disappointing last weekend, takes just five minutes to score his first for West Ham, volleying Jack Collison's far post cross into the roof of the Doncaster net. Collison is the only change from last week's Cardiff starting eleven, replacing the 'industrious' Freddie Sears.

Sears was last week's man of the match according to some of the voting Hammers fans, which proved a selection poisoned chalice. This might be as good a time as any to mention his one 'goal' for Crystal Palace whilst on loan there exactly two years ago, in August 2009. (don't waste your time heading to You Tube to revisit it; the Football League have taken it down) Referee Rob Shoebridge with his two assistant refs were the only people at Ashton Gate who didn't see it hit the stanchion inside the back of the net. Nicky Maynard scored a predictable winner in the final minute. With hindsight, further irony. And Hammer-to-be Clive Allen had done the same thirty years previously, also for Crystal Palace.

In the deep water of injury time, just when they conceded last week's Cardiff winner, Carlton Cole, shaping for a penalty area shot on goal, is manhandled by Doncaster's George Friend, but ref Scott Mathieson's sharp blast on the whistle is for full time.

After a small bout of soul searching, I have resisted a two mile walk to Doncaster Rovers' ground from the station and the sixty quid return rail fare. I feel quite confident Hammers would win, and have instead put my 'away games cash' stash into the three point promise of a visit to Vicarage Road on Tuesday. Watford have already lost there today to Derby County. I have to confess it's not unpleasant to imagine back to back away wins for West Ham. It doesn't happen in the Premiership (though, strangely, Glenn Roeder managed it at Chelsea, Fulham and Ipswich Town back in the relegation season of 2002-03).

In the following week's programme, the referee is listed as Stuart, not Scott, Mathieson. Stuart Mathieson, however, is a church organist who plays the cello, and is also (on Linkedin) a Heathcare Professional. But he ain't no referee.

The last point before this game is forever forgotten is the observation that Doncaster Rovers' starting eleven feature one Welsh and ten English players. No foreign players, but the Congolese defender Herita Ilunga will move to Doncaster Rovers in March 2012.

West Ham: 1 Green, 2 Reid, 4 Nolan, 5 Tomkins, 8 Parker, 14 Taylor, 16 Noble, 17 O'Brien, 10 Collison (19 Sears 72), 23 Ilunga (25 Stanislas 86), 30 Piquionne (9 Cole 62)

Game Three: npower Championship, 2011-12, Vicarage Road
Tuesday 16th August 2011 (14,747)
Referee: Dean Whitestone (Northants)

Watford 0   West Ham United 4

Tomkins 3
O'Brien 45
Cole 71
Parker 90

(West Ham: 5th in the table, 6 points from 9)

When was the last time West Ham won two away games on the trot? You might call yourself Stats Man, or even Stats Woman, but you're unlikely to realise it was way back in December 2007. It was on the anniversary of Alan Curbishley's first full year in charge at the club, when a 1-0 Dean Ashton inspired win at Blackburn Rovers was followed by a 2-1 victory at Middlesbrough which featured a memorable last minute winner by Curbishley's villain-turned-hero Scott Parker. It was Curbishley's 100th victory as a Premiership manager, and an echo of a similar feat (1-0 at Birmingham, followed by 3-0 at Reading) earlier that season. He'd also done it over Wigan (3-0) followed by Manchester United (1-0) the previous season, and Blackburn (2-1) and Arsenal (1-0) a few weeks earlier. Strangely it is something in the top flight, like finishing the season with a positive goal difference, that West Ham managers have always found a problem. Alan Pardew managed it just the once: Aston Villa (2-1) and Arsenal (3-2) in early 2006. Glenn Roeder managed three in the ludicrously eventful West Ham relegation season of 2002-03: Chelsea (3-2), Sunderland (1-0) and Fulham (1-0).

So returning to 2011-12 and Sam Accolade's belt, under which there currently resides the minor miniscule trophy of relegation favourites Doncaster Rovers. Sam has taken Piquionne out for Cole, the England striker playing his familiar lonely man up front role cultivated by previous managerial assignments.

Apart from an effort from Watford after just thirty-four seconds, there is little punch from the 'Yellow Army'. In the third minute a diagonal left wing cross from the perennially inspirational Matt Taylor hangs in the air long enough to be met powerfully with his head at the far post by James Tomkins. It's his first West Ham goal and for a second successive game an early strike from West Ham brings the home side out to attack.

Like an eager heavyweight title challenger, Watford fire in punches across most of the first half, few of them troubling Rob Green as much as the home fans' gleeful chant of *You Let Your Country Down!* to the old Paolo Di Canio Verdi tune. This is a 'hilarious' reference to Green's 'fumble' of a Clint Dempsey shot during the USA v England game in the 2010 World Cup. That came just over a year ago, after which the Italian England manager Fabio Capello dropped him. Capello's rather harsh 'one strike and you're out' policy was the coward's alternative to dropping Rooney, Heskey, Wright-Phillips and Crouch who didn't manage a single decent shot on goal in the full ninety minutes. Green hasn't played for England since, unlike the four forwards that night in 2010. However, he shuts his detractors up with a brilliant fingertip save on 15 minutes from Sordell's goalbound blistering shot.

Watford punch and punch to no effect, like a gnat on the neck of a Dunkleosteus. The predictable first half injury time killer counterpunch arrives from another West Ham goalscoring virgin of the night, Joey O'Brien. Arriving late from the right back position he is looking more and more comfortable in as the season progresses. Watford heads are down as they retreat from their exhausting and fruitless first half.

West Ham are out first for the second half, looking as fresh as they did at the start of the game. Watford on the other hand look like they're approaching the Mall in the London Marathon. I can't see them scoring enough goals to get anything out of this game, and it's then that I realise and remember the allure of the Championship. West Ham fans sing *We can see you sneaking out!* at the Watford fans, as early as the 70th minute.

West Ham round off a miserable night for Watford with Cole's tap-in on 71 minutes from Ilunga's overlapping cross. Parker delivers a classy finish to complete a quality co-ordinated three man move in the last minute. As with the other four goals tonight, Parker does not celebrate with the other members of the team.

West Ham: 1 Green, 2 Reid, 4 Nolan, 5 Tomkins (15 Faye 68), 8 Parker, 14 Taylor, 16 Noble, 17 O'Brien, 10 Collison (20 Faubert 76), 23 Ilunga (25 Stanislas 86), 9 Cole (30 Piquionne 74)

Game Four: npower Championship 2011-12, Upton Park
Sunday 21st August 2011 (28,252)
Referee: Michael Oliver (Ashington)

West Ham United 2	**Leeds United 2**
Cole 6	McCormack 59

Kisnorbo og 62   Clayton 90

(West Ham: 7th in the table, 7 points from 12)

A second successive Sunday home game, live on Sky, against style pretenders and Ken Bates' pocket money purchase, Leeds United. The controversy-smitten Yorkshire terriers haven't lost at Upton Park in six visits, chiefly because when they were crap and in the bargain basement divisions, Hammers were enjoying their last Premiership reign and didn't play them.

I've downed two cups of tea, a plastic cup of R White's Lemonade and a bottle of Highland Spring. This is to rehydrate after a ten mile run through Crane Park this morning. Probably the only good thing about an early kick off is how it gets me out of bed to work off some of the weekend's excesses.

'Big Sam's Claret and Blue Army' are introduced by Jeremy Nicholas - no changes from the last two (away) wins, and John Carew on the bench. Hollywood director and England manager Francis Ford Capello is in the Directors' Box with Sir Trev, so big opps for Scott Parker to prove you don't need to be playing in the Premiership to be considered for International football. Leeds are wearing all black with luminous green trim; it looks like a hastily assembled Nike range, destined for the bargain basement.

Ilunga's long throw is flicked on by Cole, and tipped over by Lonergan. The subsequent cross is headed forcefully goalwards by James Tomkins, in a similar time and position to his goal on Tuesday, but is again acrobatically flicked over by the industrious Leeds' keeper. Then Matt Taylor's corner is flicked home off the outside of his right boot by Carlton Cole on the edge of the six yard box, his second in two games, and West Ham are ahead after just five minutes.

To their eternal credit, the Leeds fans respond immediately with a stack of predictably tiresome and limited monosyllabic chants. Lifted, Leeds respond swiftly and it's soon Green's turn for the acrobatic tip over from a flick by Ivory Coast midfielder Max Gradel. From the corner Tom Lees' header is volleyed against the angle of post and crossbar by Robert Snodgrass, with Green well beaten. West Ham's defence suddenly looks a bit strudelled, but for now has survived the retaliatory rush. Leeds' manager Simon Grayson is all tightly-folded arms in the technical area, while his team are getting their shit together. They look a lot more organised than Cardiff, but then West Ham are not the same side as the hesitant nervebags of a fortnight ago. They are playing like a team of confident and slick professionals, and Noble finishes off a fine five man move with a curling shot that Lonergan has to crouch awkwardly to collect.

The Leeds' keeper Lonergan is tall, thin and wiry, like the survivor of a Tour de France peloton pile up. I look in vain for his bicycle, parked in the back of the net.

Sam Allardyce has a strange black plastic tube hanging from his shirt which could be anything from a microphone to an emaciated winger from Tony Carr's U-16 Academy side.

Leeds have a penalty on 25 minutes, awarded by referee Michael Oliver, who at 26 is almost the youngest person on the pitch. Handball in the area by Nolan. I remember the season when Green was not beaten by the first five penalties of the season and hope for a lightning strike. Max Gradel again, who embraces my dream by scuffing it wide of Green's right hand post. Green has guessed right and may even have saved it if it had been two feet nearer and on target, but no matter. I think it may be one of those seasons.

Cole is bundled over as he is put through on the half hour... But the referee gives no penalty. *You're just a shit Emile Heskey!* the Leeds' fans sing. Gradel again with a shot from twenty yards that Green palms wide. Now he fashions an opportunity, crossing to the far post but Keogh can't direct his header properly. The referee gives a corner, the pint-sized twat. At the other end Leeds number 48 Darren O'Dea is sent tumbling to the floor after an aerial tussle with the shit Emile Heskey. He doesn't get up - must be the weight of the numbers on the back of his shirt.

Season tickets are now 'eight per cent off' according to the advert, though after today that'll be only a fraction more of the season's fixtures that have passed, so not quite the bargain that it might at first seem.

I remember a game here against Leeds when Trevor Sinclair wore some kind of Frankenstein facial mask to protect his jaw. He looked like Mike Tyson's dead prison sparring partner.

Hammers are soaking up some attractive play from Leeds; Grayson has turned magician and, as his uncle might have said, has managed defensively to 'shut that door'. A crisp defensive header by O'Brien relieves the pressure in the area. Two minutes of injury time. The first half has raced by. O'Brien again, this time robbing Snodgrass of possession, probably the best in this first 45 minutes. Nolan has a rare chance at the other end, but the ball is whipped off his toes by Kisnorbo. Just the one goal from Cole separates the sides at half-time.

I note over the break that West Ham have only beaten Leeds twice in their last 26 meetings, and immediately wish I hadn't read that fact. There's something about discovering such weighty stats during a game that appeals to the superstitious in me. Hammers start the second half confidently with a corner, and Useless Heskey should do better with his unmarked header from the edge of the six yard box. The only thing identifying this Leeds United as the collective 'Leeds' is their name and their fans. You can ditch the players, you can ditch the owners, you can ditch the managers, but you can't ditch the fans. You can't ditch the name either, unless you're Milton Keynes Dons or the Chicago Twatbulls.

Leeds' howls greet a firm tackle in the area by Parker, but no penalty. Well done the child prodigy ref. Snodgrass' corner - which is all he's going to get - is wasted. McCormack, another Leeds' player in his forties (44) misses an excellent chance from the edge of the area. But those fans, that Leeds can't get rid of, they are singing, bouncing and celebrating as if they've won the match. Do they know something that we don't? I'm reminded of the perverse days of fan solidarity, when home fans often cheered opposition fans who ran onto the pitch, scarves aloft, only to be caught and taken off the pitch and out of the ground by a burly policeman, to the home chants of *Loyal supporter!*

For some reason, with only 53 minutes elapsed, I find myself wishing that the game was over. Collison is having a quiet game today after his fine performance on Tuesday. Green's handling of crosses is excellent, which is a relief as he has plenty to field. Faubert is off the bench. Collison suddenly has an excellent chance but spurns it, heading straight at the keeper. Green fields a speculative shot from McCormack which bounces out from his chest, fortuitously, to the safety of Ilunga's boot. Some excellent defensive marking from O'Brien prevents a well co-ordinated move by Leeds from progressing beyond the edge of the area. Faubert replaces Collison on 59 minutes, but Leeds are soon level. For the second home game in succession, Ilunga is asleep on the right as a swiftly taken free kick reaches Snodgrass, whose cross is eventually steered home just on the hour by the irritating McCormack. See what I mean. The pace of the game will now have to lift for West Ham to get the win that is necessary. Or perhaps not. Faubert's first touch since he's got on the pitch, a right wing cross, is viciously volleyed into his own net by Patrick Kisnorbo. Brilliant.

They might well have predicted the equaliser, but the Leeds fans hadn't reckoned on one of their own slapping it home. Leeds have a free kick, which McCockmack is taking, and like a cockerel, he slaps it over. High, wide and ugly.

I think Carew is about to make his West Ham debut, replacing the struggling Cole on 66 minutes. Are the Hammers' fans booing him? Or is that 'boo' as in *Careeeeeuhw...* Carew is wearing eleven and wins his first tussle in the air. Faubert looks hungry and a little leaner than last season. Maybe those two are linked. Tomkins has won pretty much everything that's been up for winning. Carew tries a shot on the turn which goes just wide. Faubert's run and cross, aiming for Carew, almost leads to another own goal from a Kisnorbo tackled clearance. Now Tomkins heads down Taylor's corner to Reid, but Lonergan shuffles it away for another corner. This has become a 'great' game.

Green collects the ball smartly after another protracted Leeds' move, but Leeds are not giving up. I hate to admit it, but their fans have been brilliant. They have a free kick on the right which the wall blocks; Parker brings the ball away. We approach the 76th minute. Parker's brilliant one-two with Noble ends up with his effort hitting the far post with Tour de France in the cycling sheds. Goalden McCormack is off for Ramon Nunez. Parker's performance should have demonstrated to Capello that he can cut it at any level. The Sub Loonez has a chance to break, but fouls O'Brien. Ilunga has proved something today, other than a predilection for snoozing when in possession of the ball; what a long throw he has. Tomkins meets another corner with a firm but wide header. Noble goes off eight minutes from the end to be replaced by Piquionne. Interesting substitution. Nunez's curling free kick is toe-poked over the bar to the relief of a rather static-looking Hammers' defence.

Grayson looks like a man coming to terms with another defeat. Where is Everard when you need him? *We All Love Leeds!* the fans sing, but they are not making the play like they were earlier in the first half. John Carew looks like the man for a 4-5-1 formation. West Ham man of the match as voted for by the sponsors, the England Environmentalist and Architects' Pratts Limited, is Scott Parker. We know that's only because he'll now have to spend half an hour in their private box answering all their prawn cocktail munching Directors' inanity questions, and signing the menu chits for their kids. More drama in the Leeds' goalmouth, but no third goal.

Up the other end however, in the 90th minute, Adam Clayton equalises for Leeds after Howson's shot comes back off the underside of the crossbar. Fans go cockles. Oh piss and blackberries. There are four minutes' injury time, we are informed, but West Ham don't do late home goals, do they?

Leeds now look for a winner and there's a melée in the area that the referee seems unable to control. In the end it's a free kick to West Ham. Time for one last attack, perhaps? The ref is talking to the assistant referee about something. A Leeds player is booked. Their fans pillory Green with *USA, USA, USA!*

The first Mud Mouth twin starts on one of his endless rants about 'useless' this and 'rubbish' that. It's the first time he's made any noise today. It's then I realise that it isn't to be the three points it had looked like being. That man's voice is invariably the harbinger of mediocrity. That's why I've realised I hate it so much. Somehow, the moment I read it, I knew that stat would be extending to just two wins in the last 27 meetings with Leeds.

West Ham: 1 Green, 2 Reid, 4 Nolan, 5 Tomkins, 8 Parker, 9 Cole (11 Carew 66), 10 Collison (18 Faubert 58), 14 Taylor, 16 Noble (30 Piquionne 82), 17 O'Brien, 23 Ilunga

The Leeds game, I reflect in the week, really felt like an old-fashioned top of the table tug of war. Odd, really, as this is a side that hasn't enjoyed (suffered?) Premier League football for quite some time. Their fans, however, managed to raise the game to the top level, and can take most of the credit for the point Leeds took back with them.

So amongst the stories of riots up and down the country that have become a tedious news item for the last fortnight, Sean, Mark and me set about putting together a camera and video mixer kit sophisticated enough to capture West Ham's First Round Carling Cup efforts against Aldershot Town on Wednesday evening.

We spend most of the next day preparing the kit and practising live mixing with the different cameras. Sean's position over the other side of town in Beckenham requires that he checks his kit will be okay for the mix on the night of the game. While he leans across to get the right lens, his three year old daughter brushes past his camera, set up in the garden on the tripod, and despite the contact being minimal, it's still sufficient to send it and the tripod, with heat-seeking missile precision, onto the one yard of concrete patio below. Despite a full thirty metres of grass just a few feet further out, the lens strikes the patio, revealing, on closer furtive enquiry, a half centimetre scratch right in the middle of the lens. He's on the phone to me within a minute.

Hearing a man cry is truly one of the most awful things anyone might be expected to endure in life, but if you've been unfortunate enough to own a professional hi-definition broadcast quality camera that has cost you more than £7500, and you've damaged the lens, you will understand that man's sorrow.

Armed with a spare second camera, borrowed at the last minute, we arrive at the ground at 5pm, and by 7pm have managed to get the pictures up and running on the big screens. It's then that I again remember the story of Steve Katz, the cameraman who filmed the famous 1983 record-breaking West Ham v Bury League Cup tie with his own money, the 10-0 victory, and made a killing from the video. I would be lying to you if I denied being unable to sleep the previous evening, overwhelmed by excited thoughts about a new cup tie scoring record against Aldershot; who knows, maybe 15-0? No, let's not be greedy, 12-0 would be fine. Even 11-0 would be enough to break the record. After all, Sam Allardyce will want to put out a full strength side to ensure he finally gets his first victory at Upton Park. Won't he? He will resist the temptation to put out a team of reserves on the night, most younger than the kids-for-a-quid who'll be coming to watch them.

Won't he?

Carling Cup First Round 2011-12, Upton Park
Wednesday 24th August 2011 (19,879)
Referee: Graham Scott (Oxfordshire)

West Ham United 1   **Aldershot Town 2**
Stanislas 16   Guttridge 78
                               Hylton 89

This game should have been played on the first night of the Riots, though it wasn't, because of them, if that makes any sense.

It's the first time I can remember a Hammers' game being postponed because of a riot that had nothing to do with the game. With the Millwall fixture next month, it's worth remembering that Carling Cup derby brawl a few years ago. My own experience was that I could only get to the ground that night as I had my West Ham pass on me. The police were turning people back towards the station all along Green Street. An unopened bottle full of beer was lobbed up from behind me and just missed my right shoulder, smashing open in the street in front of me. Some weeks later I was taking my phone out of my jacket pocket when I retrieved a small shard of brown glass that must have been nestling there safely since the game for almost a month. Not quite sure how I didn't slice off the top of my finger taking it out.

Aldershot FC were wound up in March 1992, and forced to leave the league. They were the first team to suffer that fate since Accrington Stanley in 1961. Despite this, just thirteen months earlier they had held West Ham United to a goalless draw in the third round of the FA Cup, before crashing out 6-1 in the replay, both games played at Upton Park.

The following year, in March 1992, a group of local supporters set up a new club Aldershot Town, and they joined the Isthmian League Division Three, five tiers below where they had just been playing. Sixteen years later, the club's new model were back in the football league, where they have remained for the last three years. Ex-Womble Dean Holdsworth is their boss. He once played under Sam Allardyce at Bolton for four years, and regards him as his managerial mentor.

We are hoping to be filming a decent number of games this season, so long as the Aldershot footage doesn't upset the Prozone team at the club. They need the footage to write up all those Opta stats of passes, incomplete passes, completed passes, girls with dark glasses kind of detailed shit. It is, however, going to be hard to impress the backroom boys with our filming of what is, even from the virtual reserve side (actually just 'virtual' side) a fairly shoddy performance.

West Ham lead at half-time through a Junior Stanislas goal, curled in from the edge of the area. Things start to go wrong in the 47th minute when Callum McNaughton is sent off for a professional foul. How weird is that? A professional foul from a player who isn't really a professional. There wasn't actually much professionalism about it, though. The only adjective you could offer to describe it that wouldn't sound vicious is 'unnecessary'. It certainly was that. A fortnight later McNaughton goes out on loan to AFC Wimbledon. He does not return.

Aldershot Town equalise twelve minutes from the end, and in the last minute, as I wonder whether we'll ever get asked to film here again, Hylton hits in a low shot which squeezes past Boffin into the corner of the net.

Despite getting the designated three copies of the edited game to Greg

Demetriou, the media maestro at the club, forty minutes later (one for the ref, one for the opposition manager and one for Sam), I know that no-one is going to be in too much of a rush to watch it that night. Even Dean Holdsworth will be too embarrassed to take it out of its box until he gets back home later on.

West Ham: 31 Boffin, 2 Reid, 3 McCartney, 4 Nolan, 18 Faubert, 19 Sears, 25 Stanislas, 37 McNaughton, 12 Barrera (14 Taylor 53), 30 Piquionne 24 Nouble 69), 11 Carew (23 Ilunga 50)

This weekend, Hammers are travelling to Nottingham Forest, these days shepherded by the 'Wally with a Brolly', Steve McLaren. Except after taking Dutch side FC Twente to their first Dutch league title in 2010, he became the 'Wally with the Bolly'. Much champagne quaffed and celebrations that should have led to his return to a Premier League club. Except people only remember the tatty newspaper nicknames, and so he becomes another pretender to kiss the sleeping frog and hope he can turn Forest into a European Princess once more.

Game Five: npower Championship, 2011-12, City Ground
Sunday 28th August 2011 (21,379)
Referee: Graham Salisbury (Lancashire)

Nottingham Forest 1	**West Ham United 4**
Findley 70	Chambers og 21
	Nolan 24
	Cole 32
	Reid 77

(West Ham: 5th in the table, 10 points from 15)

Scott Parker is not in the squad for the early kick off Sunday game v Forest, which all but ends the speculation that he might not be going to Tottenham after all before Transfer Deadline Day. Will he be forgiven? People forget that Ince left West Ham having also just been voted Player of the Season for 1988-89. But to compare Ince to Parker is clearly absurd. If West Ham were still in the Premier League, Scott Parker would not be on his way on

Wednesday.

Live on Sky, I have the delight of watching this morning's exhibition of football excellence from the City Ground live from the comfort of my own sofa. If I didn't know better, I'd say that Sky's game scheduler must be a West Ham fan, for they're getting quite a bit of exposure on the satellite box for a team that have just been relegated.

Despite their fashion for early goals, it takes West Ham a whole 20 minutes to get the ball in the back of the net, despite a very positive start. Cole feeds Taylor on the left, and his powerful low cross is expertly sliced into his own net by Forest captain Luke Chambers. Glorious, and just one week after Patrick Kisnorbo did the same in the game against Leeds. Fortune favours the knave.

Nolan is again scoring away from home, just three minutes later, flicking in Tomkins' probing header from Matt Taylor's corner into the back of the net. Both captains have scored in just three minutes, and both goals have gone to West Ham. Ever in the search for an unusual happening, I think that might be one. And almost beyond belief, a further eight minutes later Cole heads a third, after pressure from another Matt Taylor corner. The ball comes out to Joey O'Brien, whose cross is nodded into Cole's path from Winston Reid and Cole does the rest from his far post position. West Ham have had three corners, two of which have produced goals. Forest have had four, but still nothing from them.

Ex-Hammer Chris Cohen finds Lynch late in the second half when his cross finds Robbie Findley who reduces the deficit in the 70th minute. Then Reid seals it with a tap in just six minutes' later, scoring in the glory of the 76th minute. It's another Matt Taylor corner, a hat-trick of assists, though this one is a scuffer. When it comes back out to him, he steers it back in, and Reid taps it in at the far post. Yet again, West Ham have secured a comfortable victory away from home, almost at walking pace, and this against a side that they would historically have regarded as serious opposition. Out of the fifteen championship points West Ham have fought for this month, nine of the ten they have secured have come from their three successive away victories: at Doncaster Rovers, Watford and Nottingham Forest. As far as one out of six home points is concerned, Sam Allardyce will have to have a word with the Mud Mouth twins and see if he can't shut them up for good.

West Ham: 1 Green, 2 Reid, 3 McCartney, 4 **Nolan**, 5 Tomkins, 9 Cole (30

Piquionne 68), 10 Collison (15 **Faye** 75), 14 **Taylor**, 16 Noble, 17 **O'Brien**, 18 Faubert (ex-Bolton players in bold print)

So never mind about that dream of a future filming West Ham games... As we approach the end of the first month back in the Championship, and a transfer deadline day that finally took Scott Parker from our outstretched hands into the grabbing mitts of Tottenham Flotsam and Jetsamspur, let's reflect on the players who have come and gone in West Ham's transition from Premier League Prima Donnas to Championship Chavs.

West Ham United 2010-11	Where They Will Be 2011-12
1 Robert Green (GK)	Upton Park
2 Winston Reid	Upton Park
4 Danny Gabbidon	Q.P.R. (free)
5 James Tomkins	Upton Park
7 Kieron Dyer	Q.P.R. (free)
8 Scott Parker	Tottenham Hotspur (£5.5 million)
9 Carlton Cole	Upton Park
10 Jack Collison	Upton Park
11 Thomas Hitzlsperger	Wolfsburg (free)
12 Pablo Barrera	Real Zaragoza (loan)
13 Luis Boa Morte	Larissa (free)
14 Radoslav Kovac	Basel (undisclosed)
15 Matthew Upson	Stoke City (free)
16 Mark Noble	Upton Park
18 Jonathan Spector	Birmingham City (free)
19 Freddie Sears	Upton Park
20 Julien Faubert	Upton Park
21 Demba Ba	Newcastle United (free)
22 Manuel Da Costa	Lokomotiv Moscow (£1.3 million)
25 Junior Stanislas	Burnley (undisclosed)
26 Zavon Hines	Burnley (undisclosed)
27 Jordan Spence	Bristol City (loan)
29 Marek Stech	Upton Park
30 Frederic Piquionne	Upton Park
31 Ruud Boffin	Upton Park
32 Gary O'Neil	Upton Park

33 Victor Obinna	Lokomotiv Moscow (free)
34 Robbie Keane	Back to Spurs then on to LA Galaxy
36 Wayne Bridge	Back to Manchester City
37 Lars Jacobsen	Released
38 Dylan Tombides	Still on books (diagnosed with testicular cancer)
40 Anthony Edgar	Yeovil Town (free)
42 Cristian Montano	Notts County (loan
44 Jordan Brown	Aldershot Town (loan)

TOTAL EARNED FROM SALES OF PLAYERS (KNOWN)   £6.9m
(offset against £21m lost from Sky TV Premiership Rights revenue...)

West Ham made a third as much money from their end of season car boot sale, compared with what they got for the players they sold at the end of 2002-03. Bearing in mind that included Cole, Di Canio, Kanouté and Sinclair, it's not that strange a statistic. The truth is clear, which is that the bunch of clowns on the playing staff in 2010-11 were a club of loanees and mercenaries that even Brian Clough couldn't have generated any team spirit from. To look at the players Sam Allardyce has already brought in, proves that West Ham have now got a squad that are all proud to put on the shirt and won't put money before their own personal performances. The club are already three times as good as last season - just that small matter of promotion to get out of the way before the return becomes a reality.

I see out the month with a day trip to Brighton with Nick London. We are in the town ostensibly to attend a Ron Sexsmith concert at Komedia, a cosy all-standing arena in the North Laine, where Ron will no doubt be in his element. After finally securing the gloss of fame after the release of his *Long Player Late Bloomer* album, and the broadcasting of an idiosyncratic film study of his work, *Love Shines*, Sexsmith is basking in the glow of a wider interest. Consequently, it may prove more difficult to catch him at all standing venues in the future, and is pretty rare even now.

I have brought along a limited edition lithograph from the album cover photoshoot that I got from Canada, but I bring it without a bag so have to lug it around for the whole day avoiding grease stains and ice cream accidents until the gig in the evening. Luckily, his wife is on the merchandise desk, and once she sees the litho, she tells me off for bringing it loose ('You could have lost it') but sends it off to get Ron to sign it. He does, with one of his cartoon self-portraits. I manage somehow to nurse it through the gig and back on the complicated train, tube and night bus journey home, finally offering it pride of place on the mantelpiece at 2am.

Chapter 4

Ground to Zero

September 2011

I begin September journeying to Manchester for a day's training as a senior examiner for English Literature A'Level. Even this area of my work is not without controversy nowadays; examining boards have set examination questions that were impossible to answer. Everyone is under scrutiny it seems, in all walks of life. At least a midweek trip on the Virgin train from Euston means feet up, empty carriages and a travelling time of less than two hours. While I'm there I'm taking the opportunity to spend the early part of the week with my mate Neil, who has just joined BBC as an editor on 'Match of the Day' now it has moved from London to Salford Quays. Neil and I have worked together in football for over thirteen years, teaming up to deliver live match coverage at West Ham United, mainly at the end of the nineties. We also worked as a team on the West Ham 'Legends' series, the 1965 Cup Winners Cup Final DVD, the Boys of '86, Tony Cottee and Julian Dicks biography DVDs. Top of the tree stuff, as you'll know if you've seen them. With West Ham now in the Championship, I don't have the interest in Match of the Day that I would ordinarily have had, though like the final sweet in a jar of sherbert lemons, their game was usually to be found last in any edition of the programme unless they'd just been stuffed by one of the top Premier League clubs.

At the beginning of September 2006, Alan Pardew found himself with an unexpected problem back at Upton Park after an extended break for an international weekend. The programme for the live Sunday fixture at home to Aston Villa declared on its front page, 'The Two Amigos' and focused its headline with the rather threatening sub-heading, 'Why Upton Park faithful will become Latin lovers'. Apart from the lack of a definite article, it was flawed as a statement through its reliance on a massive assumption behind the implied success. Tevez and Mascherano were featured in a pullout centre spread in the national colours of Argentina at the World Cup the previous summer. I had been at the training ground for a couple of the days in the week following their signing, and had seen the evidence before me that neither of them was even halfway fit. Pardew, however, was obviously expected to put both of them straight into the first team, a team that had made such a confident start to the season, without an inkling that it was about to be broken up by the two amigos, without so much as a 'by your shirt sleeve'.

After a fairly cagey press conference during which Pardew declined to reveal if the new players would start on the Sunday, I found myself called into the manager's office on the afternoon of the game with my cameraman. I was working for the company who were running the big screens at the club, and we took our instructions from the manager. Pardew said that he wanted to film a very brief clip of him being interviewed. He would explain to the crowd why neither of the Argentinians would be starting the match. He wanted the clip shown on the big screens five minutes before kick off. We were not to tell anyone about it beforehand, especially anyone at Sky, who were filming the game. I looked behind me in the office, but it was just the cameraman, Alan Pardew and me. The fact that Pardew had lowered his voice throughout made it clear that this was his idea and nobody else's. I had been at a couple of the club's training sessions that week, so I didn't need any explanation, but the fans out there (it was now 2.30, and the match kicked off at 4pm) would expect the two amigos to be gallivanting on the pitch in their brand new West Ham shirts in 90 minutes time.

Now this was exciting. This was Alan Pardew asserting his authority as manager of the club. Who did he want to impress? Or challenge? The team had started the season well, and were bound to feel a little uneasy about the possible disruption caused by the arrival of two World Cup players into the squad. Something would have to give. Or rather, it wouldn't, as Pardew was intending to keep the same eleven that started up at Liverpool a fortnight earlier.

We filmed Pardew's 'statement', which I had to prompt with a couple of questions, interview style. He had handwritten what he was going to say on a piece of paper, and he delivered it confidently and without hesitation in one take as if he had been rehearsing it the whole morning. He had us play it back to him to make sure he was happy with the results. He again told us that the tape was to be taken to the PA room and played out over the system at ten minutes to four. I asked, not unreasonably, what we might do if nobody in there believed us. After some time considering, he told us to tell whoever needed to know that they could check with Miranda, who would verify the story if necessary. Pardew then looked at me very seriously before smiling and patting me confidentially on the shoulder. The Upton Park faithful will have to wait a while before they become Latin lovers, I thought.

The message went out live at exactly ten to four, just before the teams came out. I wondered if Tevez and Mascherano knew the announcement was being made beforehand. The team sheets had arrived late in the Press Room, so there was already a buzz around the press room about both players only being on the subs' bench. The ground fell silent when the message was delivered, and there was a hum of excited chat amongst the fans when it finished. The Sky coverage was on an advert break, and the show's presenter sheepishly announced the details of Pardew's message when they went back live, but didn't have the time they obviously would have wanted to debate it with the pundits in the studio, and had to go straight to the commentary team. Was this Pardew's plan, leaving it so late that he would minimise any potential fuss? I looked at him on the TV pictures, smiling from the dugout. He hadn't looked that confident since the day before they had signed for the club. It was a problem he was going to have to sort out in due course, but there was no question that he had made the point about who was in charge of the team selection, for the moment.

Five years later, and the first full September league programme of football takes place after the madness of the last minute transfer window rush and International weekend. England had barely broken sweat overcoming a timid Bulgarian side, and Wales beat Montenegro, which means with England beating Wales on the Tuesday, they're virtually certain of clinching the group's top spot to secure a Euro 2012 place.

The BBC are sending a crew down for the Portsmouth game, we are told early in the week, so my company will not be making its Saturday camera debut at Upton Park. Strangely enough, I am phoned on the Thursday by Manchester United's cable channel MUTV to ask if I'm free to direct their live away fixture at Sheffield United that Saturday morning. And I am free, but - I'm already thinking - can I get back in time to catch the Portsmouth game?

Then again, more importantly, can I actually direct the game in the first case? Most of my life in football, like most of my life in my life, has been something of a blag. Here is a golden opportunity to earn a decent wedge for a couple of hours graft and maybe even get back to catch the second half at Upton Park. Trouble is, if I say I've never directed a three camera shoot - and is it very difficult? - it's hardly going to endear me to the selective stable of Manchester. You already know how precious they will be even about, no, *especially* about their U-18 side. They won't want any fly-by-night southern softie chancer coming up to press the wrong knobs, as it were, and make their lovelies look anything less than the pirouetting geniuses they believe them to be. So, of course, I do the only thing I can do in the circumstances.

I ring them and tell them I'd *love* to do it. Just that, as I'm driving up from London... Could I...

I get offered another £50 for petrol. It's only five minutes after I'm off the phone that it occurs to me that £50 is not going to get me to Sheffield and back in the car unless I push it for fifty of the 360 miles there and back. But the director's fee is more than reasonable, and I know and love football, so pressing a few buttons shouldn't be beyond me.

Unfortunately, Friday night is not going to give me the surfing 'rehearsal' on the internet I'd like before directing the game, as I've promised to take my old iMac round to my brother's in Borehamwood and install it for him. He's been a Windows aficionado (though, like anyone with a PC, he complains about the virus-ridden operating system) all his life, and I need to show him the Steve Jobs way, even though Mr Jobs is unlikely to be showing anyone any way for the foreseeable after his recent various brushes with death due to organs shutting down like failing hard drives. After all that, I'm hardly going to be getting much sleep as the call sheet has me at the Sheffield United training ground by 8.30 am.

Being me, I can still find some solace from the situation as I haven't really given myself any time to even worry about how I'm going to set about being a director for the day.

So just what exactly does a director do?

The Match Director sits in the truck in front of a bank of screens and never sees a blade of grass but his role is important, creative and when it's done well, fulfilling. With a dozen cameramen out there, training their lenses on the pitch, the job of the director is to weave the shots that the cameramen are providing into the coverage seen on TV screens. A good director is an artist, who weighs up his options in a trice and is part of a seamless process. He'll also plan ahead... the main cameras may be on the action but as he switches between them he instructs the steady-cam to get close on the coach. Once the ball goes in the net, straight after the players' celebrations, the shot of the coach is available for use. These things don't just happen... it's a mixture of planning, quick reactions and judgement.

Once, at West Ham, the rain was falling hard.... in August. I heard the director in my cans ask for a shot of the rain, caught by the floodlights. The cameraman stayed on it for about 5 minutes until the director felt he had a suitable break in the action. Then he switched to the shot and, "Ahh, summer in London," I said, and the aside was complete. Back to the action with nothing missed, and a bit of atmosphere for the viewer. In twelve years of regular live commentary at Upton Park and various other grounds, I have worked with some of the best. And this is what I am thinking about as I drive up the M1 from my brother's, first thing on a very dark Saturday morning.

Bruce Thomas wrote a marvellous book about touring, as a bass player, with Elvis Costello which he called, for some reason, 'The Big Wheel'. In it he referred to Elvis as *The Singer*, Pete Thomas was *The Drummer* and Steve Nieve was *The Keyboard Player*. 'Bruce Thomas' was just the first person narrative for the book, though he is, if the truth be told, a quite exceptional bassist, very much in the Paul McCartney mould. By the end of the book, however, he perhaps should have been referring to himself as *The Sore Loser Who Got Chucked Out Of The Band*.

And each person working on a live football edit also has their role. In this kind of situation, there are what you might call the Big Three: the Producer, the Director, and the Replay Man, or the man operating the EVS (Écriture Video Simulation, or Elvis for short) replay machine. If it was the Jam, you'd have Paul Weller on guitar, Bruce Foxton on bass and Rick Butler on drums. Except today, though they don't realise it yet, they've got Basil Brush on bass.

In life, there will be many moments like these for the chancers.

The first date you go on to move beyond a kiss and a fumble. Is it best to be relaxed or frantic? Finger soft or tearing off clothes?

The first fight. Do you punch or kick? Do you wait to see what the other guy (or girl) does? The class clown puts you down with a smart quip. Is there enough time to practice a little line in repartee? Should you have a line prepared? Mine was always, *'Your dad should've had a wank,'* but I never got to use that one. Then there is the first questioning of your authority at work, once you've been given some. To be cool, or callous. Incisive or ranting. Gregarious or taciturn.

Once you're past 40, there shouldn't be too many more of these moments, if you know what's good for you. But I obviously don't know what's good for me, or for Manchester United's U-18 team.

In my efforts to 'gen up' on directing, I read about how Italian football coverage prefers the personality shots - lots of pitch side close-ups, even in the heat of the action. Then there is the German way of covering a game. They are more into tactics and rarely depart from camera one, the wide one, as they like to see how a game is shaping up; the players are just the pawns in the game. The Producer, however, does not like too much tight. As he tells me twenty minutes into the game. Stay with the wide camera and concentrate on calling the replays in right. I start to worry - have I been calling in the replays... But nothing's really happened in the game, yet. There's no atmosphere to speak of, even though there are a hundred or so watching the game. If these supporters are parents, they're not acting like the overbearing types you'd expect, swearing at the ref or their son, or both.

There are several brief videoed features to pad out the production, as well as the need to go backwards and forwards between the commentator and summariser and previewing the United first team game later that afternoon. I won't mess up the links to Sir Alex Ferguson in case he's sitting at Old Trafford, watching.

I get better in the second half, but as there is no objective correlative for me, I can't know how well or badly I'm doing. I look for some audio or visual clues out of the corner of my eye... Is the Producer shaking his head at the EVS guy, or is he reacting to an e-mail on his phone? I just heard it gently buzzing. Paranoia is the natural state of the human when he doesn't know what the fuck he's doing. It's perfectly natural. Silently and painfully I begin to take stock of what it is I should be doing, so that, eventually, I will start doing it. Unfortunately, I can only know how to do something right by witnessing the almost imperceptible body winces the other two express when I do something wrong. Sometimes I do two things wrong at once - or was that an extended wince?

Just when I begin to take stock of the EVS man's time counter, which, if I'd noticed it before, would have told me when to go back to the studio rather than asking him to count me in, the game finishes. It's all over, Manchester United's U-18s have won 2-0, and just before I've got into a comfortable stride. I cut from camera to camera to gather shots of the teams shaking hands, and eventually dissolve to the commentator on the gantry to sum up the game.

So what have I learned about directing this afternoon?

1. by all means cut between camera shots for open play BUT
2. use dissolves with replays and when going to and leaving the presenter and summariser
3. never go to a replay unless you can be sure there is enough lull in the play to accommodate it (this one is actually impossible because of the nature of football - and if you keep to it, you'd only get about half the replays the fans like to see...)
4. the Producer is in charge of all decisions (until you are...)
5. the guy on the EVS (replay man) is the unsung hero of the whole kiboosch
6. you need THREE good camera operators for a three camera shoot... two good and one okay is a nightmare, two okay is... what you get when you pay them peanuts...
7. you need a degree in Diplomacy as everyone on the shoot can hear *everything* you say *all the time*
8. I have a raised admiration for the Presenter (who in this case was also the Commentator) for dealing with all the detritus in his ear throughout the broadcast - his summariser, an ex-United Scottish international, apparently insists his is turned off!

I probably could have done with knowing all of the above before taking the job, but at least I know it now, in case they ever employ me again...

Game Six: npower Championship, 2011-12, Upton Park
Saturday 10th September 2011 (33,465)
Referee: Roger East (Wiltshire)

West Ham United 4	**Portsmouth 3**
Taylor 9	Varney 8
Lansbury 53	Norris 60
Nolan 72 (pen)	Halford 90 +7 (pen)
Cole 76	

(West Ham: 4th in the table, 13 points from 18)

While I am motoring back down the M1, West Ham are about to win at Upton Park for the first time this season. In fact, for the first time since they beat

Stoke City in early March, over six months ago. Do you ever get that feeling that the only reason your team can't win at home is because you are there jinxing them? The likelihood of this, of course, is usually then emphasised when you have to attend a funeral, a wedding or a graduation ceremony and your side ends the hoodoo and slaughter someone 4-0. Then you are in a bit of a quandary. What if you go to the next game and they lose? Which they will, of course, because they were on a losing streak just one game back, which isn't going to be overturned by one lame victory.

So I'm already sure that they'll win today. Which means I can't go to the Peterborough game in a fortnight.

New signings a-lordy! Well, not quite. Despite the transfer window slamming shut on the toenails of several players as they squeezed into the West Ham back room, only one makes the starting eleven. On loan from Arsenal, step sideways Henri Lansbury.

No, he's not French, idiot. He scored three times for England U-21s during the international break just gone. But he could hardly spell his name 'Henry' as an Arsenal player. It would just be too confusing.

But the other new signings, David Bentley (on loan) and Sam Baldock (who's already scored six goals this season and who describes West Ham as a club 'caked in history'), are on the bench. Which raises another of those interesting points. Before substitutions, a team survived with eleven players for ninety minutes. Leg breaks, toilet breaks, whatever... the team carried on with whoever was left standing on the pitch. Then, the substitute. Supersub. But that was a few years in coming. Subs initially were just that; substitutes. Rarely on unless someone was injured. Hardly tactical, as there were no Kieron Dyers in those days. But then someone twigged that you might change the game around by bringing the twelfth man on to replace someone who was flagging, or useless, or both. Flagging useless. This was the advent of the modern footballer. The sulk. *You're taking me off? Why? Who'll put the winning goal in if I'm off the field? You surely don't think that pipsqueak is likely to do any better than me?* And so supersub replaced supersulk.

40 odd years later and whilst there are those who want to leave the pitch - remember Paolo Di Canio pleading with Harry Redknapp to be taken off because he'd been refused three blatant penalty appeals? - few players actually like chewing on the potential insult factor of being substituted. It's a word that carries a pejorative judgement. Even worse when a substitute gets substituted themselves. And of course it's now possible that a side

might be almost 30% different in the second half to the one that took to the field in the first. And so we wonder, on a bright September afternoon, will Sam bring on the whole bench?

Alan Pardew probably had the toughest substitution dilemma of any West Ham manager. Bad enough that, like the callously discarded girlfriend, he seemed to be one of the last people at the club to know that two brilliant (but out of practice, overweight and non-English speaking) Argentinians Carlos Tevez and Javier Mumbletwat had been signed to play for East London's finest. Four days later facing Aston Villa in a live Sunday Sky game, he has to decide whether to field the slightly crocked South Americans or incur the wrath of the fans by not playing them. It's unlikely that anyone on the terraces will know he wasn't the guy who brought them to the club. But they really aren't fit, and those of us who've been at the training ground on Friday are well aware of the fact.

In the end, Pardew elects to play the political card of filming a short piece to camera to be broadcast over the big screens ten minutes before kick off. We are all sworn to silence and even Sky, the live hosts, are not to know. And we film his piece, as he chews reflectively on what seems to be a small brick. It's just one take, and he asks us if we think it was alright. No-one offers an opinion, so I nod. Did he mean his performance, or what he actually said? He is delighted (he says on the piece to camera) that two such world class players have come to the club, but they won't be starting today as they're not quite fit. He says.

Wind forward five years and Sam's out there mixing it up with his 4-3-3 and an Arsenal player on loan for g-d's sake! You have to say (as John Motson would preface) that unlike the freshly relegated side of 2003-04, this one is starting to look better that the one that got relegated, both on paper and in the flesh. Let's hope we do see some of those new players in the second half, even if they are injured.

After all that, it's Portsmouth who take the lead, wearing a kit with shirts half-red and half-black. The Hammers' defence find themselves caught out in Pompey's first meaningful attack, marking half men and half biscuits, and hence a wrongfooting daisy cutter corner from Liam Lawrence is hit home by Luke Varney, the ball pinballing in off Carlton Cole's knee. Not quite one for the dodgy goals panel on Monday, but commentator Tony Gubba, fired by a new pacemaker battery, and the delight of being back on a football programme that isn't a repeat, still declares, 'It's the first goal Portsmouth have scored in the first half of a game this season.' Does that even *mean* anything? But then he's from the seventies is our Tony. Hasn't quite mastered the modern sports coverage obsession with statistics.

No worries, though. West Ham are soon up the other end and Matt Taylor whacks in a left-footed free kick from twenty-five yards, scoring against his old club, again with the aid of a deflection. The ghost of Avram Grunt, not quite a ghost yet, but a man whose office has been usurped by both managers on show today. It is Taylor's first goal for the Hammers, and it's been a while coming, considering his role in the side as the most positive and attacking force amongst the newcomers. A few minutes later he sets up O'Brien, whose spinning cross beats the goalkeeper but also the Portsmouth crossbar before landing behind the goal. Liam Lawrence reacts with an over the top tackle on Lansbury that gets him booked, but a minute later he finds Benjani from a deep corner and forces Green to make a reaction save to keep West Ham in the game.

The second half is even more open, and an early cross from Noble puts the defence under pressure. Lansbury, on his debut, hits the ball home via yet another deflection to put West Ham ahead. He looks quite pleased with his goal. Maybe someone can persuade him to change the spelling of his name back to Henry. Five minutes later, Varney brings the ball away for Pompey and sets up an attack that sees Norris' header half-cleared, but the ball is shown to have already crossed the line before Benjani forces it back into the net. One hour gone, and it's 2-2. The Upton Park hoodoo looks to be in force again.

Bentley, like Lansbury, another promising Arsenal youngster who failed to break into the first team because of the multitudinous international purchases, comes on for Faubert, and there is a sense of incident in the air. Bentley is like another David for West Ham, David Connolly, from the Championship season of 2003-04. These are two players who both have a very high opinion of themselves, but neither seem to think they need to perform to their potential. Bentley's career was particularly delightful to watch at Tottenham, who paid £15m to sign him from Blackburn in July 2008, only to see the England international (yes, *England*) fail spectacularly at White Hart Lame. (Just 5 goals in 62 appearances) Even a spell on loan at Birmingham (another chance to 'resurrect' his career) failed. Fail fail fail. So why might he fare any better on loan at Upton Park? Rather typically, West Ham fans can claim that they have snatched a £15m footballer for a budget price, ignoring the counter-position that they've given a drowning man in the bargain bin division a last chance. And they've given him Scott Parker's shirt, too. That's a compliment. Or more money saved, if you prefer.

Bentley's first real contribution is significant, as victim to an over-the-top tackle by Liam Lawrence, and the ouch factor has the ref waving a red card for the first time in the game. You could of course claim that maybe Lawrence hadn't been told Parker had left the club, and was trying to put him out of the rest of the game to save Pompey's arse.

West Ham soon make the extra man count, and Lansbury's tight control in the area leads to a handball that gives Noble the chance to put Hammers back in the lead. He does, from the penalty spot. The Pompey keeper guesses right, but Noble's strike is true. He's a pretty sound spot kicker, having buried two against Manchester United at home in the last relegation season, when most penalty takers would have needed oxygen after the shock of the Red Devillers having two penalties awarded against them in the same game. See, there are still a few brave referees in the Premier League - that time it was Lee Mason.

That's all three goals scored or set up by new boys. The Allah Dice Man can be more than happy. And there's one more to come for the Hammers, a deep cross from Matt Taylor picking out Carlton Cole who heads in superbly, despite the difficult angle. Even more significantly, it's West Ham's second 76th minute goal of the 2011-12 season.

You know, Bentley *has* got that slightly low centre of gravity thing going on, like Scott Parker and Paul Gascoigne before him. I wonder if he just might prove another Di Canio bargain... if West Ham were ever able to afford him. We'd have then done a Harry on Harry. Lansbury hits in a low skidding shot just past the post before ex-Pompey Piquionne, who came on some time earlier when no-one was looking, is just as anonymously sent packing with a red card. Even Tony the Gubbster has missed the incident. The replay man finally discovers the reason, captured by a camera behind the Pompey goal. Piquionne pushed a defender who got in his way. Portsmouth immediately exploit the return to man parity; Ben Haim dive bombs into the six yard box over Mark Noble's outstretched leg to earn his side a penalty. This is a man who was once on loan to the Hammers to earn his reported £38k per week, *plus image rights!* Greg Halford nets to flatter Rompey Pompey 4-3, but the referee mercifully blows the whistle before the black and red blurs can force home what had seemed an unlikely equaliser. I'd call that a close call (another goal conceded at home deep in injury time), but the home fans go home happy.

West Ham: 1 Green, 2 Reid, 3 McCartney, 4 Nolan, 5 Tomkins, 9 Cole (30 Piquionne 85), 14 Taylor, 16 Noble, 17 O'Brien, 18 Faubert (8 Bentley 63), 22 Lansbury

At this point in football time I am in the kitchen at home, delighted at the news and reflecting on my brief career as a football director. I didn't get back in time for the game. My report is culled from the highlights package on BBC's Championship programme that evening. Two days later a message is left on my phone by the company that cover the Liverpool U-18 games, asking if I'm free the following weekend to direct their game at Barnsley. Somewhat flattered, I ring back to accept, twenty minutes later, only to find they've already found someone else. Maybe Manchester United tipped them off...

On Wednesday it's a trip to my New Zealander dentist for a checkup. This is the man who has been sorting my teeth out since he himself was a student back in 1970, strangely enough the year I saw my first West Ham game, that 2-2 draw against Chelsea. He's semi-retired now, which means I had to make a tough financial decision if I wanted to stay with him. Going private has potentially serious remunerative consequences for a man in his fifties with a mouth full of teeth in need of love, but I'm old-fashioned in that sense, and don't want any other pretender to the title of Defender of the Teeth anywhere near my pearly yellows. As a consequence, a couple of waves of the metal molar mover, and that's £65 please. With the promise of two fillings and a clean, it's a forthcoming visit next month that's unlikely to yield much change out of a decent wad. But this Kiwi's more than just a dentist. He owns the practice now, and can pretty much do whatever he likes - except work five days a week, or do any work on the NHS, now he's over sixty. His receptionist is as hard as nails and plays falsetto to his baritone, her cockney accent gritting against his gentle marsupial drawl. I try to get to the surgery twenty minutes before my appointment to hear her insulting the patients with fake smiles and wounding understatement. He, on the other hand, applies a more direct coat of schmooze with classic FM or one of his Richard Clayderman CDs stuck on repeat, what the psychoanalysts lazily term passive aggressive. See, I'm not just paying for the work on my teeth.

Game Seven: npower Championship, 2011-12, The New Den
Saturday 17th September 2011 (16,078)
Referee: Lee Mason (Bolton)

Millwall 0   **West Ham United 0**

(West Ham: 5th in the table, 14 points from 21)

Well, what do you know? We have Lee Mason as the referee his afternoon, a man who's not frightened to award a penalty. Yes, that one.

Lansbury nearly scores from the kick off, noticing that Millwall keeper David Forde is still fiddling with his gloves and out of position, but Henri's forty yard chip sails just wide of the unguarded net. Second half substitute David Bentley also comes close to scoring, in the magical 76th minute, but as Forde spills Faubert's cross into his path, the not-so-supersub somehow manages to screw the ball wide rather than breathe confidently on it to ease it into the net.

West Ham: 1 Green, 3 McCartney, 4 Nolan, 5 Tomkins (2 Reid 30), 9 Cole, 14 Taylor (8 Bentley 59), 15 Faye, 16 Noble, 17 O'Brien, 18 Faubert, 22 Lansbury (7 Baldock 74)

I have lived with Jules in our house in West London since May 2001, and if it seems like I have several vocational interests, hers profoundly outnumber mine. Apart from being an artist and a university art lecturer, she has recently taken up karate and retrained as an arborist (that's tree surgeon to you) and her week is spent oscillating between the different activities these areas of interest and expertise offer her.

On Wednesday it's her birthday; she's 46. We rarely get the chance to spend time outside home together, but today we get along to the John Martin 'Apocalypse' exhibition which opens today at Tate Britain, and we meet up with some of her old friends from backintheday at Chelsea College. The exhibition is about Martin's nineteenth century visions of heaven and hell, which anyone with an Upton Park season ticket in the twenty-first century would understand with intimate empathy.

I've found a stash of old films including an exhibition of Jules' work from 2000, a film from her studio around the same time and a digital recording of her one woman art show in Osterley from July 2001, over ten years ago. Being able to edit is a handy skill for making birthday presents. I compile a DVD of the different events which we watch that evening when she gets back. The best thing about today is that as her birthday falls on a Wednesday, we can indulge our greatest extravagance, the single malt. Since the discovery of this velvet substance, we have invented the concept of 'Whisky Wednesday' to enjoy it. Whatever we've been up to and wherever we've been, we always meet back at the ranch by eleven, and retire for a double measure of whatever Scottish single malt might be by the bed. This ritual breaks up the working week perfectly, and in addition guarantees a perfect night's sleep. This evening it's a choice between a Jura and a 15 year old Dalwhinnie. No contest. The Dura wins. Happy birthday, Julesy.

Game Eight: npower Championship, 2011-12, Upton Park
Saturday 24th September 2011 (29,895)
Referee: Tony Bates (Staffordshire)

West Ham United 1   **Peterborough United 0**
Noble 10 (pen)

(West Ham: 3rd in the table, 17 points from 24)

Reid is in for Tomkins, but it's otherwise the same side that turned up for the Millwall non-event last Saturday lunchtime. Nolan is definitely on a bonding mission, splitting first from the 'respect' team pack to race down to the Bobby Moore end and wave high clapping hands at the home supporters, while Rob Green looks on behind him, perplexed.

The game kicks off at 15.03; a Championship kick off time - there's no Sky TV Director bawling into the ref's headset to cue his whistle. This is the closest West Ham are going to get to the Ferguson family hair dryer treatment this season, his son Darren's Morphy Richards quick dry less likely to invoke tinnitus.

It's my first game at Upton Park for a month, having last seen them in their reserve team flesh lamely slipping out of the Carling Cup against Aldershot Town in front of our two man camera team. Sadly for my pocket, Sky are sending a team over to cover the game, so our cameras will remain in their 'pocket brace' bags back at Woodland Towers.

From Grant McCann's brilliant first minute near post corner, Tommy Rowe heads straight at Green, point blank - some start that would have been. McCann again proves troublesome down the right wing, and it's now that I remember where I've seen him before. Harry Redknapp signed him as a sixteen year old for the Hammers in 1996, and he made his second of four appearances for Glenn Roeder as a substitute in a 1-7 thrashing at Ewood Park, managing to get on the scoresheet on debut after putting the ball in the net for Blackburn. Not a great day for West Ham all round as later that evening Roeder got a speeding ticket after dropping Paolo Di Canio home. The Italian had refused to fly back from the North West with the team in a post match sulk.

As the tenth minute passes, Lansbury is pushed over in the area following a cross by Faubert, and Noble slots home the penalty to the left of Jones after a diagonally perpendicular run up. No wonder the keeper had no idea which way to move. The season's anthem rings out round the ground - *How shit can you be, we're winning at home*... Posh fans' minimalist riposte is *You're not famous anymore*... They choose not to punctuate this with, *The bears are defecating in the forest*...

Ah, fame, the ephemeral one.

The Allah Dice Man now has an 'exclusive' column in the Evening Standard. In terms of the history of other West Ham managers fingering the digits, I suppose it is 'exclusive'. Quite why he's writing about Arsene Wenger in it becomes clear by the second paragraph, with the introduction of the collective noun for managers, 'scapegoat'. He's putting in a good word for his old French pal. The reason for this 'exclusive' column (I'm beginning to think it's 'exclusive' as it may be the only one he ever writes) seems to be for the opportunity it's presenting Sam to plug the 'Kids for a Quid' offer at the Peterborough game. Yes, like many of the articles in London's favourite free evening paper, it's a glorified ad. Not only that, but it's giving Sam as a Championship manager the opportunity to boost his 'PR Profile' down South.

George Boyd's curled left foot effort on the half hour drops just wide of Rob Green's left hand post and wakes up the crowd. Abdoulaye Faye at left back is proving a very tidy defender, effortlessly cutting out threats from McCann and Rowe throughout the half. I notice Spurs are winning 2-0 at Wigan. Maybe a year off from the Premier League isn't a bad thing after all.

On their big day out, Peterborough have taken up about three-quarters of the lower Sir Trevor Brooking stand, more than most Premier League teams north of Watford last season managed. O'Brien and Faubert link up well to give Cole a headed opportunity that skids wide. Nolan and Lansbury also fashion some neat interplay, leading to a powerful effort also hit narrowly wide, this time by the Arsenal loan striker.

Not sure if it's all this World Cup rugby combined with Winston Reid at number two for the Hammers, but I keep thinking we're playing the All Blacks. Peterborough's kit (as well as the build of their back four) does nothing to lessen this image. Even so, West Ham see it though to half-time. I find myself longing for a second goal to make the last fifteen minutes a little more bearable. Each of the other four teams West Ham have played at home this season have scored goals deep into injury time, Cardiff and Aldershot Town finding winners and Leeds denying Hammers the two extra winning points in the final breath of the game.

'Derby 2 Millwall 0' is the kind of scoreline that would always be likely to raise a cheer at Upton Park, but when Jeremy Nicholas delivers it, deadpan, in the context of the Championship, it gets the loudest cheer of the afternoon.

The ground is a little like a morgue in the early part of the second half until Rowe and then Boyd miss good chances. Even Mud Mouth and his twin shout monosyllabically at Carlton Cole, in an attempt at encouragement I guess. G-d help their poor deaf relatives, if either has been able to persuade anyone with low enough self-esteem to commit to having a family with them. Faubert produces a brilliant byline cross that Cole gets to on the edge of the six yard box, but heads over. He is soon substituted for John Carew, who gets an early shot in with those luminous yellow boots of his.

Peterborough had started the second half well but are now on the rack. Possession for the Hammers but few and far between on the chances tally. Then Carew breaks and turns to produce a yard of space into which he hits a fierce bending effort that beats Jones but dips too late to hit the target. Gabriel Zakuani is doing a real man to man shirt-tugging / marking job on Carew, but referee Tony 'Norman' Bates is upholding none of the Norwegian's complaints.

A Noble corner is headed out by Little. McCann hits a skidding thirty yarder at Green, who fields the ball uncertainly, to recall last summer's world cup shocker, but there's no-one near to capitalise on his spillage. Bentley replaces Faubert in the 68th minute, the Frenchman going off to rapturous applause. Ferguson calls the limping McCann over to disseminate a little advice - this'll add to the injury time. I can already picture the Peterborough players celebrating a late late equaliser in about twenty-five minutes time...

Another Posh player goes down. This one wasn't too posh to be pushed.

I can see two cameras on the gantry, but only one camera is feeding the big screens. Bizarre. This means that the BBC and Sky have both sent ONE cameraman to get the pictures from the game, the same 'wide' set of pictures. If they shared resources, they could do a two camera feed with a mix for two angles on the action. Allies and the Russians. All trust has been fucked. It's the BBC not trusting Sky, I suspect, as Sky are more than capable of sending six cameras here if they felt like it. Having watched the 75 minutes of this game, however, one camera would have been quite enough to catch all the interesting action.

Throughout the majority of last season, the backs of seats at Upton Park would become increasingly visible around the 75 minute mark. This despite the possibility of late goals and late points in the fading minutes of a game. The police at the tube station would rig up the queueing barriers ten minutes before the final whistle, such were the columns of fans departing from the ground at ten to five on a Saturday.

This season, however, with its Peterboroughs and Doncasters, has had very little of that. The majority of the 29,895 remain obstinately in their seats. I've never been too certain quite why someone might pay up to £50 for ninety minutes of football and then bin the last fifteen. It's effectively like cramming the better part of a tenner down the drain. And why...? To save queueing at the train station? Someone help me with this one...

Faye is still looking like the last line of defence, but even when he is beaten, Green is thankfully up to handling the crosses comfortably.

West Ham have only played Peterborough here once before in a league game, back in the early nineties, a game which finished 2-1 to the Hammers in Billy Bonds' first promotion season.

Bentley has a superb shot tipped round the post by Jones before Norman blows the final whistle inviting relieved sighs all around for 'winning ugly'.

West Ham: 1 Green, 2 Reid, 3 McCartney, 4 Nolan, 9 Cole (11 Carew 56), 14 Taylor (5 Tomkins 90), 15 Faye, 16 Noble, 17 O'Brien, 18 Faubert (8 Bentley 67), 22 Lansbury

Scrolling through nonsense on the iPad in bed early on the Monday morning, I notice with amazement that one of my favourite bands of the late 70s, the Roogalator, led by guitar wizard Danny Adler, are playing a 'reunion' gig at the 606 Jazz Club in Chelsea that evening. This is quite a 'double': a band

I haven't heard of for fifteen years, and a club I haven't been to for at least ten.

A singer/songwriter I never got to see was the great French genius Serge Gainsbourg, but I did the next best thing and formed a band in late 1992, Faut Parler (translates as 'we need to talk'), a year after his death, to cover a wide selection of his songs on the North West London pub circuit. After rehearsals and gigs most of the band would invariably drive down to the 606 to catch the last set of whoever was there. And of course, as members, we could drink out of hours. Singers performing in those days included Stacey Kent, Ray Gelato and Diana Krall. Great music, great atmosphere and decent food if you got there early enough. And Roogalator are playing there.

I'm sure I read that Danny Adler now lives in Cincinatti, so they must have flown him over for the gig. I manage to ring the club and book a table, even though it'll only be me going. This band released their 'With The Roogalator' EP in 1977 on the Stiff label that boasted artists such as Nick Lowe, Elvis Costello, Wreckless Eric and Ian Dury. I meet up with a mate for a beer in Fulham before moving on to the club to catch their set with a handful of equally sad music punters with long memories. They play *Cincinatti Fatback* and *Get Ready (for the Get Ready)* and I treat myself to a little lean cuisine and a couple of beers, so I'll go home happy.

The Big Fat Gypsy Gangster Movie, as with most Big Fat Movies, features a Big Fat Person, and this time it's a Big Fat Gypsy. Ricky Grover is the Big Fat One, and a man currently starring in Eastenders. For a West Ham fan, it's surprisingly not a soap I have been a particular aficionado of, so he might as well be Kate Middleton's equerry for all it means to me. However, my mate from the DVD world, Andrew Palmer, needs me to sort him and a guest a seat for the midweek game v Ipswich Town. Andrew's had a pretty shit year so far, with a stroke, and embollism on the lung, but he has a never-say-die attitude and refuses to let any misfortune get the better of him.

Game Nine: npower Championship, 2011-12, Upton Park
Tuesday 27th September 2011 (27,709)
Referee: Keith Stroud (Dorset)

West Ham United 0   **Ipswich Town 1**
                               Bowyer 89

(West Ham: 4th in the table, 17 points from 27)

This is about as attacking as it gets. On paper it looks like a 4-2-4 but I am reliably informed that we will be playing 4-4-2 with a diamond shape. Sounds a bit Percy to me. It's not that I don't understand the concept, but if this was a firmament of Hammers' players up in the sky at bedtime, then I wouldn't see any diamond shape, even if I'd dropped a couple of tabs of acid.

On four minutes Carlos Edwards moves into the six yard box as Michael Chopra pulls back a brilliant low cross and he meets it sweetly only for Green to beat it out point blank. Who are Ipswich? 13th in the table, seven points behind West Ham, but almost ahead in the first five minutes. Faye clears well with an overhead - and then gets an elbow in the throat for his troubles.

There is a great atmosphere here tonight, the first evening league game of the season at the Boleyn. No-one who was here in 2004 will forget the brilliant play-off semi-final second leg between these two sides when Christian Dailly flicked home a goal after being slapped in the gonads. Lee Bowyer is here yet again, this time for Ipswich, and they have a corner. The tractor boys are in town. Another ex-Hammer Jimmy Bullard takes it, but it comes to nothing.

Finally, a West Ham attack; Nolan's effort is cleared off the line with Stockdale beaten. Cole breaks away to cross and earns a corner, which Bentley takes. So much for the diamond shape. Ipswich find no problem cutting a way through, and Bullard is the man doing the cutting, but it peters out as Jason Scotland fails to control a pass intended to put him clear. Bowyer picks up a loose ball across the area and chips Green who fingertips the effort against the post behind him when the shot has looked goal bound all the way. Up the other end on 22 minutes, Lansbury sees his effort skid past Stockdale, but just wide of the upright. A corner from Bentley is headed just over by Carlton Cole.

Is Ipswich more likely to have farms than any other English town? Just that this Tractor Boys thing is beginning to irritate me.

Bullard is playing quite deep in midfield for Ipswich; you might even say he was at the back of the diamond, if they say that at all. Looks like that early Suffolk pressure has lacked punch, though just as I say that, Bowyer sprays another cross-come-shot across Green's goal face. Half an hour gone and the crowd are getting restless. This four attackers thing isn't working, as it seems to have reduced the options of distribution. Loads of targets but few bullets.

I've already decided, as it's almost Jewish New Year, that if Abdoulaye Faye makes an error tonight, I'm reserving the right to scream out, 'Oi Faye!' in exasperation.

On 33 minutes Chopra breaks clear down the right and hits a dipping volley over Green that he saves brilliantly. It was offside. McCartney hits a hopeful long ball forward. Is this where it's headed, after all that talk about 'playing football'? Cole robs Bullard and breaks away to feed Lansbury, but the Arsenalite slips over in his attempts to control the ball. It's pitiful. Great team on paper. Shame we're playing on grass.

Ipswich free-kick. Bullard takes it and it flies across the goal too low to head, too high to connect with. Where has this half gone? You get the impression that a single goal would win this game, the later, the more likely. But Hammers have maybe had one in six of the efforts this half and that's not good. Now we move into injury time. Bowyer has a booking at the end of a relatively foul less first half. Bentley punts the free-kick into Stockdale's chest and that's it.

Second halves spent attacking the Bobby Moore end always seem to inspire greater confidence. Perhaps there is some metaphorical wind powered from the Sir Trevor Brooking home of the North Bank. Burnley are beating Nottingham Forest 4-0 at half time, taking the gloss over Hammers' recent win up there... But we have a free kick which Bentley is shaping to take - over the top for another corner. Ipswich break out with Bullard. Now Cole breaks away in the opposite direction, keeps possession, but his low shot is easy pickings for Stockdale. The big screens tell me that West Ham have a store in Westfield. It's clearly nearer than Lakeside, but how busy will that be at Christmas? Depends on whether they can grab something in this second half. Poor ball in from Tomkins. The delivery in has been pretty kak for most of the evening. Now the best move all match is punctuated by a skier from Joey O'Brien.

An hour gone. An Ipswich player is down on the edge of his area. Lansbury is ticked off and yellow-carded for the incident, where he is seen to have left 'a bit of himself' in the challenge. Would either of these sides score, even if they were to play for another couple of hours?

Allardyce takes Carlton Cole and Henri Lansbury off and brings on Wales and Norway's finest in Collison and Carew. They have just twenty-five minutes to impress. Collison is my bet for raising the bar - maybe his extra bit of class will make the difference.

Carew's first pass goes awry. It's all getting a bit desperate. Aren't we supposed to be getting out of this division at the first attempt? At least Ipswich are playing like a side who'd prefer to get a win than eke out a draw. Bentley sees his effort at the far post come back off the upright. He looks in vain at the big screen for a replay. It's all a bit *Pard who?* at the moment. Mud Mouth and his twin start growling their poorly choreographed moans from behind the press area. Oh for a West Ham Cantona to leap off the pitch and into the stands to throttle both of them, one with each outstretched hand.

Bentley corner. Nothing.

Was football better when I was a kid, or was it as half-arsed as much of this has been tonight? Someone remind me. Take me back then so I can check.

We have just a quarter of an hour... Fifteen minutes somehow to turn this into three points. We enter the magical seventy-sixth minute. Will it send us the goal we need? Er... Ipswich have a corner. Green collects! Big clearance. This team that has seemed so much better than last year's overpaid hopeless hopefuls, is looking absolutely clueless. Carew lets fly, but the ball ricochets away into touch.

Cresswell then fashions a piece of magic from thirty yards that Green fingertips over the bar. Still a brilliant keeper, he must wonder what happened to the top flight and the guaranteed pair of England gloves. If Capello had played him in the game after his World Cup blunder against the Yanks, it would have been a smart, confidence-inspiring move for him, and he wouldn't have made another slip like that. Instead, the Italian knee-jerker finished Green's international career and effectively left the side marooned with a rookie, a granddad and a passenger. Great man-management.

A minute to go now, so any winner will be theirs. And, as any cynic and Mud Mouth might have predicted, it has to be Bowyer. Bullard's corner is headed onto the post by Keith Andrews and there is the spoiler to tap in the rebound. Only good thing is that Brighton have surrendered to our weekend opponents Crystal Palace, conceding three in the last ten minutes, and Hammers will still remain in the play-off places in fourth position.

West Ham: 1 Green, 3 McCartney, 4 Nolan, 5 Tomkins, 7 Baldock, 8 Bentley, 9 Cole (11 Carew 63), 15 Faye, 16 Noble (18 Faubert 89), 17 O'Brien, 22 Lansbury (10 Collison 63)

The last day of the month sees the Bible's 25th Anniversary Concert at The Grand in Clapham Junction, a band whose history has interwoven with mine over all this time. I first saw them in 1987 playing in their birthtown, Cambridge, where my then girlfriend lived. Their lead singer Boo Hewerdine is a masterful songwriter having penned *Patience of Angels* and *Joke (I'm*

Laughing) for Eddi Reader as well as the Bible's *Graceland, Honey Be Good* and, in their second incarnation, the soulful *Dreamlife*.

It's quite a month to have caught Roogalator's gig at the 606 and to have that almost trumped with The Bible at The Grand. I'm not expecting to see a horde of teenage fans, and I'm not disappointed, but the place is full. For a seminal band who were very poorly marketed by their myopic record label Chrysalis, this could have ended up feeling like a celebration of what could have been, but no-one here seems to feel that way. The band play songs that cut across the whole of their diverse output with all the passion and joy of those early gigs back at the Cambridge Corn Exchange nearly 25 years ago.

So much good live music around for the picking. Now that musicians can raise very little revenue from their recorded material, they've been forced to come back out onto the street to peddle their wares. Almost the reverse of what happened to the Beatles who were forced away from performing live to virtually camping out permanently in the studio to make their music. Studio time, long forced through expense to be rehearsed for and argued over, became less revered. Nowadays young singers can make their own lavish sounding personal symphonies on Garageband.

Professional football, however, remains a tiny playground for the rich and talented few.

Chapter 5

Mr Stadium Has Left The Moon

October 2011

My brother is getting married.

At least he was in October 2009, and my delayed wedding present to him, and his wife Dorota, was an edited DVD of their wedding video. Two years on, they have a beautiful daughter, Phoebe, named after our maternal grandmother.

Looking at the wedding footage I shot a couple of years later, it's clear that he has done things right. He will be 50 next April, so he's got his feet off the procrastination stool and under the procreation table. Proof, if it were needed, that you never can tell. I had always imagined when I was younger that I would be a parent one day, but had never positioned my brother in that role. Now there he is, changing nappies, burbling baby talk and reading up on parent psychology. It's the equivalent of Barnet taking the lead at Internazionale in the first leg of a Champions League quarter-final.

Game 10: npower Championship, 2011-12, Selhurst Park
Saturday 1st October 2011 (20,074)
Referee: Kevin Wright (Cambridge)

Crystal Palace 2	**West Ham United 2**
Ambrose 6	Nolan 16
Murray 52	Carew 80

(West Ham: 4th in the table, 18 points from 30)

West Ham also played Crystal Palace on 1st October 2003 after relegation from the Premier League, and it was also their tenth league game that season. This one was at home, though, and they won it 3-0, with two goals from the 'occasional' Neil Mellor. Hammers had also dropped a point against Millwall at this stage in the season, but after winning, they had 20 points out of 30. If they win today they will have a parallel total of 20, but this game is at Selhurst Park, and Palace are fresh from having beaten the early league leaders Brighton 3-1 at their own new ground, all three goals coming in the last ten minutes.

The last time these two teams met in any form of league competition was in the Championship play-off final at the Millennium Stadium in Cardiff in May 2004. That day Neil Shipperley's goal sent Crystal Palace, managed by ex-Hammer Iain Dowie, into the Premier League and condemned West Ham United to another season chasing rainbows in the Championship.

Today these two sides are both lined up to move to athletics stadiums which will have ramifications for all of their supporters well into the twenty-first century. They are also both rebuilding sides with new managers and may provide a very interesting afternoon's football on a day historic for a completely different reason. With temperatures of 30 degrees centigrade in the capital this afternoon, it's the hottest October day in the UK since thermometers began.

West Ham have a new goalkeeper in Manuel Almunia, thanks to Rob Green sustaining a midweek knee injury that's likely to put him out of action for six weeks. The Arsenal reserve, signed on loan by Allardyce, has been the target of much mocking and divisive slurs over the years by my good friend and Arsenal fan Richard O'Dwyer. I won't bother texting him just yet for fear of what he might have to say on the matter. I gave him a bit of a caning over Arsenal's recent 8-2 reverse at Old Trafford, though at least the Arsenal keeper on the day (and wearing number 13) was Wojciech Szczesny. What - Arsenal with a bad / foreign goalkeeper? Surely not! Remember David Seaman? Bob Wilson? (Or was he Scottish?)

Sam Allardyce has his second column in the Evening Standard, to prove that first one was only 'exclusive' in that he isn't writing for anyone else. This one is an apology for Kevin Nolan's performance on the previous Tuesday against Ipswich, which Allardyce puts down to Nolan not yet having settled in London because his wife and kids are still oop North. It is humorously (but not very economically) headlined, 'Kevin will be on song for us once the rest of the Nolans are with him'. Just when I'm beginning to sympathise with the argument, Allardyce ruins it by comparing Nolan's predicament to that of Benni McCarthy who apparently experienced something similar at Blackburn when his wife and kids went off to live in Spain. That and his Weightwatchers' subscription running out, I guess.

Tom Cross, a lifelong Palace fan and season ticket holder has commandeered my ticket for this afternoon's game. This means in short that I'll have to sit in the Palace end with the Palace fans on a ludicrously hot day, unsheltered from the sun. The problem with getting tickets for away games these days, with so few on offer, is that you'll often find yourself with the home fans. Hardly a problem in London, as you won't give yourself away with anything you say. A journey to Sunderland, however, which I made back in December 2004, saw me right in the middle of the Mackems. Not only was I the only person in eight rows of fans not wearing the red and white striped club shirt, but everyone there kept asking me what my opinion was about the match, politics, even the weather. I had a few cod geordie phrases to get me by, all taken from Roger Mellie's Profanisaurus, but when West Ham scored, unexpectedly, and then a Sunderland player got unfairly (well, that was how I had to look at it) sent off, I had to stand up and wave my arms in frustration. And it was genuine frustration - there we were, a goal to the good against the league leaders, with them down to ten men - and I couldn't celebrate!

Tom can't help me today as his season ticket seat is on the other side of the Holmesdale Stand. And I need help. I am next to a guy who wants to talk football. What is this, a test? It's, 'What do I think about this player? or Did I go to the Brighton game? No, of course I didn't go to the Brighton game, you idiot. I support the team who are about to whip your arses, so shut up and prepare for defeat. Except I say, 'Yeah, I think Parr's good enough for the first team. No, Dougie's got his team selection right this time. Darren Ambrose's goal at the Amex was brilliant.' Thank g-d I read the programme in the bar.

Palace are attacking our end, and it doesn't take them long to put the ball in the back of the net. Classic route one. A long clearance from Julian Speroni is headed into Lee Hill's path by Glenn Murray, and his cross finds the Palace number seven Darren Ambrose. He buries it in the bottom of the net for his career fiftieth. Like I care about his achievements (but I have to as I'm at the Palace end, remember, and these things matter to the home fans). This is Palace's first attack, and in a game where they aren't awarded a single corner (we get 15), it still takes West Ham ten minutes to get level.

Neil Ship-per-ley! Neil Ship-per-ley! the Palace fans taunt. I forget where I am for a moment and start working on a response. How badly did Palace do in their one season back in the Premier League? The guy to my left laughs - has he read my mind? No, he's still laughing at the Shipperley comment. Limited imagination, these *Sarf* Londoners.

Lansbury is playing at the base of the diamond (does that sound right?). He finds McCartney overlapping on the left, who puts over a measured cross which Cole heads over to Nolan who flicks it in. He was in the same far post position earlier in the season when he scored his match-winning goal at Doncaster. If you are in possession of the footage for this goal, it's well worth checking out how, in his determination to pick out Nolan on the line, Carlton Cole whacks David Bentley on the head. He's the only one not celebrating a minute later. It's a 'double whammy' as Bentley was looking to take the chance all for himself to pocket his first West Ham goal.

I struggle to find Tom at half-time, so we miss out on the third pint - just as well in this heat, what with me still having to remember to stand up when Palace attack, and applaud when they score. My hopes that class will eventually tell in the game are thwarted when Palace regain the lead just seven minutes into the second half. Wilfried Zaha plants a hopeful ball into the box which Glenn Murray has time to control and steer into the corner of the West Ham goal net, past a slow-motion dive from Almunia. Despite plenty of possession, there's no getting past the stubborn Palace back line, but each time they break out, Faye is there with a perfect collection of well-timed tackles and intelligent distribution.

The guy to my right starts another philosophical conversation predicated on how Palace always manage to beat the top teams, but capitulate in their tussles with the league's minnows. But you haven't won this yet, I'm thinking. In reality I just nod and smile. I'm looking at him thinking *I'm a West Ham fan, you wanker...* Eventually I realise this bloke can't read minds.

Allardyce has this afternoon given a first start to Papa Bouba Diop the popular Sengalese international who famously scored for his country in a 1-0 win over World Cup holders France in the opening game at the FIFA 2002 World Cup. Coming in at 33 he is the oldest player in the squad, but with his 63 international caps and John Carew's 89, that's quite a high level of experience out there for West Ham. Carew is brought on for Collison in the 68th minute, and the second part of the double substitution is Baldock for Cole. There are just twenty minutes to turn this round and preserve the unbeaten away record. Finally with ten minutes left the domination produces a goal. Again it's the left boot of George McCartney that picks out Carew, and with a subtle twitch of his right scaline neck muscle, the Norwegian diverts the floating ball past Speroni's left hand for the equaliser. I restrain myself and look at the floor with the row of disappointed fans either side of me. With any luck they'll all go home in disappointment and I can celebrate on my own. Although that doesn't happen. Within two minutes there is a replica move, but this time although Carew's header again beats Speroni, it also misses the far post by a couple of inches.

There's been a rumour this week following Carlos Tevez's refusal to come on in a Champions' League game for Manchester City, that we might in a cartoon moment of madness be allowed to sign the Argentinian for duty in the nPower Championship. *There's only one Carlos Tevez!* the fans sing. Now that *is* funny. The last minute sees a brief appearance by Freddie Sears replacing Bentley. He gets a very generous welcome from the Palace fans and for the first time in the game I can stand up with them and clap without irony.

Hammers though haven't managed to grab all three points, which means they finish their tenth league game of the season with two points fewer than they had at this stage of the 2003-04 season. They will need to get into a winning habit to push ahead and prove the predictors right about retaining them as their favourites for automatic promotion at the end of 2011-12.

West Ham: 13 Almunia, 03 McCartney, 04 Nolan, 05 Tomkins, 08 Bentley (Sears 89), 09 Cole (Baldock 68), 10 Collison (Carew 68), 15 Faye, 18 Faubert, 21 Diop, 22 Lansbury

Tuesday night provides yet another foray into the magical music world of the outed live performer. Having seen Todd Rundgren perform his 1973 album *A Wizard, A True Star* in February 2010 at the Hammersmith Apollo, I am now off to see him perform his greatest hits at the Jazz Cafe in Camden Town with friend and fellow music aficionado Nick London.

Just imagine one of your favourite musicians performing live in front of you and a few hundred standing staring fans, playing word and instrument-perfect renditions of the songs that you grew up on but never for one living moment imagined witnessing live. Moments from your youth resurrected in front of you, decades after you first heard them. That's Roogalator, the Bible and Todd Rundgren, all playing in London, over just eight crazy magnificent days.

The cricketer Graham Dilley, at just 52, his age resonating at a year younger than me, has died suddenly 'after a short illness'. How short can an illness be to kill a 52 year old man? This is an England bowler who is still remembered for what must have been the innings of his life against Australia at Headingley in July 1981, scoring 56 while Ian Botham pillaged 50 odd at the other end, a total of 117 runs for the eighth wicket in just over an hour that put England ahead after having been put in again. Eventually this helped them to an unlikely victory. It was the first time since 1895 that a test side had won a game after following on. I still remember watching the game live on a television in the science lab at Ernest Bevin School, Tooting, with about twenty other members of the teaching staff all as fortunate as me to be ending that historical day without a timetabled lesson.

The second loss is another man in his fifties, Steve Jobs. At 56 the recognisably emaciated ex-CEO of Apple's computer company has finally died. He had been suffering with cancer of the pancreas for over seven years.

I bought my first Apple product, a Mac Book, in April 2007, followed by iPods, an iMac and finally an iPhone. While Jobs didn't actually invent these, he pioneered the ideas behind them and worked the company that delivered them to perfection. It was because of him that the Blackberry and Android phones developed as they did, and he's a key reason for the stunning advances in communication and technology in the last ten years. In fact I would argue that Apple has now eclipsed Microsoft in design, content and world importance. Jobs was said on his death to have a net worth of $7billion, which would take even Carlos Tevez almost a year to earn.

The final and most depressing loss is the Alaska Republican Sarah Palin, who has finally announced that she won't be running for US President next year. This has denied the world a year of public imbecility by someone who proved she was a genuine and serious rival to George W Bush, and her running would have ultimately improved Barack Obama's chances of a second term in office. Like Tony Blair, and before she had even managed a decent political career, she has succumbed to the lure of the green-backed monster. And they are both devout Christians. *Ouch*.

The second weekend in the month offers one of those football vacations that replace the senior league fixtures with a vastly inferior and increasingly irritating international schedule. FIFA has now decided that such games should be played on Friday evenings, and though this weekend's fixtures have conjured up a few qualifying deciders, it'd probably be more entertaining to watch one of the kids' matches down the park.

On Saturday, following a feeble draw with Montenegro that nevertheless qualifies England for Euro 2012, England's rugby team slip feebly out of the Rugby World Cup, after failing to beat a French team who lost their last qualifying match to Tonga. That's the football equivalent of England failing to beat Montenegro twice in the Euro 2012 qualifiers, as if anything like that could happen.

At lunchtime Tony Cottee pops round before his appearance on Sky's 'Soccer Saturday' to pick up a few boxes of his 'Career Goals' DVDs to flog at some of the forthcoming 'Boys of '86' evenings. This is a rather timid and disappointing end to the life of one of the best DVDs I have ever had the pleasure to have been involved with, and the story of which probably merits a book of its own. If you are a West Ham fan, and chances are that if you're reading this you are, (or hopefully will be by the end of chapter twelve, especially if it is spent celebrating promotion), you will know who Tony Cottee is. In a club with over a century of history, this man with 146 goals is their fifth highest goalscorer. In the list of the highest scorers in the football league from 1888, Tony makes the top twenty, with 217, two places above Geoff Hurst.

I first met Tony when I interviewed him after he had returned with Everton to beat West Ham at Upton Park in April 1994 and he had scored the only goal of the game. Having just beaten Spurs 4-1 at White Hart Lane, and with Everton in one of their many relegation crises, it was a surprise result. I found Tony an astute and intelligent interviewee, and someone who clearly still loved the club, even though he'd been at Everton for over five seasons. When I fed on the enthusiasm and asked TC if he could ever see himself playing for West Ham again, he smiled, but delivered a typically diplomatic response. Little did I know I'd be interviewing him in the same spot five months later to discuss his late goal for West Ham that had beaten Ron Atkinson's Aston Villa 1-0. Same spot for the interview and same spot for the goalscoring position, on the corner of the six yard box.

Our paths crossed many times in the next ten years, leading to the occasion I was entrusted with filming the 'Boys of '86' evening at Upton Park towards the end of the 2005-06 season. I was working on a 'Boys of '86' DVD for the club and had been given the chance to help staff the 20th anniversary evening celebration of the 1985-86 season, when West Ham finished 3rd in the top division. This is still, at the time of writing, their best achievement in 115 years, the closest since then being Harry Redknapp's 5th place finish in 1998-99. TC had retired from playing a few years earlier and put to me the idea of making a DVD of his career. I looked at the issues behind such an ambitious project. Cottee had played for West Ham, Everton, West Ham again, Selangor, Leicester City, Birmingham City, Norwich, Millwall and finally Barnet as a player manager. Luckily TC was contracted to Sky Sports, an employee of Sky. They could help with a lot of the footage, especially the obscure stuff, so we got cracking. Three years later we were ready to go, having got all and sundry on board, and Russell Brand (TC's biggest fan) to front the programme.

There were an absolute stash of goals on the programme, and interviews with Alan Shearer, Ray Winstone, Jeff Stelling, Graham Gooch, Trevor Brooking... the list went on. We called it 'Career Goals' and were ready to launch it at the end of 2009. For the uninitiated, the idea of such a project seems to be a no brainer. Make the copies, get the DVDs and sell them. No. You have untold difficulties getting new interviews, collecting footage of acceptable quality, revoicing those with a muffled (or no) soundtrack, and getting all the clubs on board to get their official product licence. Then you need PR and a decent, reputable and sympathetic distributor. Our PR was Paul Mace, an experienced and intelligent football man with plenty of ideas and lots of patience. The problem was, the timing. It was the summer of 2009 and nobody wanted to touch new products. 'Bobby Charlton, Geoff Hurst, Jimmy Greaves, but *Tony Cottee?*' I'd often hear.

'He scored more goals than Geoff Hurst,' I would say. 'He's a celebrity on Sky, and played for England. He's a footballer with a brain, and the whole thing is compered by Russell Brand for G-d's sake. He'll sign copies in your store.'

I could have been offering them a week in New York at the Plaza with Keira Knightley and Scarlet Johansson; it wouldn't have made any difference.

Paul Mace did a sterling job with the PR. He got the DVD coverage in the Sun, the Mail, the club fanzines and got TC onto the BBC, Talk Sport and BBC London Radio. However, the killer was not being able to get a sympathetic distribution company. We found an experienced one, but their lukewarm response to the product when TC and I went there for a meeting should have told us it was a bad idea. Despite a year on the job, as it were, the company have yet to make us a farthing. For all I know, they could be single-handedly responsible for the current financial crisis in this country. We gave a goon squad the opportunity to sell a profoundly marketable DVD, and they pooped.

We also did what we could our end, even putting together a product-based website (www.tonycottee306.com), but despite an earlier release, reduced price, the offer of signed copies and an appearance at the club, we sold relatively few. I put it to Tony that an affair with a politician or someone with a terminal disease might shift a few shelf loads, but he preferred the more orthodox sales approach. He's taken a crate or two today, so I hope his optimism is justified. It's a DVD that features over three hundred goals and a breathtakingly brilliant performance by Russell Brand, who makes some unexpected revelations about his love of the club and Tony Cottee in particular. By the time you read this we will have hopefully released it again for 2012, and got some people who know what they're doing on the case to sell a few copies.

Today brings more developments in the Olympic Stadium debacle. Having been led to believe it was done and 'dusty' with concrete, it now appears that the trawl of legal complaints and harassment that Tottenham Hotspur and Leyton Orient's lawyers have fabricated have worn down the owners of the stadium to a new position of 'no sale'. Fearing that it will be decades before such legal time-wasting comes to any kind of resolution, financial or of tenure, the owners decided to lease out the ground. This means the London Borough of Newham's potential £50m loan to West Ham will not now be needed. The taxpayer will now almost certainly have to fund the redevelopment of the venue into a football stadium. Short term saving, long term loss? Will the stadium owners ever replenish their input from the initial investment if they are only able to rent it out?

West Ham seem pleased by this development, which must mean they are still optimistic about securing the ground for themselves when it comes up for rent. The morning news is only giving them a 60% chance of ever playing there. Do you now understand why West Ham fans hate Spurs? They aren't even an East London team - they're *North* London. Why don't they move to Edmonton or Enfield? Or Preston? That's more North in the UK than Stratford, which is just over two miles from Upton Park.

Game 11: npower Championship, 2011-12, Upton Park
Saturday 15th October 2011 (31,448)
Referee: Andy D'Urso (Billericay)

West Ham United 4   Blackpool 0
Carew 12
Baldock 47, 51
Collison 55

(West Ham: 2nd in the table, 21 points from 33)

Ian Holloway's Blackpool side started their first season in the top division for forty years with a stack of surprise results, precipitated in the main by their decision to travel to away matches with the intention of scoring as many goals as they could, and winning. Unfortunately for the detractors of this deliciously cavalier approach, they eventually got found out and, despite efforts to tighten up at the back, dropped with West Ham into the Championship at the end of the 2010-11 season.

West Ham were one of the few sides who failed to score against Blackpool at home in the Premier League last season, but then they were also one of the few to stop Blackpool scoring on their travels, that game at Upton Park finishing goalless. In the 'lightning, she no strike twice... unless it's in our direction' world of West Ham football, I figure there will be goals today. As I sign in at the Press Lounge door, I ask around for a few predictions. No one I can find is prepared to offer me better than a score draw for West Ham this afternoon, and I am the lone predictor of victory, suggesting a 3-1 win for 'Big Sam's Claret and Blue Army'.

Out go Cole and Lansbury as the starting strike partnership, and in come Carew and Baldock. I sense an optimism around the ground for Baldock's inclusion, even though he is yet to score in a West Ham shirt. He is a striker in the mould of Tony Cottee or Paul Goddard. West Ham have been waiting for an effective six-yard box finisher like that for over a decade.

There are obvious nerves in the opening five minutes, concluding with an Almunia 'drop' in the area that Nolan rescues with a neat dribble out of the danger zone. Two minutes later he is in his predictable far post position testing Gilks with a volley into his chest. Matt Taylor receives a worryingly early booking from Essex ref Andy D'Urso, sure to incapacitate him in the tackle for the rest of the game. Does Carew's first start mean that he's proved his ninety minute fitness in training? The answer comes after just twelve minutes with a cross that he meets perfectly with a perfectly timed header to find the bottom corner of the Blackpool goal. 1-0! Just forty seconds later and Baldock is through after an error from Southern. Sensing the virtue of surprise, he hits the ball on the volley in the direction of the goal without even looking up - Gilks spills his effort, but no West Ham player is much past the half-way line to benefit from the potential chance. In the 17th minute Collison is booked for an innocuous-looking challenge. I wonder what price D'Urso is for handing out a first half red card?

Jeremy Nicholas has finally got himself back into the match programme after four years of trying, but he's had to write a book to do it. 'Mr Moon Has Left The Building' is selling well in the shops, and Rob, the programme editor, has deigned to give him a page to plug it. There's an extract covering West Ham's victory in the first round of the UEFA Cup in Croatia back in 1999, taken from his second season behind the microphone at Upton Park. The programme is a little thinner in content this season, the balance between text and pictures shifting towards the latter, the focus for the club's voice and history softened. In the same way, clubs have allowed a 'cut and paste' mentality to staff a league full of identically designed bland websites, different only in name and colour. They all look very pretty and professional, but are all ultimately shite.

There is no budget for football programmes either these days, and all of the available 'creative' content has to be offered free of charge by the contributors, most of whom have three or four other jobs to do before submitting their weekly copy on as an e-mail attachment. When the News of the World's Phil Hall joined West Ham as an advisor back in the 2006-07 season, he changed the shape of the programme to a square (shame on his pin-striped trousers and slip-ons) and threw out many regular features that had given it an oddbeat and humorous feel. Instead came a format that was predictable, professional and dull. Hall left at the end of the season, but his legacy remained. So much of the club's money now goes into the pockets of the players, that once-major concerns like the match programme have been allowed to become secondary budget items. Money only talks to the players, and hasn't had much of a conversation with the fans in the last ten years.

'You Arsehole!' Mud Mouth screams behind me. D'Urso has just awarded a foul in the centre circle as Baldock was breaking free of the Blackpool defence. Faubert's free kick sails harmlessly over both sets of players for a goal kick.

I've realised something else about the Mud Mouth twins that annoys me. Perhaps it's being at the back of the Press Pen, where they are barely six inches from the back of my head. They have this knack of producing spontaneous volleys of profanity from nowhere. The only warning is a perceived error, usually by Carlton Cole or the referee, and out come those ear-shattering yells.
'You're bloody useless Cole!'
'Fucking referee!'
'Put it in the bloody middle you wanker!'

What I've realised this afternoon though, being so close to them, is that they can carry on a generally civilised conversation throughout the game, pontificating about the performance of the opposition, their place in the table, how entertaining the game is, and then... the profanities. They can even fit one into their discussion as if it's arrived there from a different game.

'He's strong in the tackle, but I don't rate him good enough to play for his country. *Baldock, you fucking wanker! Why don't you hit the ball, you piece of shit!* Did you see Pearce called up Tomkins for the U21 squad next week? I've put it on my Sky Plus.'

Baldock and Carew are beginning to look like a decent starting bet for the rest of the season. Carew almost scores a second on the break, but Gilks beats out his low effort. The Norwegian shows some intricate touches for the oldest Hammer on the pitch. McCartney then gets mugged in the area, but Tom Ince (yes, the son of *you-know-who*) gives the ball straight back to him in his excitement, and the panic subsides.

West Ham have been battering Blackpool pretty solidly for half an hour, and Ian Holloway's side look a little distraught. He's standing in the opposition technical area fingering his chin with his right hand. McCartney blasts the ball out of defence but Southern's boot loops it into touch where Taylor still lies since receiving a kick in an earlier challenge. Without warning he leaps up from his supine position, catching the ball, and takes the throw in. Brilliant.

The Blackpool fans have taken about two-fifths of the Lower Sir Trev, and are clapping a lot, but are currently unable to hold any audible tune. Their team has a free kick about thirty yards out which fifty shades of grey-haired Gary Taylor-Fletcher plants a few yards south of the big screen over the illuminated scoreboard. That is very possibly the worst free kick ever seen at Upton Park.

Carew again forces Gilks into a save with his feet, and from the rebound Nolan finds Baldock whose instant shot goes just over. Is it Blackpool making West Ham look good, or has Big Sam finally found the right chemistry after ten games? Jonjo Shelvey tests Almunia from twenty-five yards with a daisy cutter that the Arsenal man thankfully shields cleanly. The two minutes of injury time pass uneventfully.

I meet Jamie on the steps, ADI's 'Mr Fixit', who helped us set up the equipment for the filming of the game against Aldershot Town back in August. I realise he's the one who must have put me in the frame for the MUTV job last month. I keep my head down.

Just 90 seconds into the second half and Sam Baldock is put through one on one. It seems to take him forever to draw the keeper - will he go round him? - he places the ball deftly under his body for West Ham's second. A two goal cushion... what luxury... and Sam's two new starting strikers have a goal each.

Within a couple of minutes it's three! Carew has a chance inside the six yard box but loses possession, and as two Blackpool defenders attempt to clear, Baldock runs between them and flicks the loose ball into the net! Two minutes later Jack Collison sees a deflected clearance drop at his feet just inside the area, and he gleefully rams it home! A delightful start to the second half with three goals in ten minutes... And it's almost FIVE as Baldock runs free again, but Gilks saves well. Now Matt Taylor hits a rising pass just over... It seems unlikely that Holloway's men will stop Baldock getting his hat-trick. Carew though, breaking down the left, does just that when, with Baldock screaming for a pass, the thinning-haired one chisels a shot that clears the bar. Baldock favours the Norwegian striker with a few choice epithets to describe his disappointment.

Blackpool are, of course, the side who almost forced West Ham to sign Robbie Keane, allowing him to score in the 3-1 away Premier League victory earlier this year. Part of the loan deal from Spurs was that West Ham would have to sign him if they stayed up. As it turned out, Keane's proliferation for wasting several 'gilt-edged' opportunities in key home games against Aston Villa and Blackburn meant another 'escape to victory' was not possible, so relegation. At least the club saved 7 million quid! In the end Keane had to go to LA to find a club who 'wanted' to sign him...

James Tomkins leaves the field on the hour to be replaced by Abdoulaye Faye, who must consider himself the most unlucky player in the Championship to have been dropped after his four successive 'man of the match' displays. Matt Taylor (did Jeremy say 'Mark' Taylor?) now leaves the field to be replaced by Freddie Sears, saving Taylor from a potential red. Maybe he should sub Collison too for the same reason. It seems unlikely that Blackpool will score four now...

Triple substitution for Blackpool: Off Ince, on Ormerod, off Shelvey on Lua Lua and off Phillips and on Bogdanovich. Kevin Phillips? He has been on the pitch for nearly 75 minutes and I didn't even notice... John Carew gets a welter of applause as he goes off ten minutes from the end, to be replaced by Mark Noble.

Faubert's brilliant run ends with a pass laid perfectly into Baldock's path, but Gilks is just able to fingertip the striker's effort round the post and again deny him his well-deserved hat-trick. Now Blackpool have a chance as Stephen Crainey gets through on the left after a quick one-two, but Almunia beats his shot out. Blackpool have a corner! Is it their first? Well, they now have a second. Their fans applaud and cheer ironically. And let's face it, that is some distance to travel to see your side tonked 4-0! As in the seventies, and not forgetting West Ham's FA Cup 0-4 thrashing at the Seasiders in 1971, 'Loyal Supporters!'

After the interval of Blackpool action, normal service is resumed, with Hammers on the attack. The action comes to a halt as the mighty Bouba Diop has been slain like a giant oak, unnoticed (or ignored) by Andy D'Urso. In the chicken run, the fans sing directly at him, *The referee's a wanker!* I'd love to know just what referees think when they hear that.

This has been a good win for West Ham, who seem to have got more out of the fortnight off than Blackpool. Why is that? Maybe we'll discover at the Media Conference. It'll be good to see Sam Allardyce with something to celebrate. The sponsors have finally chosen a worthy man of the match, we hear, over the PA, it's Sam Baldock. Now can he get his hat-trick in these last five minutes? And will we have gone up to second place in the table by the end of the game?

Blackpool still attack, forcing three corners, but never seriously threaten the West Ham goal. Andy D'Urso finally blows the whistle, and the theme tune pumps out round the ground. Bubbles has rarely sounded so good.

This is West Ham's biggest home league victory since September 2005, when Marlon Harewood hit a hat-trick in a 4-0 win against Aston Villa.

West Ham: 13 Almunia, 2 Reid, 3 McCartney, 4 Nolan, 5 Tomkins (5 Faye 60), 7 Baldock, 10 Collison, 11 Carew (16 Noble 80), 14 Taylor (19 Sears 62), 18 Faubert, 21 Bouba Diop

Game 12: npower Championship, 2011-12, St Mary's
Tuesday 18th October 2011 (32,152)
Referee: Darren Deadman (Cambridge)

Southampton 1   West Ham United 0
Hooiveld 45

(West Ham: 2nd in the table, 21 points from 36)

This is the first evidence that it is going to be a long, long season. Sam Allardyce plays a 4-5-1 with Carew up front, and it's a long long ball game. Lansbury and Baldock play behind Carew with limited effect. Noble hits the post with an early effort, but after Taylor limps off with a damaged calf after twenty minutes it's clear that the best West Ham can hope for is to stop Southampton scoring and nick a point.

Championship relic David Connolly is in his second set of red stripes, having played for Sunderland, prior to Southampton, in 2006-09. In just one season for West Ham the player Roeder christened the 'Angry Ant' managed 39 appearances and scored 10 goals. He chalked up the same number of appearances for the Black Cats, over three seasons, scoring 13 goals in all that time. George McCartney's career has also seen him play at the Stadium of Shite. Do players who have played over two periods for a team with red and white stripes become confused when they face an opposition wearing those same colours? Apparently not. But have there ever been any colour blind players? What would be the worst teams they could play for, kit-wise? This after Spurs turned up to play Newcastle at St James' Park on Sunday in an all purple kit. *Why?* I texted my fellow Hammer fan Professor Jason, who replied less than five seconds after I'd pressed 'send' with the response, *'Because they're all dickheads.'*

Just before half-time Daniel Fox's inswinging corner is headed home by on-loan Celtic defender Jos Hooiveld. In injury time West Ham almost grab an equaliser off the boot of a Southampton defender, but then referee Deadman denies a second Southampton goal for a free kick that he has blown up for too quickly instead of playing advantage. The free-kick is wasted, but the final whistle follows swiftly. 'Sam Allardyce will be a less than happy chappy,' says Phil Commentator of BBC London 94.9 who, for some reason, I want to punch. He has been calling Faye 'Abdullah Fye' throughout the game, when any fule no it is *'Faye'* as in 'too much *pay'*. He calls Sam Baldock 'Bulldog' and has twice referred to Jack Collison as 'Cullison'. It's not his fault, I'm sure, but I'm glad he's out of range of any cull of sputum I might be able to summon from the back of my throat.

Despite losing their unbeaten record on the road, West Ham are still second in the Championship partly thanks to Middlesbrough's less impressive goal difference. With the Brighton and Leicester fixtures approaching, we'll see if Big Sam can decide playing 'the West Ham way' might be a good idea after all.

West Ham: 13 Almunia, 2 Reid, 3 McCartney, 4 Nolan (capt.), 15 Faye, 7 Baldock, 11 Carew (17 O'Brien 78), 14 Taylor (30 Piquionne 20), 18 Faubert, 21 Bouba Diop (16 Noble 66), 22 Lansbury

The game scheduler at Sky Sports has again made the right choice by sending a crew down for the Monday night game to Brighton to cover the top of the table clash at the Amex (or American Excess) Stadium. Jeremy Nicholas has kindly invited me over to spend the evening with him and his missus watching the game in the hope of three points over an Indian and a clutch of Stella Artois 'Cidres' (a drink I've taken to since I quaffed a couple of pints with Tom earlier in the month at a pub just outside Selhurst Park). Jeremy and I are often pilloried for living in West London, but I always put it down to an accident of Geography rather than anything the trolls might nail up. It's true that my father followed Chelsea and Queens Park Rangers, and would often say how he felt he'd failed as a father the moment I declared my allegiance to the Hammers. Even if I lived in the Outer Hebrides, open up my arteries and I would still bleed claret. And blue.

Game 13: npower Championship, 2011-12, Amex Stadium
Monday 24th October 2011 (20,686)
Referee: Kevin Friend (Leicestershire)

Brighton 0   **West Ham United 1**
                                    Nolan 17

(West Ham: 2nd in the table, 24 points from 39)

After last week's fruitless trip to the coast, Big Sam's crew step it up on a very wet American Express Brighton pitch, coping better with the conditions than their hosts. I've asked Jeremy to announce the West Ham substitutions for me, if there are any, with the TV sound down. A personal reading, you might call it.

He and Jeanette have ordered a take-away that's enough for six people, but we're all ravenous, so that shouldn't be a problem. It arrives just as the match kicks off, which might have been difficult to serve up if we were at Upton Park, but Jeremy has taken care of business on the plates and cutlery front, so with one eye on the food and the other on the telly, we begin.

Neither side is making much progress in the driving rain, so conversation in the room addresses the Anton Ferdinand v John Terry incident at Loftus Road yesterday in the live game between QPR and Chelsea. The Guardian and lots of other papers have learned that, unable to deal with criticism of alleged details of his alleged personal life, Terry is alleged to have called Ferdinand a 'fucking black c**'. My point is, with the aid of some lip reading of the incident now available for general consumption on 'You Tube', that Terry may have called Ferdinand a 'Black Cat', in reference to his erstwhile career at Sunderland before joining QPR. (Sunderland are sometimes referred to as the 'Black Cats' according to Mackem folklore)

The conversation peters out as Kevin Nolan dispossesses Liam Bridcutt and breaks free of the Brighton defence. He lets fly from twenty-five yards with a shot that skids off the wet turf past Harper into the back of the Brighton net. One-nil after just sixteen minutes; poor Steve Harper only joined the club this morning on loan from Newcastle United. Away from home the lads. And Alan Pardew said less than a week ago that Harper was still a key player for Newcastle, despite being kept out of the team by Tim Krul. Six days later and he's at Brighton. I suppose that's 'key' in a financial sense...

Hammers are under increasing pressure as the half develops, but still look strong in defence. I wonder if Phil of BBC London is getting Faye's name right tonight? He's playing well enough to deserve it. The conversation turns to the value for money Manchester United's fans are getting from their season ticket this season, having already witnessed an 8-2 victory over Arsenal, followed by a 1-6 home trouncing from rivals Manchester City. Seventeen goals in two games, but only one in this frankly disappointing Amex fixture. At least the result has gone the right way, and the food is excellent.

Jeremy's loo, which I'm off to visit at the break, is a shrine to the Hammers. It features an unexpectedly vast library of West Ham literature (including a couple of my efforts, I'm glad to see), and I miss the first few minutes of the second half nosing through John Northcutt's 'The Claret and Blue Book of West Ham United'.

I needn't have worried, the second half isn't much of an improvement on the first. Sears is on for Papa Bouba Diop, but in a cidre-induced haze I forget to ask Jeremy to announce it. John Carew comes close with a well-struck shot on the turn that Harper does well to keep out, and Hoskins comes close in the last few minutes for Brighton. In the end it's three well-earned points, and after a quick chat about the book I'm writing (this one, actually, which is a little surreal, as you're currently reading it) I make my way downstairs to the car. Jules has come to pick me up on her way home. How civilized is that?

West Ham: 13 Almunia, 2 Reid, 3 McCartney, 4 Nolan, 15 Faye, 10 Collison, 11 Carew (30 Piquionne 65), 16 Noble, 17 O'Brien, 18 Faubert (7 Baldock 90), 21 Bouba Diop (19 Sears 54)

News is coming through about Carlos Tevez and the tribunal's conclusion regarding his punishment for refusing to come on as sub for Manchester City in some Champions League game. He has apparently been fined just four weeks wages, though that does come to a few bob over a million pounds. City have since beaten Manchester United 6-1 at Old Trafford, and tonight have massacred Wolves 5-2 in the League Cup at Molineux with their reserve team. It doesn't look like they're currently missing him.

I can't help but reflect on events on the last day of August 2006, when he and his Argentina World Cup compatriot Javier Mascherano signed for West Ham United. This is ultimately another (unheeded) warning about all that glitters, or glisters... or festers...

Game 14: nPower Championship, 2011-12, Upton Park
Saturday October 29th 2011 (30,410)
Referee: James Linington (Isle of Wight)

West Ham 3	**Leicester City 2**
Baldock 21, 71	King 58, 74
Faubert 22	

(West Ham: 2nd in the table, 27 points from 42)

Rob Green is back, and this afternoon's ref is from the Isle of Wight. Just how much excitement can one West Ham fan take?

Ex-Hammers Paul Konchesky and John Pantsil (on the bench) are at Upton Park in Leicester shirts this afternoon. Leicester are wearing an all-blue Chelski-esque kit. Two good omens there, the first being the fact that Chelsea have just lost 3-5 at home to an improving Arsenal. The second is that Leicester City have tended to 'roll over' in that all blue kit whenever they've played at Upton Park. The last time the two sides met was ten years ago, in 2001-02, on a cold January Saturday, when a first half goal by Paolo Di Canio divided the teams. This was just three weeks after a 1-1 draw at Filbert Street when Di Canio scored from a penalty that was, equally incredibly, a contender for Hammers' Goal of the Season that year, so cheeky was his chip from the spot to wrong foot Ian Walker.

In the present, however, Leicester have just sacked their manager Sven Goran Chequeriksson 'by mutual consent'. It's another expensive payday and they're already looking for a replacement, currently thought to be Martin O'Neill. He is supposedly about to return for another stint at the club to follow his successes at the end of the 1990s when the club achieved their highest league finish yet and won the League Cup. I don't think so.

Rob Green's return, sooner than the Doc expected, is met with great cheers from the crowd who have quickly recognised the shortcomings of Arsenal's cross-shy Almunia. Hammers are second in the table, and if Middlesbrough win at Southampton and West Ham beat Leicester, they could be top tonight (on goal difference). Leicester's keeper is Kasper Schmeichel, son of the great Peter. His father, with his mixture of Danish brogue and Manchester vernacular, memorably secured a two million pound four year contract with the BBC in 2003 as a Match of the Day punter only to swiftly reveal his inadequacies in front of the camera. After much failed effort at PR training and several media courses, the amiable Dutch import was offered an end of contract payment to terminate his appointment two years short of its planned date. I wonder what he spent that million pounds on... good old BBC.

The first real action in the game occurs on fifteen minutes with Faye's near post header from Collison's cross cleared off the line from under the bar by Leicester's Sol Bamba. Leicester's technical area is filled this afternoon by stand-in managers John Rudkin and Mike Stowell. They sound like extras in some limping 70s' US detective series.

Nolan is booked for a debatable foul just inside the West Ham half. Carew's hopeful far post cross is bundled over the line by Sam Baldock on twenty minutes. The pressure has counted, though few genuine chances have been created so far for a full quarter of the game. Now the explosion... as Collison's wide run and pull back for Faubert sees the Frenchman coolly steer the ball into the far corner for two goals in two minutes... Southampton have taken the lead against Middlesbrough. Carew now finds Baldock in the 26th minute and the diminutive pint-sized cliché-ridden striker curls a shot from the edge of the area past Schmeichel but against the post. The referee pulls the action back for a foul by Carew. The camera work from the gantry is shaky and poorly framed, but free. We can't really compete with that kind of quality, on any level...

Baldock and Carew have been tearing the Leicester defence apart, but something is clearly wrong with Carew, who is substituted on the half hour by Freddie Piquionne. It's somehow sobering to hear Jeremy making the announcement from the touchline, free of his plate of take-away and cider glass. Nugent gets up for a header that is blocked for a corner. Wellens' corner is expertly handled by Green. Good to have you back, Rob.

The guy in front of me is logging the game for someone, probably West Ham. He has 'West Ham United' stitched into the upper arm of his jacket. Faye is a tower of strength in the defence, restored to his rightful position as starter in the back four. Peltier nutmegs McCartney and his cross is hit towards goal by St.Ledger (footballer or horse race?). The ball strikes Reid's boot and loops wide with Green committed and beaten. Middlesbrough have conceded a second. Abe's far post cross is headed over by Jermain Beckford. McCartney clears with St.Ledger looking for a tap-in, but the corner is again wasted. Ex-Villa star Darius Vassell is crocked but the half-time whistle goes before he can be replaced by Lloyd Dyer. More evidence that Leicester City has become a care home for pensioned off Premier League players.

With the Bristol City home game on Tuesday and a potential three points today, the season is thickening nicely. This courtesy to the media continues to fascinate me. It is, after all, they who are after something (a story in this case) but the food, drinks (non-alcoholic) and general hospitality is all provided free by the club. I have a round of brie and cranberry and tomato and hummus sandwiches that wouldn't look out of place in Marks & Spencer.

The second half starts as falteringly as the first, but it's Leicester who are chasing the game, with the West Ham goals already in the bag. The sun has hidden behind some scabby grey clouds that threaten cold and rain. Beckford steps off for Steve Howard in the 57th minute. That was something Jeremy pointed out about the matchday announcer. When the substitutes go on, you announce opposition names, 'Coming on for Accrington Stanley is Number 26, George Thump,' but with home players it has to be 'Will you please welcome...' Then again, if Judas' son had come on as a sub for Blackpool the other week and Jeremy had given it, 'Will you please welcome...' he'd have been lynched.

Konchesky shields Piquionne's attempt to put Baldock through and puts the ball into touch, just a few yards from where I interviewed him for the club the week before the 2006 FA Cup Final. Happier days.

Leicester's goal has been coming, and it does on the hour, Wellens' left wing cross is headed home by Andy King, Jack Collison's Welsh team-mate. A minute later Leicester have another corner and St.Ledger squirts his far post effort wide when it looked like the equaliser. At the other end, Baldock forces a good save, low down, from Schmeichel. Reid now gets in a terrible tangle in the area with Wellens, but referee Linington waves the Leicester penalty appeals away. The sun creeps out again just as the floodlights tinkle on. Sub Lloyd Dyer breaks free wide on the right, but his shot is smothered by Green. This is worrying.

Abdoulaye Faye (correctly pronounced 'FAY' - thanks, Jeremy) is substituted by James Tomkins in the 65th minute. Swansea are 2-0 up against Bolton. Might mean we don't have to play them again for a while if we take their place, a thought of poetic dimensions, especially in the Nigel Reo-Coker department. A subtle flick on from Piquionne puts Baldock through and the expletive deleted striker strokes the ball into the net for a 70th minute West Ham third. Baldock now has four in his last two home games and looks a good bet for top scorer in 2011-12. Lloyd Dyer becomes one of those rare football victims, a subbed sub. In the seventy-fifth minute, recent arrival Andy King spanks a blistering strike, his second for Leicester in just twenty minutes on the pitch, past a well-beaten Rob Green. The two goal cushion vanishes almost as suddenly as it had returned.

For a moment it seems as though we might be heading for one of those 'goals conceded in injury time' moments that this season has been full of, but after a couple of corners and a run on West Ham's tested defence, Leicester run out of steam and time.

West Ham: 1 Green, 2 Reid, 3 McCartney, 4 Nolan, 7 Baldock (19 Sears 86), 10 Collison, 11 Carew (30 Piquionne 30), 15 Faye (5 Tomkins 64), 16 Noble, 17 O'Brien, 18 Faubert

I discovered running when I was 34. As anyone who has been there will tell you, it will change your life in the same way that 'getting religion' can do to people. But then running is a religion. Nearly twenty years on from my conversion, it has become a way of life for me. Every Sunday morning I go out at around ten, either round Richmond Park (7.5 miles) or on my three parks run through Osterley Park, along the Grand Union Canal and back home through Syon Park (9 miles). I also nip out another two or three times in the week for slightly shorter runs.

The effect of a decent run where you push yourself is that your body produces endorphins that take you on a natural high. The experience is neither life-threatening nor wallet voiding, though in evangelical runners, it can produce an irritating intolerance to obesity. My need to get fit came from a gradual awakening to the DNA future ahead of me, starring Anne Gina, Hart to Hart Attack, Colless Stroll and Sammy Stroke. I got fit the quickest way I could, given a gentle push in the weight loss direction by a serious bout of shingles, during which I lost nearly two stone.

With running come niggles and injuries. I have a clicking left leg around the knee joint, given to sudden collapsing when walking, so Jules has put me in touch with the guy her karate mates use in times of trouble, Reg the Physio. For thirty quid a pop, Reg has been working on the knee joint, by giving me exercises to build up my glutes and by connecting me to an electric gizmo that gives the muscles in my left thigh the necessary current to relax them. If you want this kind of treatment on the NHS it might take a few months to even get a date set. If you run and you're injured, you'll rather go without food for a week than forgo the appointment at the physio.

On Halloween, the last day of the month, it is my eighth wedding anniversary, and time to celebrate eighteen years with Jules, who I met back in 1993. Midnight in Paris, Woody Allen's latest, is a good choice.

They say that relationships are about growing together, celebrating differences and adjusting with time and change itself so that each day still offers something new. Or some such bullshit. But it still feels like that. You may not be making lurve every time you get a private moment together after 18 years, but there will still be magic enough for two. Come on, are you that cynical that you can't embrace that simple little conceit? If you're a true West Ham fan, you must be a romantic at heart.

I know I am.

Chapter 6

New Bubbles

November 2011

Game 15: nPower Championship, 2011-12, Upton Park
Tuesday November 1st 2011 (27,980)
Referee: Mark Haywood (West Yorkshire)

West Ham 0   **Bristol City 0**

(West Ham: 2nd in the table, 28 points from 45)

Top plays bottom, and David James, surely the first keeper to play at Upton Park in a white shirt, gets a fantastic reception from the Bobby Moore end. Glenn Roeder's first big signing at £5 million, James immediately set about paying back the investment by damaging his knee ligaments at White Hart Lane and sidelining himself for six months. What is he now, 41? I think you get my drift. Retire for g-d's sake, before it all gets embarrassing. James is a year older than the City manager, Derek McInnes who, it says in the programme, *enjoyed a successful playing career*. With whom? West Bromwich Albion. No, mate, I think you'll find that was Jeff Astle.

Bristol City boast a squad of 32 players. West Ham have 24. But who has the bigger wages bill, I wonder?

Winston Reid is crocked in the fourth minute and replaced by Abdoulaye Faye, who, let's face it, should have been starting in the first place. Why *isn't* he starting? I'm hoping this isn't some kind of squad mentality arrogance. Play the best eleven, *purlease*.

I've had the biggest paper plate of chips and beans you've ever seen, and am sitting here like a total pork-u-pine. Meanwhile, out in front of me, Sam Baldock has missed two quite difficult chances, both shots on the turn. Sears hits a sweet curved effort from outside the area which thuds back out off the foot of a post to safety. The journo to my left is old school, writing up his report in a spring bound lined notebook, the centre of each page providing a pitch shape for logging moves and moments from the game. Cute.

Bristol's number 36, Ryan McGivern, on loan from Manchester City, has a ludicrous fry up of peroxide blond hair about his person. He's been on loan at Morecambe, Leicester City, Walsall and Crystal Palace, but he has at least made his debut for City, back in April 2011 against Sunderland.

Halfway through the first half and not much to shout about, I look up at the gantry to check out the Sky Reporter sending his filmed reports back to Jeff Stelling every ten minutes or so on Sky Sports News Gillette Soccer Tuesday. Earlier he was in the Press Lounge telling his cameraman how he's looking for a house in Weybridge. 'But it's so *pricey* there,' he says. 'I'm playing for a local side now,' he says. 'In Ewell. Just a minute from the house. I get changed at five to ten and I'm on the pitch five minutes later,' he says.

'Where do you play?' the cameraman asks, grinning.

'Centre mid,' he says.

Centre *what*?

'I love it,' he says.

Why would you? I keep thinking. Wouldn't you rather be playing for Ewell FC?

West Ham are trying to walk the ball into the net allowing James the opportunity to make one completely unnecessarily acrobatic save. And there's another. Hard to believe that there's only ten minutes left of the half. I have just noticed the ground is full tonight. In anticipation of a 6-0 drubbing? Or the kids for a quid lure? Last year West Ham played Oxford United at Upton Park in the Carling Cup, Rumbelows League Cup, whatever it's called... and who should stroll up with his son into the Press Lounge, *I am the One and Only*, that's who! Chesney effing Hawkes! A major Hammers' fan, I have it on good authority. We only get to see him at Upton Park when it's Kids for a Quid night, but a great fan. He's probably here with his son tonight. One quid only for a one hit wonder?

Bristol City almost score when Rob Green lets a shot from Marvin Elliott pass him and bounce away to safety off the foot of a post. Good leave. City are getting into the game now. A header from Elliott with just Green to beat is directed straight into his midriff. West Ham fans have gone very quiet. At least the illusion of a major slaughtering has evaporated.

Faye slots a ball through the City defence to give Sears a real opportunity, but Freddie pulls it back across the box instead of going for glory. The sign of a player currently without confidence, and there are plenty of those signs tonight. The fourth official says four minutes of additional time. Noble finds Faubert down the right whose pinpoint cross is headed straight at the keeper by Piquionne. Noble skies an opportunity a minute later. Southampton are beating Peterborough 2-0. We should have got something at St Mary's that night. They are the super soaraway Sun Champions at this moment. Ref puts us out of our misery and it's time for a cup of tea. Could this end up a goalless farce? Well, of course it could. This is *West Ham*, remember?

Amy Childs from *The Only Way Is Essex*, no doubt a lifelong West Ham United fan, is going to be talking to Jeremy during the interval. Definitely time for a cup of tea elsewhere.

In the first 30 seconds of the second half, Piquionne is sent through wide, but scuffs his shot into the hoardings. Some delicate skills from Tomkins and another header just wide from Piquionne. The sound of Bubbles is launched up into the rafters of the stadium. West Ham are now attacking the Sir Trevor Brooking end. Mark Noble, uninspired by the giant poster picture of Sir Trev, wastes the first free kick of the half. At the other end, only a last minute interception from Faye prevents City taking the lead as he takes the ball off the toes of Nicky Maynard.

McCartney steps too quickly into the breach and puts the ball into touch instead of finding O'Brien. Legend West Ham player, Noble, all heart and determination, but he looks majorly off the pace this evening, and without the requisite skill to make such a facet of his game unimportant. Another free kick. A free header for Tomkins, but he's too far out to get any real welly on it. Good tackle from McCartney as Skuse steps up. Well *Skuse* me.

The Hammers fans are starting to get a bit nervous. Noble gives the ball away in midfield. West Ham need to be patient, and at the moment they are anything but. Fantastic piece of play from O'Brien, great turn and cross, but just too high for the the head of Piquionne. We have a corner. Noble will take. Soon the ball is back with Green. Didn't think I'd say it, but we are missing John Carew. And yesterday evening Demba Ba scored another hat-trick for Newcastle. Alan Pardew has raised his Toon Army side above Chelsea in the Premier League, for now at least.

Elliott brings down McCartney. Sam Allardyce prowls around his technical area like a nervous undertaker at the house of the deceased, awaiting the cortège. Collison can't take the ball past anyone tonight. It's so-*oh* frustrating. Baldock is through but fires straight at James. The shaking camera covering the action on the big screen looks like it was filmed from the deck of the Titanic. Who hired that cameraman? No wonder they're free. They should be paying for the thrill of filming this non-event! Baldock shoots over, he can't keep his shot down. I am thinking that he may well be a sell by date situation.

Carlton Cole is on the bench, I notice, as we pass the hour. City replace Martyn Woolford with Yannick Bolasie. Ominously the Bristol City fans start singing his name...

Baldock is taken off. Sam can't let any more chances go begging. He brings on Carlton Cole in the 68th minute. Middlesbrough are 3-1 up at Doncaster. Julien Faubert seems to lose his way and chips his cross up into the rafters. The 'old school' journos at the end of my row have decided to call it a day and are leaving twenty minutes before the end. When did we last play Bristol City here, I find myself wondering...

The cameraman has lost his bearings and is pointing his camera at the roof over the chicken run. About time James made a mistake. The truth is West Ham haven't really tested him at all this evening. Bristol City appear to have already settled for a point. Sears pokes a ball through a crowd of players that tamely makes its way through to the keeper. But a corner arrives. And goes. Nolan has been remarkably quiet this evening. Have only just seen him out there.

Freddie Sears is replaced by Papa Bouba Diop, but no-one sings, *You don't know what you're doing...* The cameraman, who the chant could also have been directed at, appears to have left a small badger in charge of his camera. Ten man Peterborough have grabbed a goal back against Southampton. Come on the Posh!

As I said at half time to a mate of mine from the Press Lounge, this one had 'goalless draw' written all over it from the moment they kicked off... Those two shots against the post is all they'll be able to parade for the highlights. Faubert suddenly finds Cole, but he drops his head back and skies it on the edge of the six yard box...

There are very few goalless draws at Upton Park these days. Hopefully that's the one for the season.

West Ham: 1 Green, 2 Reid (15 Faye 7), 3 McCartney, 5 Tomkins, 17 O'Brien, 18 Faubert, 4 Nolan, 16 Noble, 7 Baldock (9 Cole 68), 19 Sears (21 Diop 76), 30 Piquionne

Game 16: nPower Championship, 2011-12, KC Stadium
Saturday November 5th 2011 (21,756)
Referee: Nigel Miller (County Durham)

Hull City 0   **West Ham 2**
                                   Baldock 49
                                   Collison 57

(West Ham: 2nd in the table, 31 points from 48)

Hull have just had a seven match unbeaten run ended at Barnsley, but at home it is an enviable four straight wins. Sam starts with Baldock and the returning Carew, with Cole on the bench joined by the dropped Sears and Piquionne.

The forthcoming Remembrance Sunday, a week away, draws the standard one minute's silence before kick off, 'lest we forget,' says the stadium announcer. Since 1980 it has become a remembrance for any who have given their lives for peace and freedom.

West Ham wear the old 70s' away kit of the two maroon hoops on a light blue kit, but it's Hull who have the best of the first half, despite the kit, and a vigilant Faye clears off the line from Koren after Green has only half parried the shot. Cole comes on for a tired looking Carew at the beginning of the second half and stokes up the Hammer power to earn an early Noble corner, from which his header finds Baldock on the far post to give West Ham the lead. It won't be the first time this season the fans are wondering why Allardyce doesn't start with Cole. There again, bringing him on when he does has done the trick. Eight minutes later and Cole is again the architect with a measured through ball for Collison to make it 2-0. The second goal knocks out Hull and the BBC commentator John Roder, who refers to them in the second half as 'Nigel *Worthington's* team' as opposed to Pearson's. Not a great compliment, as Worthington was sacked last month as Northern Ireland manager and isn't on anyone's to hire list at the moment.

By the end of the day, Hull City have dropped out of the play-off zone, and West Ham remain in the automatic promotion places with Southampton.

West Ham: 1 Green, 3 McCartney, 5 Tomkins, 15 Faye, 18 Faubert, 4 Nolan, 10 Collison, 16 Noble, 21 Diop (19 Sears 83), 7 Baldock (30 Piquionne 87), 11 Carew (9 Cole 46)

Three years ago, on 15th November 2008, my three month reign looking after the microphone for Jeremy Nicholas, while Scott Duxbury worked out how to reinstate him without losing face, came to an end. It was put to me at lunchtime by the new man in charge of the PA Room since the sudden and unexplained departure of Nicola Lord, that he had commissioned a new version of 'Bubbles' and that he wanted it playing that afternoon before the teams came out. I looked at him in disbelief. 'Change' is a tough word in any world, but in a world as designed and decided as that of a West Ham fan, it's nigh on impossible. Remember the Bond Scheme? Remember Lou Macari? Remember the Poll Tax? I feared the worst. But I asked him for a copy, and he handed over the CD. It had 'Bubbles - New Version' written on it, rather ominously. He smiled at me and left hurriedly, as if he'd handed me an unexploded bomb. He had.

I listened to the track in headphones in the PA Room. As the noise from the whirling CD struck my ears, time seemed to stand still. The way I had run the job since getting it involved turning up at the ground at 9.30am for a briefing with Nicola and the team at 10. There we would confirm the music tracks and check we had all the video sequences and the running order with strict timing perfectly in place. Then it would be down to the main office to collect the birthday wishes and celebration requests. Back up to the PA room and once the TV companies had completed their pre-match interviews, I would give the system a final test by announcing memorable West Ham teams from the 1970s, ('Number 4: Peter Eustace' a favourite) and then, before you know it, the turnstiles had opened. Once we got to ten minutes to three we would play the Prokofiev Romeo and Juliet 'Dance of the Knights' theme followed by 'Bubbles' as West Ham came out onto the pitch, fading it out for the fans to sing *Fortune's Always Hiding*, always the moment to raise the hairs on the back of your neck. The piece of crap I was listening to was unlikely to even raise a laugh. It was shocking. I could taste blood in my mouth after gnawing at my lip. I took a deep breath and got on the phone to the PA man. He wouldn't listen to my pleas, and said they'd spent a lot of money on it, so they had to put it out there. The fans would get used to it in time. I still have a copy of it (which hasn't been played since that afternoon).

Jeremy has related bookloads of nightmare experiences he has had behind the mike at Upton Park, including several that didn't make the final cut of his announcer's autobiography 'Mr Moon Has Left The Stadium', so I know some of the insane things he's been expected to do. Then, I could only think that this might be my last time behind the mike at Upton Park. And how right I was. As the teams came out, Robin (the sound man) pressed 'play' and the dirge of the 'New Bubbles' theme dribbled out of the stadium PA like a shot of phlegm. As I read out the teams for the second time, I could sense unease in the crowd. It had nothing to do with the names of the Portsmouth players.

A couple of Wednesdays later, the call I had been expecting came. For the next month the West Ham blogs and dogsites were filled with several intimidating comments about me, and how I had been sacked for playing my own version of Bubbles. Naturally enough at the next home game the original version was played, so the apocryphal rumour became a truth, and nothing I could do would change it.

In the end you have to just accept such social shitework things and move on. Many times prescribed fate will approach you like a bad plotline in a cheap American detective series. Another such moment was at the local youth club when, aged 15, I was clumsily dumped by a new girlfriend of four weeks. I hadn't even managed a full calendar month before I was to hear her line: 'Things aren't really working out, are they?' Hard to contradict that kind of prescribed wisdom. That line is the forerunner of today's disingenuous equivalent, 'It's not you, it's me.' Such an excuse has been spectacularly switched by Lily Allen to 'It's not me, it's you', which of course is what it meant in the first place.

I'd done the job of stadium announcer for a third of the season, and I'd done okay; just the one gaffe, missing the chance to be sacked for disobeying a harebrained instruction. It's a very public experience. Jeremy Nicholas I would never be though. I was only ever keeping the seat warm for his return. I was delighted when it happened swiftly after two further stand-ins were tried out and replaced. Bill Remfry was the announcer who was the MC when I was a teenage supporter, and for me he's the only one who can even lift a hammer to Jeremy, a man who really does live and breathe West Ham, every time he gets behind that microphone.

Finally it's time for me to take a break, having failed to get away over the summer. I've tracked down a cheap flight to New York and will be stealing away over the international weekend to spend a few days with my mate Mike Legrand. I have West Ham to thank for Mike's friendship, having got him a ticket for a West Ham v Liverpool game as a favour for one of my mum's friends, and later discovering he was from the Big Apple. He's since put me up there on many occasions, and this time does the usual, loaning me his room in an apartment on Spring Street, smack in the middle of Soho, while he spends more quality time with his girlfriend.

This is the best time to visit the city that never sleeps. It's not too cold, Central Park gets those autumn winds that blow leaves across the grassy walkways, and the nights are drawing in to give that melancholy sense of outdoors heading home. A coffee on the third floor of Barnes and Noble in Union Square, a pizza at John's or a movie at the Angelika Film Center with the subway trains audible in the quiet parts. These are all things I love, and why I go back there whenever I can.

Towards the end of my stay I visit another mate, Englishman Nick Bullard, who recently married Erin, a music therapist, and they've since had two sweet children, Briony and Gabriel. They live in New Hope on the New Jersey / Pennsylvania Delaware border, but are moving nearer to Erin's family in Cincinatti very soon. Nick's had some eventful months, having recently delivered his second child thanks to a delayed midwife. Then, despite finally getting his green card, the poor guy finds himself in the current economic climate still without a job. He has money, but his accumulated pile is beginning to dwindle. He and his missus introduce me to the beautiful music of Regina Spektor whilst I'm there; she is a kind of cross between Tori Amos and Anna Calvi. It's all plinkety-plonk tunes, star-struck love stories and a liberal sprinkling of mental health issues. I love it.

Before loading up with two giant tubes of red cinnamon toothpaste (can't get it in the UK), a year's supply, I buy the Beach Boys US Box Set of their hitherto unreleased 1966 album *Smile*, 45 years on from when it was originally due out. It's full of pictures, vinyl pressings, unnecessary takes and retakes, in short enough to keep my musical tastebuds satisfied until the end of the year. Thank g-d I didn't fly Ryan Air – I'd have had to book another seat to take this one back.

Back in the UK, and a fantastic opportunity to check out AFC Wimbledon in their first season in the Football League since rebirth less than a decade back in 2002. Of course I've picked their home fixture against the league leaders, Swindon Town, managed by footballing West Ham legend Paolo Di Canio. The odd thing is, the police have decided the game has to be all ticket as travelling Swindon fans have started to petition the club for advanced bookings. As a result I'm forced to go to the club on Thursday evening to try to convince them I am a fan, from London, and not a member of the Wiltshire Warriors, determined to wreak havoc and mayhem in West London. So how do I do it? In the end I decide to take a copy of my 'Our Days Are Few' book along to the ground. In Chapter Six of the book I describe an AFC Wimbledon game against Walton Casuals in the Premier Challenge Cup that I attend, which they win 5-4 after being 3-0 down. I offer to read the section from the book out loud, but after a quick flick through, the woman in the ticket office at Kingstonian takes my word for it and sells me two tickets.

AFC Wimbledon 1   **Swindon Town 1**
Hatton 6*   Connell 73
(*actually an 'own goal')
Attendance: 4581

AFC Wimbledon are in the football league, and have requisitioned Milton Keynes Dons claim to Wimbledon FC's history. It's an incredible story, but here they are after beating Luton Town on penalties in the Blue Square Premier Play Off Final at Manchester City's ground earlier in the year.

Going to matches still has that seventies feel about it, and I'm on the terrace behind the goal AFC Wimbledon are attacking in the first half, not that they get very close to us much in the first half. Wimbledon start out the better of the two sides, and take the lead in the sixth minute with a deflected shot, preventing Swindon's run of clean sheets going to a record 7th game. I note with interest the number 22, Callum McNaughton, defender on loan from West Ham United. Yes, the one sent off against Aldershot Town back in August. Small footballing world.

We are in debilitatingly bright direct sunlight, and the Wimbledon goalie wears a cap, much like Leeds' Gary Sprake used to. Di Canio gets a few ironic taunts of 'fascist' from the crowd, harking back to some unguarded moments at Lazio when he voiced his support for Italian right-wing lunatic Benito Mussolini. The GMB Trade Union withdrew their sponsorship of Swindon Town after his appointment as manager in May 2011. Di Canio has hardly improved matters with his Swindon team turning out in their away kit of black shirts.

I'm not really reflecting on such matters at this moment, preferring to revel in my pre-match purchase of veggie burger and programme, at just £3. The whole 'fan's club' image is further embraced when the match announcer dedicates a song to Matt Cooper on his 40th birthday, revealing that he was once a Plough Lane club mascot.

Halfway through the first half a fan behind us holds up a mobile phone - 'Anyone lost a blackberry?' A man a few steps further back up the terrace claims the phone with embarrassed relief. It's difficult to imagine such a happening at Stamford Bridge even though most people attending Chelsea matches are likely to have a phone in each pocket.

In the second half Swindon have clearly had the hairdryer treatment from the hair-thinned Di Canio, and fill the field like paparazzi hunting a young royal. Chances start to rain in around the AFC Wimbledon goal, and after striker Connell misses his third golden opportunity, a wag alongside us calls out, 'Hope he and his wife aren't trying for kids...'

Finally Connell puts an even better chance away, and the game ends up one apiece, the fairest result. Di Canio's side remain top and favourites for promotion. AFC Wimbledon may not go up this year, but it surely can't be long before they finally get to meet their criminally mendacious brother from Buckinghamshire in that new Milton Keynes stadium or Stadium:MK. If I have to write a 600 page book about their struggle to get back into the league and reclaim their name, I'll do it if it gets me a ticket for that game.

Game 17: nPower Championship, 2011-12, Ricoh Arena
Saturday November 19th 2011 (20,524)
Referee: Keith Stroud (Dorset)

Coventry City 1   **West Ham 2**
Platt 33   Cole 69
                             Piquionne 76

(West Ham: 2nd in the table, 34 points from 51)

Coventry are almost twenty points adrift of West Ham at the start of the day, second from bottom of the Championship table, but they take the lead towards the end of the first half with a goal from Clive Platt.

Repeating his tactics from the previous game, Allardyce brings on Cole for Carew, and again, West Ham start to look threatening for the first time in the game. With a hilarious example of the very football West Ham fans have complained about under Allardyce, the 69th minute brings a spectacularly route one goal, and the equaliser. Green's gigantic punt downfield is chased ambitiously by Cole, who finds himself able to stroll through and prod the ball home from just twelve yards. West Ham then hit a second goal in the magical 76th minute, with Piquionne nonchalantly slipping over and his head dropping into the path of Faubert's cross, and it's all over for Coventry, who have easily had enough of the game to have grabbed something from it.

West Ham: 1 Green, 3 McCartney, 5 Tomkins, 15 Faye, 18 Faubert, 4 Nolan, 10 Collison, 16 Noble, 21 Diop (30 Piquionne 62), 7 Baldock (17 O'Brien 80'), 11 Carew (9 Cole 46)

Game 18: nPower Championship, 2011-12, Upton Park
Saturday November 26th 2011 (27,864)
Referee: Colin Webster (Tyne & Wear)

West Ham 3	**Derby County 1**
Cole 44	Priskin 35
Nolan 64	
Noble 74p	

(West Ham: 2nd in the table, 37 points from 54)

Igor Stimac is guest studio summariser for Sky, I notice before treading the 130 steps up to the Press Area.

With only two home games in December and Southampton losing for the first time this season at Bristol City, a win this evening will take Hammers to within two points of the leaders. Hammers have proved that even a live Saturday evening game, usually an attendance killer, has not affected the gate, which is a healthy 27.864.

Derby County haven't had too many happy visits to Upton Park, but the last time they were here was for a Championship fixture back in the promotion season of 2004-05 for a live game that Hammers lost 1-2. I recall Alan Pardew bringing the young Mark Noble on as a substitute in that live game for his home league debut, a player who six years later is at the heart of the West Ham midfield.

Hammers have a couple of promising attacks in the first five minutes, including a chance for Collison set up for him by a sneaky Carlton Cole header. Sadly he wafts it over the bar from the edge of the six yard box. Next it's McCartney with a skidding shot just wide of Frank 'I' Fielding's left hand post. Then another neat header from Nolan, which sets up Baldock for a decent chip that finishes up just wide. Derby have a half chance at the other end from a speculative effort from James Bailey, the other half of a great partnership with Robbie Savage from last season. Plenty in the first ten minutes to please the television audience.

Jamie Ward, the Northern Ireland international, looks tricky, and sets up two wasted chances for Derby. Cole, on the other hand, is more productive at the Bobby Moore end. His flicks and touches send the Derby defenders off balance and ensure that Baldock is likely to improve on his five goals from seven starts Championship record for the Hammers. Ouch! Really should shut my mouth. Baldock gets a knock in the twenty-first minute and is replaced by Freddy Piquionne. Now we have the two goalscorers from last weekend's Coventry game. John Carew remains on an attacking looking Allardyce bench, also featuring Matt Taylor.

One thing that has quickly become obvious is that Nigel Clough's Derby aren't here to eke out a draw. This means the goalless end stat from the Bristol City game is unlikely to be repeated. The cameras show Allardyce sitting between Downes and Neil McDonald, offering reflections on why Hammers have yet to score after 30 minutes. The 'Mousse' has put the Dammers on Derby's loan star defender Kevin Kilbane by interviewing him for tonight's programme. Kilbane, as it happens, isn't even on the bench tonight.

Now a smash and grab break for Derby as Tamas Priskin cuts through on the right to take a perfectly timed through pass and fire it past Rob Green. Derby have the lead on 35 minutes, with a goal scored by a player new enough not to be mentioned in the programme.

McCartney is booked for arguing with the referee as Derby look to capitalise on their sudden superiority. West Ham finally get out of their own half, but seem to have lost their edge since Baldock went off. Nolan is the only one who is still up for it and, for the first time at home this season, seems to be enjoying the fit of the captain's armband.

Noble stands over the ball, ready to take a free kick in the last minute of the half. The ball is headed out, but O'Brien yanks it back in on the full and Carlton Cole heads home a vital equaliser seconds before half-time. Collison is playing his best this season, twisting and turning in the hole behind the strikers.

As the teams come off, the director picks out Tamas Priskin, his forearms adorned by tattooed scribble. Carlton Cole is all smiles, his sixth goal of the season pulling him ahead of his sidelined strike partner Baldock. He's competitive like that is Carlton.

I've just noticed that if Harry Redknapp's Spurs win their game in hand over Manchester United, they will go second behind Manchester City. When did Spurs last occupy second place in the top division? Harry, this will be a terrible thing you've done if you go on and win the League for the sc*m. It can't happen...

Cole wins an early corner for West Ham at the start of the second half. Noble takes, but seems to have lost his corner prowess from a few seasons ago when they regularly tallied as assists throughout the Premier League season. Faubert takes one now and Piquionne is inches away from contact. Whatever Allardyce has put in his players' tea during the half-time break, seems to be doing the trick. Another corner. Noble again... The goalkeeper is impeded.

The ref stops the play after Piquionne has accidentally back-headed Derby's Shaun Barker's head. He looks concussed, but half of them do tonight, even standing up, so that doesn't mean much. The dropped ball is slammed back down the pitch to Green who returns it back along good old Route One. O'Brien gives away a free kick in front of the chicken run. Derby loiter. Great defensive header out in the end by the very man who gave the free kick away. Piquionne turns from hero to villain in a couple of seconds, brilliantly pulling down the through ball only to dither at the trap door and allow Fielding the chance to recover and block his effort for a corner. Irons! Irons! Irons!

The genius moment we've been waiting for is here now, provided by the captain. A neat build up with Cole and Collison ends with the ball spinning up into the Upton Park night sky into the path of Nolan, who crashes it sweetly on the volley past the helpless Fielding.

How shit must you be...? We're winning at home...

Nolan has now got five goals in 2011-12. It's a novelty to see three Hammers' players all vying for the position of top scorer. Recently it's just been a matter of will anyone manage to get into double figures over a forty-plus match season?

Faye brilliantly blocks Ward's shot after Tomkins has dithered outside the penalty area. Still plenty of time. The Sky cameras pick up Carew tightening his laces. I'm betting Cole will rest for the last quarter of an hour. Ward's corner is brilliantly headed out by Faye who launches an attack that sees

Piquionne bundled over in the area by Craig Bryson. Nolan wallops the penalty home and a delicious two goal cushion emerges to everyone's relief. 74 minutes played. Cole is off, as predicted, to a full round of stadium applause, in the 76th minute. Derby make two substitutions too, but it seems unlikely this will prove to be anything but door stopping the goal difference. Carew is straight into the action, despite the unlikely hope of catching an overhit through ball that is almost out before he begins his sprint.

Matt Taylor comes on for the last ten minutes, and Carew has a couple of half chances towards the end. The score remains the same and it's an important third successive win that keeps Hammers up with Southampton at the top.

I'm left with enough time gently to consider that if there had been a goal in the 54th minute, that would have been five goals, each scored at exact ten minute intervals. I really must get out more.

West Ham: 1 Green, 3 McCartney, 4 Nolan, 5 Tomkins, 7 Baldock (30 Piquionne 21), 9 Cole (11 Carew 76), 10 Collison, 15 Faye, 16 Noble, 17 O'Brien, 18 Faubert (14 Taylor 82)

I am woken from sleep on Sunday morning by an early morning text from my editor friend Neil, now working at Salford Quays, editing Match of the Day highlights for the BBC. The text informs me that Gary Speed is dead. Watching Speed on Football Focus the previous day, in a charade of ordinariness, the news arrives with the power of a defenestrated bucket of cold water. Five minutes on the Net, and the story is fully digested, in all its confusing curiousness.

Game 19: nPower Championship, 2011-12, Riverside Stadium
Tuesday November 29th 2011 (18,457)
Referee: Mike Dean (The Wirral)

Middlesbrough 0   **West Ham United 2**
                          Piquionne 9
                          Cole 90+4

(West Ham: 2nd in the table, 40 points from 57)

Four successive wins is a statistic, as far as West Ham are concerned, that you would have to go back four years to find at any level, in any competition. Add to that the fact that Middlesbrough have not lost at home for sixteen matches, and you have a pretty impressive all-round performance for the Hammers all told on a cold Tuesday night north of the Watford Gap.

The goals come at each end of the game, the first, a novelty goal from Piquionne, hit in single minute figures, strangely common for this season; the second is an injury time sealer from substitute Carlton Cole, who has come on for Piquionne. He extends his tally for the season to seven. It's a fantastic end to a very positive month for West Ham, one draw and four wins; 13 out of 15 points in November.

West Ham: 1 Green, 3 McCartney, 5 Tomkins, 15 Faye, 18 Faubert, 20 Demel (17 O'Brien 79), 4 Nolan, 14 Taylor, 16 Noble, 21 Diop, 30 Piquionne (9 Cole 68)

From my days as a full time teacher back in the 80s, I have a strong memory of determined union action, organised to combat the government of the day's unsympathetic attitude towards the spiralling injustice of lousy public sector pay. Fast forward over twenty years to November 2011 and we have the second day of action by my union this year in response to the intended tearing up of decade long agreements on pensions, to fund the bankers' bailout from a few years' back.

The day of union action has been organised for the last day of the month, and although it is not a teaching day for me, I join my colleagues up at Westminster to register support for the action. The government's intentions and their similarity to Robert Maxwell's theft of pension funds from the workers at the Daily Mirror in the late 80s is not lost on most of the quality press, but the day is under-reported and it looks as though the dispute will drag on into the new year.

Chapter 7

Goodbye Kim Jong-Il

December 2011

It is said that your path in life relies on making wise choices throughout the journey. That, of course, was the way of thinking before the advent of the Sat Nav. The element of choice has again been raised. The road less travelled will be just that. In an effort to simplify our lives we strip them of the tiresome demands of individuality. With only one league defeat each month so far, and 37 points from a possible 54, the Sam Nav looks to have been a good decision. West Ham are nipping at the heels of Southampton and six points ahead of the pack, looking odds-on at this stage for an automatic promotion place.

The beginning of December is a good time to organise pipe dreams for the following year. You'll know after smoking them for four weeks whether they're still full of flavour or as likely as a Premier League title at Upton Park. The last dreaming pipe I made a genuine effort to smoke came my way a couple of years ago courtesy of an Egyptian magician. This man, for whom I had a lot of time and respect, offered me the opportunity to travel with him to China. This was to deliver media training to enthusiastic Chinese diplomats looking to work in prominent positions in the West over the next few years. I was guaranteed 26 days work if I could commit to joining him overseas to become part of his media circus. Stripped of the cynicism I ordinarily carry like so much skin, I bought in to the project with a firm handshake. The promise of easy money had settled under my nose and I'd had a good old sniff. Working on the simplistic principle of having to be in it to win it, I began December 2009 looking East.

The work placement came at the end of July, when I'd just about given up on the enterprise, and took the form of three trips to China. The hotel, travel, food, pocket money and sartorial presentation were all catered for. My boss' sister was a presenter on an international cable tv news programme, and travelled with us on two of the visits. She delivered several effective but unwaveringly identical lecturettes on how to present well on the small screen. I was told by my boss before my first seminar not to talk about myself, not to try and pronounce Chinese names, not to act surprised, point during presentations, name books or information sources, try and be funny, say anything that could be construed as anti-Chinese... I started to make a list of the things I could and couldn't do and carried it round with me. There were thirty-nine 'don'ts' and two 'do's' – 'do use your initiative' and 'do read books about China'. The people we worked with were high up in the CCP (Chinese Communist Party), but invariably sociable and pleasant, and not deserving of patronising or fawning behaviour. The paranoia at our end of the room was uncomfortable and often palpable.

I was grateful for the chance to see what is an amazing country, with its beautiful gardens and parks. On my days off I saw the art districts around Beijing and the Great Wall and met people who were generous with their time and very interested in how their country was viewed abroad. Any prejudices I had about the Chinese dissolved fairly promptly with each new person I met.

On one of the trips we travelled to Inner Mongolia on the Russian border, just a mile or two from Siberia. It was unseasonably warm out there, the temperature clocking 40 degrees centigrade on one of the days, with the equally unusual experience of shop mastheads laden with both Chinese and Russian script. Both the boss and his sister were confident that their efforts would be rewarded with an exponential supply of work, but there were enough Chinese officials taking notes at the back of each lecture hall or seminar room we worked in to suggest that they would shortly be running the show themselves.

Unsurprisingly, the work dried up after that and, slightly worryingly, so did the Chinese honouring of the invoices my boss had put in for payment. I eventually received about a fifth of the earnings I had been promised. I wrote off the rest as an important reminder that easy money is like immortality: a nice idea, but only a reality for dreaming imbeciles.

On the subject of dreaming imbeciles, the month opens with a chance for West Ham to close the gap on Southampton. They have a tricky fixture at Doncaster, while Hammers face improving Burnley, sat navved by 34 year old Eddie Howe, another championship manager younger than many of his playing staff.

Game 20: npower Championship, 2011-12, Upton Park

Saturday 3rd December 3rd 2011 (26,274)
Referee: Fred Graham (Stanford-Le-Hope, Essex)

West Ham United 1	**Burnley 2**
Nolan 52	McCann 57
	Vokes 75

(West Ham: 2nd in the table, 40 points from 60)

The minute's applause for Gary Speed with every spectator standing is a respectful yet sober start to the afternoon's events. The Guardian's 'secret footballer' column has ruminated over the issue of depression in sport amongst the elite players, and how ten in the top flight are said to have contacted mental health specialists after Speed's death last Sunday. The Leveson enquiry into press standards, started last month, is the only reason the poor man's demise hasn't generated another obscene tabloid frenzy. Give them time, though...

West Ham Historian John Helliar and I have had our usual pre-match chat, lingering over the improved form of James Tomkins and the seemingly unnoticed talent and defence-strengthening performances of Abdoulaye Faye; these two may well be connected. Faye seems slow, almost lazy, on the ball, but very rarely makes errors. Tomkins has shown greater decisiveness under pressure, an improvement from previous Premier League seasons. We end our chat with predictions - he goes for 4-1, whereas I am optimistically up for the increased goal tally of a 4-2 finish.

West Ham have a goal difference of plus twenty, a points total of forty and all of this in the twentieth championship game of the season, holding second place in the league with a stunning away record.

In the first genuine Hammers' attack, O'Brien puts over an excellent cross which just evades the head of the diving Matt Taylor, lurking at the far post. Burnley have a leaky defence away from home, having conceded fifteen in nine games, but they've scored eleven and none of their nine games away from Turf Moor has ended in a draw. With twenty-four points they are four points from the drop zone and five from the play-offs. It's that kind of league.

West Ham's fifth corner is another speculative effort that reaches a Burnley head first. The sixth is flicked on past Cole to Tomkins who can only head it straight at Burnley keeper Lee Grant. Two ex-Hammers, Junior Stanislas and Zavon Hines, are in the Burnley squad, Stanislas starting in the number eleven shirt, with Hines on the bench wearing sixteen. They've spent all their careers in claret and blue shirts (okay, so they're wearing yellow today) - what if they both get transferred to Villa after a spell with the not so lanky Lancastrians, and who knows, maybe a career end at Scunthorpe?

Cole runs to the touchline and puts a perfectly weighted ball into the six yard box that Nolan only has to blow gently on to place it past Grant. His touch is unfathomably lightweight and the ball spins narrowly wide. Somewhat surprisingly half an hour has already passed. Hammers and Burnley have scored sixty-four league goals this season, but nothing here yet. Burnley's travelling followers are few in number over in the far corner of the Sir Trevor Brooking Lower (809), and are perhaps already regretting their shelled out fares.

Burnley finally produce a shot at goal from around twenty-five yards by Chris McCann, their captain. It bounces harmlessly on its way towards Rob Green; this from the side who, according to the stats, have had more shots at goal in the Championship than any other. Collison hits a shot from the edge of the area at the other end, but it skids wide. Forty minutes gone. West Ham beat this lot 5-3 two seasons ago in a fast and frenetic Premier League game cluttered with errors; in February they beat them 5-1 in the fifth round of the FA Cup. But still no goals.

Faye makes a timely intervention with a masterly tackle. O'Brien runs brilliantly towards the corner flag and hits over a deep cross that deserves more than just a corner.

Champions League or Championship? You guess. At least Crystal Palace have blurred the definition slightly by winning 2-1 at Old Trafford in the Quarter Finals of the League Cup this week. It's a pleasant thought, nullified only by the referee's half-time whistle to end a rather tame first half. At least Burnley seem unlikely to score. Geoff Hurst will be seventy on Thursday. I wonder what he thought of Frank Lampard's 'goal' against Germany in the 2010 World Cup...

I'm looking on the subs' bench to see whether we might have a game changer. Who is Guy Demel? He's a defender wearing number twenty and his journey here has been fought via a career in Germany at Borussia Dortmund and Hamburg after becoming homesick at Arsenal. As a Frenchman who plays for West Ham, that seems highly improbable. The only other likely hero in waiting is John Carew, though Frederic Piquionne might have a few words to say about that...

I imagine Burnley manager Eddie Howe would be more than satisfied with a point here this afternoon. He'll be celebrating a year in the job next month and is no doubt more popular with the fans than Owen Coyle, the Bolton manager. Coyle is currently looking down the barrel of the Premier League's relegation gun, all this since hurriedly abandoning Burnley, having taken them up into the Premier League in 2009. The Burnley fans subsequently paraded a banner at most of the remaining games that season before they were relegated, adorned with the words, 'We'll Never Forget You, Ewen Coyle'.

George McCartney loses the ball down the left wing. He is not having a great game. Like the uninspected gusset of a hitherto clean pair of pants, I have just become aware of his stuttering performance. In the fifty-second minute of the match, the goal the crowd have almost given up on finally arrives. Nolan runs onto a through ball wide on the right, into the Burnley area, and lifts it expertly over Grant to put Hammers into the lead.

Matt Taylor leaves the pitch on 55 minutes, to be replaced by Fredi Piquionne. From the next attack, Burnley level from a far post Chris McCann header. That has to be only their second chance of the game. Burnley sub Ross Wallace for Keith Treacy. And now I hear Doncaster are 1-0 up against Southampton. If it stays that way, a win by two goals could put us top. Where do we get this ludicrous optimism from?

Collison on the ball shows some neat close skills to find Cole, but he takes too long over his cross and the danger passes. Burnley seem to have acquired a little confidence and are stringing a few moves together.

Cole puts Piquionne through but the French striker opts to pull the ball back unselfishly and, ultimately, finds the foot of a Burnley defender who rakes it clear. Two quick substitutions for Burnley suggest that they feel they may be in with a chance of winning this. I see nothing to suggest their manager is wrong, especially when Collison puts an 'easy one' wide from six yards out. West Ham fans sing, *You're getting sacked in the morning*, though it's not exactly clear who they are talking about.

The best moment of the game so far. A hurried poor clearance by Green is lamped back in at pace by sub Ross Wallace, and watched by Green, it skims the bar. Two minutes later Green atones with a brilliant save from a blistering thirty yard shot by Marney. From the corner, however, substitute

Sam Vokes heads Burnley into the lead.

Our predictions at the beginning of the game have demonstrated the folly of becoming confident of success after a good run of West Ham form. In the light of Doncaster's unexpected 1-0 victory over Southampton, the defeat is even harder to stomach. Hope turns swiftly to fear in the anticipation of a visit to the swiftly improving Reading.

West Ham: 1 Green, 3 McCartney, 4 Nolan, 5 Tomkins, 9 Cole, 10 Collison, 14 Taylor (30 Piquionne 56), 15 Faye, 16 Noble, 17 O'Brien (11 Carew 80), 18 Faubert

One of the tasks facing anyone trying to get some publicity for their book is to get a slot on the radio. After 'Our Days Are Few' was released, Tony McDonald got me on BBC London Radio. Then, on 3rd December 2004, on Time FM, the self-proclaimed 'West Ham United local radio station', broadcasting on 107.5 FM to Romford, Barking and Dagenham. These were the days before digital radio saturation, and there weren't too many options available to reach the prescribed audience.

Mike Goodwin was the presenter on Time FM, and with another studio guest in Geoff Pike, West Ham's industrious midfielder from 1975-87, it seemed like a useful opportunity to preach to the perverted. Unlike later books, where publishers were loath to give away free copies to the writer, let alone the press, Tony Mac had made free copies available for radio stations to give away in competitions and phone-ins, and everyone who rang in that day got a copy.

Time FM was a modest radio station, broadcasting from a top floor suite of rooms in an office block in Romford. This was in contrast to the vastness implied by its name. It was nevertheless exactly what was necessary, and a bullseye hit, as its audience were almost certainly going to be West Ham fans. The hour went by very quickly, and I did my best to answer the calls as accurately and entertainingly as possible. I was surprised, nevertheless, to be asked about the championship game the following day at Sunderland after Geoff Pike and the interviewer had predicted defeat and a draw respectively. Although I would have been happy with a draw, I said that I thought West Ham might surprise a few people and nick it. It balanced the predictions, even if it wasn't exactly the way I was thinking. It did however prove to be exactly how the game went. It was a 2-0 away victory, and I was even there to see it after a dash from the studio. Sunderland ended 2004-05 as runaway leaders under Mick McCarthy, whereas West Ham had to endure the play off route for a second successive season.

Game 21: npower Championship, 2011-12, Madjeski Stadium
Saturday December 10th 2011 (24,026)
Referee: Neil Swarbrick (Lancashire)

Reading 3   **West Ham United 0**
Pearce 66
Church 80, 86

(West Ham: 2nd in the table, 40 points from 63)

This is one of those games whose fate hangs on a referee's decision. West Ham are looking to secure an important away point with a goalless draw at the Madjeski. Then in the 65th minute, Joey O'Brien is sent off after collecting a second yellow card. Neither offence is particularly extreme. However, Alex Pearce highlights O'Brien's absence a minute later by tapping in from eight yards out. The substitute Simon Church then slots home Adam Le Fondre's chip a quarter of an hour later. Six minutes on, after some winding up before a set play, Jack Collison is sent off for the first time in his career for an uncharacteristically vicious challenge on Jimmy Kebe, after the Reading player took the Michael pulling his socks up whilst on the ball. Church then heads home Ian Harte's curling free kick to complete the debacle. It's a case of red card... goal, red card... goal. What a great pile of horse dung. Everyone in the following list should hang their heads in shame.

West Ham: 1 Green, 3 McCartney, 5 Tomkins, 15 Faye, 18 Faubert, 20 Demel (17 O'Brien 4), 4 Nolan, 10 Collison, 16 Noble, 21 Diop (9 Cole 57), 30 Piquionne (11 Carew 72)

On Thursday December 14th 2011, our e-publishing company runs off its first five titles. Driven mainly by the industry of my business partner Belinda ('Driven' is her middle name) we finally launch 'mardibooks' in time for Christmas. I had thought of 'mardi' as we began taking the idea seriously over lunch on a Tuesday at Tate Modern (pretentious), and Belinda added 'books' (practical) when we realised the 'mardi.com' website domain name would cost us £15,000. 'mardibooks.com' on the other hand would set us back just £20 (cheapskates).

I have always enjoyed writing. It was short stories when I was at school about characters like Pixie Wixie and Vince Deviney, always coveting a little dream that I would be a published writer in my adult years. Stage one of this dream was effectively ended when I failed my interview to be a journalist with the Acton Guardian as an eighteen year old. Stage two was continuing to write material that I could perhaps solicit a market for at a later stage.

I completed my first novel, 'Once in a Lifetime', in 1987, and was initially pleased with the final manuscript, but my second effort, '1909', completed in 1988, seemed a bit more likely to make the grade. In the event, after much polishing and time off to make a reasonable job as a new Head of English in a school in Surrey, I found a literary agent and sat back. And sat back. And sat back.

Despite some very positive rejection letters (or that was how my literary agent euphemistically categorised them) I wasn't getting into print. I wrote two more novels, before realising that a compromise in subject matter might be necessary. I finally managed the leap into print thanks to Steve Blowers and Tony McDonald, who published my book about West Ham's 2003-04 season. I should have learned from the Greeks that tragedy would always be more likely to sell.

I released another three West Ham books, one every two years, but always yearned to get control of my own operation, and with e-books and the emerging literary virtual world, the opportunity arose. Finding it nothing like as straightforward as I had imagined, I went at it headlong, and found new books written by other writers to ensure that we would launch something looking a little less like a vanity project and a little more like a serious business venture.

We managed to publish both the website and the books in the week before Christmas. Whether our efforts would prove more venture than vanity would only be seen in the New Year.

Game 22: nPower Championship, 2011-12, Upton Park
Saturday December 17th 2011 (34,749)
Referee: Scott Mathieson (Cheshire)

West Ham 1   **Barnsley 0**
Diop 6

(West Ham: 2nd in the table, 43 points from 66)

The last game before Christmas sees West Ham desperately looking for a win to counter the successive defeats that have proved face slappers this month. Despite our 'Dark December' the game is a sell-out. Ditto my point about tragedy.

Barnsley have just been spanked 3-5 by an out-of-form Ipswich Town. They were 2-0 up at one stage, so today there is hope in the air, filling the millions of bubbles blown into the East London sky.

My guest at today's game is floor manager to my stadium announcer from 2008, Jason Stone, invited to help celebrate his 42nd birthday. The last time Jason joined me for a game at Upton Park was for West Ham's 1-0 brilliant home victory over Spurs last season.

Hammers start well. Noble's early free kick skids under the wall but is easily saved by Luke Steele. Inspiring name for your last line of defence, even if he spent most of last weekend picking the ball out of the net. Barnsley breakaway, forcing a corner from which Jacob Butterfield heads straight at Green. *Butters*. In the sixth minute, Noble's neat inswinging corner is headed home by Papa Bouba Diop from the centre of the goal line. It's his first West Ham goal and a rare phenomenon. A footballer whose name suggests the very way he plays. We've had them before: Robbie Savage, Graeme Sharp, Robbie Fowler, Mark Fish... and who could forget Tottenham's John Pratt? Bouba Diop plays with a kind of 'Bouba' in his swagger and a 'Diop' in his finish. Even his celebration contains a delicious mixture of disbelief and delight in his shaking lowered head, the head that has just put West Ham United ahead. This is a bit early to be the only goal of the game, but if Hammers can finally patch up their leaky defence, the points will be theirs.

Three minutes later the ball drops invitingly just outside the area to give Kevin Nolan the chance to repeat his delightful volley against Derby. He balloons it into the afternoon sky. There are two schools of thought on Nolan. Both embrace him warmly as a passionate and inspirational captain, but one thinks he can't play football to save his mortgage. I find myself, as you would expect, splinter-arsed between the two.

Debutant Dan Potts, son of West Ham's omnipotent 1990's club captain Steve, whacks over two impressive left wing crosses, both which are headed narrowly wide by Carlton Cole. Potts seems to have been already blighted by family recognition problems, having appeared on the sub's bench on the team sheets in the Press Room, but starting the game at kick-off. Will this be an unrecognised game that denies him five hundred appearances fifteen years from now? The player Potts has given up his place to on the team sheet is Abdoulaye Faye, who I can't see anywhere. Did he injure himself in the warm-up? It's meant that Callum Driver is on the bench for the first time, without any teamsheet recognition at all. Steve Blowers points out to me that with both Frank Lampards and now Steve and Dan Potts, this is the second example of father and son home grown debuts at the club. Frank senior, aged 19, played his first game for West Ham in November 1967 v Manchester City. His son, aged 17, made his debut v Coventry City in January 1996, and Steve Potts, aged 17, made his v QPR on New Year's Day 1985. His son, Dan, on debut tonight, is also just 17.

Barnsley's Jim McNulty gets in a neat effort which would have caught Rob Green out but for a last minute deflection from James Tomkins. Barnsley striker Craig Davies then finds himself put through on twenty minutes, but a last minute toe in from George McCartney sends the ball out for a corner, which Barnsley waste.

Allardyce is playing Cole, Carew and Piquionne up front in a 4-3-3, but they all seem to need too long on the ball, too many touches, too little end result. Bouba Diop looks very comfortable, and Noble gets a couple of worthy shots in, but the single goal lead looks increasingly precarious. Barnsley, in their entire senior squad feature only two players who aren't from the UK. Best of the bunch this afternoon is proving to be Welsh international and 25 year old lower league legend Davies from Burton-on-Trent, who originally started his career at Manchester City several teams and contracts ago.

'Sort it out, you fucking cunt!' the philosopher behind me screams. Fair enough. You pays your money, you makes your statement.

Carlton Cole now embarks on a run during which he beats three defenders, two of them twice, before putting the ball wide of an empty net. The fans aren't sure whether to applaud or boo. I am reminded of the great, but clumsy, Roger Davies of Derby County, who beat the entire Chelsea team and two peanut vendors before tripping over his own feet and kneeing the ball wide of an empty net. Legendary miss.

Barnsley are clearly still in the game, and it's with relief that the half time whistle sounds. Will Allardyce up the ante in the second half?

The second half lights up when a cat streaks onto the pitch from the Bobby Moore end and runs the full length to the Trevor Brooking stand before turning round on a sixpence, cheered on by the crowd, and leaping into the West Stand lower seating area, evading the half-hearted efforts of three luminous orange-jacketed stewards. I return to the action to just catch David Perkins poking the ball wide of Green from a corner and, luckily, just wide of the near post.

Allardyce's decision in the second half to bring off John Carew is met rather sadly by cheers. Freddie Sears, West Ham's 'trier' seems a good bet to add a bit of inspiration to what has proved a frankly lacklustre front line today.

Barnsley have won a free kick in a dangerous position just outside the area and Hammers come back in numbers to defend. In the end Rob Edwards, yes - the Welsh one - steers it over the wall and over the Trevor Brooking Lower. I forgot to mention that I predicted a 1-0 win before the game. I'm only saying that now in the hope that Hammers will find the back of the net again before the end.

There is a double substitution from Barnsley. Ricardo Vaz Te is replaced by Jim O'Brien, while Nile Ranger, on loan from Newcastle since being banned from driving in the week and left without a car so he can't drive back, is replaced by Danny Haynes. The substitutions proved West Ham's undoing against Burnley a fortnight ago - this time the Irons reply immediately with another of their own - Faubert going off to be replaced by Lansbury, finally back from injury.

Sears now hits a blockbuster from point blank range that Steele turns over, his effort rendered pyrrhic by the assistant referee's upraised flag. Cardiff are currently beating West Ham's close rivals Middlesbrough 2-1, so it's vital that Hammers get all three points. The Boxing Day game against Birmingham, and the New Year's Eve fixture against Derby County could then prove something of a launch pad for the second half of the season.

Mark Noble, who has been letting fly from long distance for most of the game, hits one from 35 yards which just clears Steele's crossbar. Potts is receiving treatment, making an extended injury time finish a virtual certainty. A goal would ease the nervousness in the crowd but still it doesn't come. A Lansbury throw by the corner flag leads to a weak clearance which Daniel Potts slams wide of Steele's left hand post. His father's five hundred odd games (if we include Anglo Italian Cup appearances – and I do) yielded just the one goal, a wrong-footing deflection against Hull in a 7-1 annihilation. It would be great to see his son score on debut. Hammers once beat Barnsley 6-0 here in the FA Carling Premiership, in January 2008... but not today. But then again, Samassi Abou isn't playing.

Freddie Sears breaks free of the defence in a run on goal only to lose his footing at the key moment. He looks back in vain to the referee who waves play on. Sam Allardyce, however, begins a rant from the technical area that sees him eventually sent off to spend the rest of the game in the stand. The nature of the ground design above the tunnel ensures that it is only a few yards away from where he was previously standing. It's a reminder to the fans about showing passion. Avram Grunt's passion was only finally made evident to me by a friend in the removals trade who was responsible for organising the transportation of his personal magazine collection from his home after he left the club last season.

Jeremy Nicholas announces the corporate West Ham man of the match decision, which is Kevin Nolan. The second half of the Nolan Society now raise their voices to laugh, hiss, moan and yell in frustrated disbelief at the decision. I, and most of the fans around me, would have chosen Dan Potts who has been impressive throughout in his first game and looks a brilliant bet for the future. Him or Bouba Diop, who had also had a cracker and scored his first goal in English football for six years.

Four minutes injury time. Short of a ludicrous error or misjudgement, the three points should be West Ham's. Tomorrow Southampton play their arch-rivals Portsmouth away, and may end up with nothing. Incredibly, if that is the case West Ham will be second, and only by goal difference. The final whistle means we will occupy that position for at least a day.

West Ham: 1 Green, 3 McCartney, 4 Nolan, 5 Tomkins, 9 Cole, 11 Carew (19 Sears 55), 16 Noble, 18 Faubert (22 Lansbury 67), 21 Bouba Diop, 30 Piquionne, 48 Potts

The win over Barnsley and assault on the top position is tempered by the revelation that West Ham's Media Manager Greg Demetriou is leaving the club next month for a job with the FA. Greg arrived at the club from his previous job at UEFA some time after the departure of Peter Stewart back in 2006, and has since been my first point of contact with the club in the last few years. He will be sorely missed.

Straight after the game, Jason and I decamp to Camden Town, where we wolf down a quick pint and a Wagamama before marching on to the Fiddlers Elbow in Kentish Town. I'm playing Cliff Richard in a forty minute set that starts at 9.30. I'm backed by Shadows' tribute band the Silhouettes, who fire off seven songs before I'm up to join them for *Apron Strings* and *Please Don't Tease*. I have a quick drink with Jason before the set, and we head out straight afterwards, without a chance to share a word with the band. The modern world, eh?

On Sunday Portsmouth force a draw with Southampton, who have now not won a game in the whole of December, suggesting that the elite clubs in the division might well end up bunching at the top into the New Year. The two who end up getting those automatic promotion places might currently be elsewhere, ready for a late run at a promotion place.

Jules and I celebrate Christmas with our usual run round Richmond Park on a mild and damp morning. It's probably the best day to do it, with much of the run spent in a kind of splendid isolation, not a single human being or deer in sight. Does this explain just why venison is such a popular festive offering in Richmond?

My mum, brother, his wife Dorota and their new daughter Phoebe, born back in April, come for lunch and the Queen. Jules cooks an 'Indian' Christmas meal of sag paneer parcels and chana massala with typical Christmas veg. Not surprisingly, I have asked for – and been given – the Amy Winehouse 'seconds' CD and Kate Bush's latest *50 Words for Snow*. It's said that there are more successful women solo singers at the top of their game than at any time in modern music history. First time I typed that last sentence, my inappropriate auto correct function app (another Christmas present) changed 'said' to 'sad'. Lucky I checked it.

Game 23: nPower Championship, 2011-12, St Andrews
Monday December 26th 2011 (20,214)
Referee: Darren Deadman (Cambridgeshire)

Birmingham City 1	**West Ham 1**
Murphy 81	Cole 4

(West Ham: 2nd in the table, 44 points from 69)

The Boxing Day game features yet another early goal from West Ham, and Carlton Cole is the scorer. Finding himself abandoned by the two Birmingham centre halves, Cole heads left and slots his left foot shot right of Myhill prompting a lap of honour in front of the festive celebrating West Ham fans.

I'm at home on the sofa, lapping up the live Sky game.

Cole's first half goal here back in January, the last time the clubs met, built a seemingly impregnable 3-1 lead in the semi-final second leg of the Carling Cup. Two late Birmingham goals and a subsequent third in extra time meant falling at the penultimate hurdle for West Ham, much as it had done some forty years earlier against fellow midlanders Stoke City.

My drawn out point here is that an early goal means nothing. That said, Hammers spend most of the first half camped around the Birmingham goal, Julien Faubert in his new striking position unlucky not to score three and to have earned a penalty for a handball that saved his header from ending up in the back of the net. In the minute of injury time at the end of the first half, Myhill makes an impossibly brilliant save on the line from Cole just four yards out, and as the half time whistle goes, I'm wondering if there will be a big plot shift in the second half.

There is.

Sam Allardyce holds ex-Hammer Jonathon Spector in a friendly bear hug on the touchline, preventing him from taking a quick throw to get Birmingham on the attack. This is the young American who left West Ham last season, finding himself unable to play central midfield, and has joined Birmingham City in the hope of consolidating a permanent place in his preferred team position. Today he is playing right back at St Andrews, covering for absent defenders. *Plus c'est la même chose.*

Sam is mixing it up, bringing on Henri 'Angela' Lansbury for the slightly ineffective Piquionne on the hour and then Carew, a quarter of an hour later, for Cole, who has been unlucky not to add to his early goal at the top of the game. Neither substitution has the desired effect, as a second goal does not come. However, Spencer appears to have given West Ham a gift penalty when he handles a dropping ball in front of Lansbury. Incredibly referee Deadman again misses the offence. If Birmingham had a giant video screen for messages to the crowd, 'Late equaliser' would now be running across it in bright neon letters. And so it proves, nine minutes from time when Burke's far post corner is headed on by Caldwell for David Murphy to plant the ball in the corner of Rob Green's goal. Thankfully the recidivist Marlon King's last minute header is kept out, tipped over by Green. Another plus is the second consecutive promising performance by young number 48, Daniel Potts.

That's half the season gone, and in terms of Sam Allardyce's stated aim of recruiting two points for every game, West Ham now have 44 from 69, just two away from that target. Back in 2003-04 at this stage they only had 37 and in 2004-05, 38, so an automatic promotion place looks more likely this time... providing they can start winning at home and score a few goals in the process. Middlesbrough have drawn level with West Ham on points, and are only behind on goal difference.

West Ham: 1 Green, 3 McCartney, 4 Nolan, 5 Tomkins, 9 Cole (11 Carew 74), 16 Noble, 17 O'Brien, 18 Faubert (19 Sears 84), 21 Diop, 30 Piquionne (Lansbury 58), 48 Potts

When West Ham were relegated from the Premier League in the 2002-03 season, they decided they wouldn't be needing me as club commentator any longer. Although I had fulfilled the role home (and sometimes away for beambacks) for eleven successive seasons, clocking up over 250 Upton Park commentaries, it looked like I would finally be putting away my Coles commentary lip mike. That was until a year later when I noticed an advertisement from Trans World International (TWI) on the Grapevine website pages looking for experienced match commentators to help fulfil their three year contract with 3G and Vodafone to deliver bespoke two minute Premier League match highlight packages sent straight to mobile phones just minutes after the games had finished.

Could I do it? Brian Blower, West Ham's Commercial Manager, had hired me back in 1991 to give out a 'completely biased' commentary to a West Ham audience. The TWI job would require moderation, thought, reflection and, ultimately, fairness. So long as I could keep away from West Ham games, it wouldn't be a problem. The Irons, of course, would now be playing in the Championship for at least one season, so the partisan concerns wouldn't be an issue.

I was asked to attend a one hour training session, and met up with Gary Bloom (C5 and Eurosport commentator) and Peter Brackley (ITV) in the foyer for the run through. In my time at West Ham I had worked alongside most of the top commentators, but had never gone into a head-to-head with them for a position behind the mike. I'm a confident and irritating individual at the worst of times, but this was Brackley and Bloom for g-d's sake. Two of the very best. Any West Ham fan worth their drachmas will know that it was ITV Legend Peter Brackley who was the man behind the mike on the day the Hammers thrashed Chelsea 4-0 at Stamford Bridge in the memorable 1985-86 season. He was also, I discovered later, the Spitting Image puppet voice for Jimmy Greaves. Tempted as I was when I met him to ask that he recount the exact commentary for each of the four goals from the Chelsea annihilation, I kept shtum and wondered what chance I might have in such esteemed vocal company.

I met the man in charge, Martin McGahon, who put me in a small commentary booth with one of the editors. I was given an Arsenal v Middlesbrough match from the previous season that had ended up 4-1 to the Gooners. I voiced it, but was not completely comfortable with the format or with what I finally put down as commentary, especially as I could hear Brackley and Bloom barking out suave clichés in the adjoining booths. It was not easy to feel confident in such company, but I sat swigging on a coffee at the debriefing and was told they'd call us in the week before the games if they needed us. I read it as a polite rejection, but in the second week of the new 2004-05 season, I received a phone message to turn up the following Saturday to put a commentary on Everton v West Bromwich Albion.

At each game, we would be working with an editor who would be editing the match as it developed, like clay on a potter's wheel, chopping up action with replays to maintain an organic two minute bite of the match. This changed as the match developed; penalties and sending-offs were deemed essential, along with the goals. As for anything else, it was down to the editor and the commentator to pick and choose as the game went on. Five minutes before the final whistle, we took the two minute segment we had and then laid down the commentary. As we did so we had to keep one eye on the live action to see if anything was happening that would require a re-edit. Hilarious commentary, Freudian slips and spooneristic tongue glitches were likely to occur whilst trying to do all three things at once. Surprisingly few games I did required more than a couple of changes, though the poor commentator who got Arsenal 4 Spurs 5, ended up laying a different commentary track down four times!

It was brilliant working with, amongst others, Jon Champion, Tony Gubba, Gary Bloom and Peter Brackley, all of whom had many football stories from their years in the game that they were only too willing to share over lunch or dinner and cake before the games. My favourite of these remains Peter Brackley's Boxing Day story.

Brackley was moving into semi-retirement but as an establishment commentary voice, could command plenty of work when he was up for it. His son was now living in his house in West London, and Peter had moved to Spain for the cooking and the weather. He had booked a football season's worth of cheap easyJet return tickets from his corner of Spain to Luton, and flew in whenever he was offered a decent weekend gig. If things went well, he might get a Friday night live game followed by a Saturday 3G commentary and a Sunday live world feed match, flying back first thing Monday morning into the sun. If there was nothing worth getting out of bed for, he'd tear up the tickets. They'd only cost a few quid, after all. What a great life.

The first year of the 3G contract had proved a very busy one for Brackley. Not only had he been in demand for football commentaries, but he had also put his voice on a couple of football computer games, one of which was the now legendary Pro Evolution Soccer. This proved a most lucrative challenge, and Brackley soon found himself known as the 'voice of the game'. The computer game, that is, not the whole of football. But it was still something not to be spat at.

On this particular Boxing Day 2005, Brackers flew over first thing, commentated on a game, and then stayed over at the West London house that evening. He was on his own, so he had a couple of whiskies and slipped off to bed at ten o'clock, ready for an early lunchtime commentary at TWI the next day.

He was rudely awoken by the shrill bell of his son's phone jingling a merry midnight tune inside his head. He had already decided not to answer, knowing it wouldn't be for him, but instead of going to answer phone, like any decent phone might do, it carried on ringing, regardless. Eventually, he got up (Brackley got up as he was telling us the story to re-enact the moment) and staggered down the stairs.

'Hello?' he said, now almost awake.

'Is that Peter Brackley?'

'Yes,' said Brackley, devoid of the consciousness that admits improvised rudeness.

'What does 'upping the ante' mean?'

'What?' Brackley asked, not unreasonably.

' 'Upping the ante'. On one of your commentaries you say it. On a couple of the commentaries, actually. On Pro Evolution Soccer.'

'It's,' said Brackley, struggling for an appropriate expression that might provide a synonym. 'It means… taking a risk. Raising the stakes…'

'Oh,' the caller said. 'Right. Thanks.' And put the phone down.

Brackley's face as he told the story was a picture.

'And that was it!' he said. 'This man has somehow got what is now my son's number - I haven't used it for five years – and he is ringing me at *midnight* to ask me some technical question about my commentary on a *computer game*. He doesn't explain who he is, how he got the number… and what's even more ridiculous is… *I don't ask him*! I've just taken the call and answered his question, just like that, and I don't even ask him *who he is*!'

'Very polite of you, considering…' I said.

'I don't know this man, and he's ringing me *at midnight* on *Boxing Day* in a house I haven't lived in *for five years*, to ask me what I mean by *upping the ante*!'

Maybe you had to be there, but the tears were streaming down my face.

My last evening out before New Year's Eve is spent at the Young Vic watching Michael Sheen as Hamlet. A challenge that most serious actors take sometime in their career, this production is set in a lock-down unit with Hamlet as an 'inmate' and the tickets have told us to get to the performance half an hour early, when we are treated to a tour of this 'establishment'. Our tickets are in the front row alongside the main action, which is in the round, and it proves to be a breathtaking event, with Sheen excelling. What a year it's been for him. The performance covers nearly three and a half hours, but the time flashes by, the acting mesmerising right across the cast.

Earlier in the year I have enjoyed Michael Sheen as Brian Clough in The Damned United, a decent link to the final game of the year, away at Derby County. If I am honest, I am not feeling too optimistic about this one.

Game 24: nPower Championship, 2011-12, Pride Park
Saturday December 31st 2011 (28,067)
Referee: Jonathan Moss (Yorkshire)

Derby County 2	**West Ham 1**
Ball 2	Nouble 42
Green 10	

(West Ham: 3rd in the table, 44 points from 72)

Derby go into the game having won two of their last three, including turning over Leeds United, and this on New Year's Eve sits ill with West Ham's eight-player dearth. Kevin Nolan, Julien Faubert, George McCartney and Jack Collison are all on the self-inflicted suspension list, whilst Faye, Demel, Taylor and Bentley are just plain old-fashioned injured.

Derby waste little time racing into the kind of quick lead normally reserved this season for on the road West Ham. Nathan Tyson sets up Callum Ball who smacks a firm shot efficiently into the corner of the West Ham net. Before you can say 'for g-d's sake don't concede another one,' defender Gareth Roberts races down the wing and pings over a classy cross that Paul Green heads crisply down past West Ham's namesake keeper into the bottom corner of the goal.

Noble and Papa Bouba Diop go close in the next quarter of an hour before Frank Nouble, set up by Piquionne, hits home his first goal in a West Ham shirt, with a powerful twenty yard effort. Just as I'm beginning to slip into dreaming imbecile mode, the referee blows for half-time, and the chance to take advantage of the shift in play is lost.

I have texted Jason to see if he knows of some North Korean website that might be covering the game live, but no luck there. I'm directed to Radio Five Live Sextra, where BBC radio commentator Jacqui Oatley is describing the action. I'm guessing it's been a better year for her than Richard Keys and Andy Gray. It hasn't been much of a month for West Ham, however, despite an excellent debut from substitute Robert Hall. They don't threaten Frank Fielding's goal in the second half and have now only won once in December. That's good news for Nigel Clough and my clutch of Derby relatives, but nowt for Hammers' aficionados hopeful of a fillip before the New Year. Despite a goal difference of +16, they have conceded the second automatic promotion place to Middlesbrough, who have drawn 1-1 with Peterborough. The fans have their first opportunity to practice the term 'play off place' since the end of September.

West Ham: 1 Green, 2 Reid, 5 Tomkins, 17 O'Brien, 48 Potts, 16 Noble, 21 Diop (46 Hall 79), 22 Lansbury, 32 O'Neil (9 Cole 61), 24 Nouble, 30 Piquionne (7 Baldock 61)

Chapter 8

Fifty-Four and Counting

January 2012

One of the gifts I received for my fiftieth birthday four years ago was a framed display of celebrated events occurring on my birthdate in 1958, most of which I have become accustomed to seeing in similar lists over the years. It was, however, the first occasion that I had realised I share the same birthday as Rowan Atkinson and Joan of Arc. It doesn't reflect too well that I am forever linked with Mr Bean and a woman who was put to death for her beliefs. Just my luck when a couple of days either way would have secured permanent Capricorn calendar links with Elvis Presley, David Bowie, Michael Stipe or even Shirley Bassey. It could have been Ron Atkinson, though, so I shouldn't complain.

Game 25: nPower Championship, 2011-12, Upton Park
Monday January 2nd 2012 (34,936)
Referee: Simon Hooper (Wiltshire)

West Ham United 1   **Coventry City 0**
Nolan 67

(West Ham: 2nd in the table, 47 points from 75)

Always imagining that December was just a 'blip' month, West Ham were hoping to begin 2012 in style against bottom side Coventry City, one of three in the Championship yet to record an away win. Yes, it's a worry.

Daniel Potts is rested after three successive first team appearances in which he proved himself to be calm, assured on the ball and able to kick with both feet, just like his father. That's one less position West Ham will need to fill in the transfer window.

The suspended crew are back, including Collison, who plays in a very advanced position in the opening five minutes. An early Noble free kick is flighted in intelligently, but Coventry's defence handle the threat with confidence. They are wearing their famous green and black striped away kit, the one they wore when Frank Lampard made his debut here as a substitute in January 1996 with Gordon Strachan also coming on for one of his last appearances for the club.

Coventry left back Chris Hussey suddenly finds himself twenty yards out with a free shot at goal. He misses the West Ham left upright by two or three inches, Green staring at the passing ball like he's just seen Chris Moyles in a dinner jacket. West Ham fire back and first Collison, then Cole have shots turned away, before Tomkins' tenth minute flick from the ensuing corner is spooned out from under the bar by Joe Murphy, the busier of the keepers by some distance. Gary McSheffrey is then twice robbed last gasp in the area by Tomkins as Coventry play with a vigour well above their current league position.

Today the club has a decent cameraman doing a superb job on the gantry, all crash zooms and tight midfield action, yet still managing the wide shots for the approach play. Gary Deegan takes the ball off the toes of Carlton Cole as the 50 goal West Ham striker prepares to shoot.

We are West Ham's claret and blue army!, the fans in the Sir Trevor lower sing. Papa Bouba Diop can't find Baldock with a speculative long ball, but there is more industry in this opening twenty minutes than we've seen from the side in weeks. Nouble's goal at Derby has still only earned him a place on the bench, and with Lansbury and Carew there, it's quite clear how Allardyce sees the match developing. But still no goals.

There has been much talk over Christmas in the sporting media about Sam Allardyce not playing football 'the West Ham way', his approach perceived to be an increasing reliance on long ball tactics. If Hammers had managed a single decent season in the previous three, this might cut a little ice, but as the last seasons have only produced a couple of irrelevant cup runs and the brilliant form of Scott Parker (who has now left for *you know poo*), such critics ought to hush their mouths.

Coventry's squad of 30 features: 21 Englishmen, 5 Irish, 1 Scot and 1 Welshman, with two foreign players. This is a side without cash, not unlike Barnsley. Putting a decent squad together presents phenomenal financial difficulties for sides compared to the cash-backed Premier League over the road. Coventry win their first corner on the half-hour, but waste it. George McCartney goes close with a deflected shot which the keeper does well to turn away. Hammers need a goal before half-time to calm the nerves, but it's not coming. There are too many long distance shots and speculative crosses.

Lucas Jutkiewicz (English) is beaten in his chase for a through ball by Green, who races swiftly off his line to avert the danger. Players I haven't yet noticed, 35 minutes into the game: Winston Reid, Kevin Nolan, Sam Baldock. Perhaps I should rewrite the book and call it 'The Damned Statistics'.

There, Nolan touched it. But he broke up a three man move by hitting a short pass to... Not actually sure who it was to. It didn't reach him, whoever it was meant for. A free kick is awarded to West Ham on the edge of the box. Dangerous. Collison and Nolan hover. It's eventually flicked back to Baldock whose shot pinballs off the wall. Reid (there he is) fails to turn in a decent cross from the rebound. Now it's Faubert's turn to have a twenty yard shot fly just wide of the upright.

Carl Baker plays in McSheffrey, but a superbly timed tackle from Tomkins stops the away side from taking the lead. We're into first half injury time now, and with only a minute of it, it looks likely to be a fraught second half. Collison's corner is clueless, and that's where we leave the action after forty-five frustrating minutes. I can visualise another season in this division if West Ham don't start getting three points from their home games. With only one other match at Upton Park in January, Sam Nav Allardyce needs to conjure some second half urgency from his team.

Julian Dicks is in the Press Box, summarising the game for BBC London. He looks a little cold and slightly miserable, but not a day older than when we filmed him for a DVD biography out in Cartagena, Spain, in July 2006. Playing off scratch, Dicks' golf talents are well-known, and my bosses at ILC took this into consideration when deciding to travel there for a couple of days and interview him in his new surroundings. His apartment backed onto a golf course, which was where he was spending most of his days, practising for the tournaments he competed in. For a footballer with one leg (left), I was surprised to see that he played golf right-handed. What I wasn't surprised at was the litany of stories he offered up during the interview. Starring in most of these was a gang of likely lads, including Frank McAvennie, Mark Ward and Phil Parkes. The fall guy in most of the situations was then manager Billy Bonds, whose relationship with Julian over the years has deservedly achieved legendary status.

We learned a great deal about the pre-Liverpool Dicks, with the routine petulance, wall-to-wall sendings off, and friendship with the local milkman whom he and Frank McAvennie would regularly cadge a lift from to skip two-thirds of the cross-country course Bonds set his team to keep them fit. Bonds was always suspicious at how his two Olympic skivers always managed to get back to base near the front of the group, but never clocked the trick. We heard some graphic tales about the cartilage in the knee of his left leg being scraped out of the joint like cheese off the base of a pasta dish; how he loved Graeme Souness and hated Roy Evans. Dicksy? I could have spent the whole week out there chatting if they'd rolled out the budget another two hundred yards.

St Albans are winning 2-0 away at Hemel Hempstead in the local derby. Sounds exciting. I'm starting to wonder whether or not I can get back home in time for the start of the second half of Fulham v Arsenal. Quite fancy Fulham to grab at least a point.

A few stray bubbles find their way over to the Press Box at the start of the second half, one popping on my lapel as I hit the stop watch app on my phone for the start of the second half. Jutkiewicz catches Faubert out, chasing back to goal, but the striker's looped header drops just over the bar. Collison and Baldock link up in midfield, but the move breaks down. Coventry have a corner. Their away support are making themselves heard, despite being barely 700. Green rises above the strikers to claim the ball.

I'm starting to look at Allardyce's options on the bench. Lansbury looks the best of these and I guess we'll be seeing him in a few minutes. Collison has earned a corner with a well timed run down the left hand side. It's hit to the far post where Cole is waiting, but he can't work a way through the Coventry defenders who hold firm. At the other end, Green holds a testing long range effort from David Bell. Now Baldock gets on the end of Cole's cross but his touch flashes inches wide of the far post with Murphy beaten. From the corner, Baldock's flick is turned away by Murphy, who denies his header less than a minute later with a brilliant point blank range save. More bubbles. Hammers are cooking now.

Can I get through the next couple of paragraphs without using the word 'Alamo'? 62 minutes and no sign of Lansbury. Coventry are playing six men deep in their own half, and almost pay the penalty when Baldock seems to have been brought down in the area - but no penalty says Simon Hooper. Well, 'gestures' is more accurate.

Now, guess what, a 67th minute goal from Kevin Nolan. He may well be criticised for rarely putting in 'man of the match' performances, but there he is, timing his run to the far post perfectly, to head in a rare George McCartney right wing cross, headed on by James Tomkins. Another of McCartney's many assists this season. Coventry quickly make two substitutions, indicating their desire to, as Peter Brackley would have it, 'up the ante'. Mark Noble gets into a fracas with Gary Deegan, and both are booked, despite a theatrically staged effort at hand shaking. West Ham make a 73rd minute substitution with the tiring Sam Baldock being replaced with Frank Nouble.

Back in defence, Winston Reid puts in a couple of good tackles, as Coventry push upfield for an equaliser. This would be a great win for the Hammers with Southampton and Middlesbrough now losing. Jason has texted to tell me that Alvin Martin's son Joe has been sent off for Gillingham for a second bookable offence against... Aldershot Town! That's what I call keeping tabs on the Irons.

Frank Nouble is looking like a contender for 'part time man of the match' with two close efforts in succession, looking like a player with the January transfer window in his rear view mirror. Coventry string together a couple of decent moves before a terrible defensive lapse again lets in Nouble whose shot is brilliantly fingertipped out by Murphy, only for Noble to steer the loose ball wide with the goal gaping open like the mouth of a juror at a James Murdoch trial.

The last five minutes feature a pivoting effort from Carl Baker which is deflected onto the bar and over. The honest cockneys in the crowd, even the ones leaving ten minutes before the end, would probably give the man of the match award to the Coventry goalkeeper Murphy for his second-half performance. Allardyce manages to waste the third minute of injury time by bringing Joey O'Brien on for Carlton Cole. If only there was an international cap at stake.

West Ham: 1 Green, 2 Reid, 3 McCartney, 4 Nolan, 5 Tomkins, 7 Baldock (24 Nouble 73), 9 Cole (17 O'Brien 90+3), 10 Collison, 16 Noble, 18 Faubert, 21 Diop

Shouldn't I be feeling elated? West Ham are now joint top of the Championship on points, thanks to Southampton's 0-3 reverse at Brighton, and Middlesbrough's similar misery at Blackpool. With Southampton at Nottingham Forest and Hammers at Portsmouth in a fortnight, this might be the chance to go clear at the top of the division. How predictable was that after the misery of December 2011? The problem is, West Ham are not scoring goals at home, and if they do, they end up hanging on like Buster Keaton round the minute hand of the Town Hall clock.

FA Cup Third Round 2011-12, Hillsborough
Sunday 8th January 2012 (17,916)
Referee: Keith Stroud (Hampshire)

Sheffield Wednesday 1   **West Ham United 0**
O'Grady 87   Baldock (missed pen) 49

Irritating but significant. Last year's irrelevant cup runs were a reminder
that no run of form in a domestic competition is a substitute for securing
Premier League status. This one amounts to confirmation that Sam Baldock is
officially yesterday's flavour, his 49th minute penalty miss unsurprising for a
man who has not scored in his last nine games.

Ex-Hammer Stephen 'B-Y-W-A-T-E-R' is on the bench for Sheffield
Wednesday, where he has been on loan from Derby County since
September. His is a story worth recounting for its twists and turns. Signed by
Harry Redknapp as a sixteen year old from Rochdale, for whom he'd already
played in a 6-1 Autoglass Trophy defeat against Carlisle, Bywater went on to
feature in West Ham's 1999 FA Youth Cup winning team alongside Joe Cole
and Michael Carrick. He finally made his debut for the first team in February
2000, coming on as substitute for Shaka Hislop who had the misfortune to
break his leg in the first five minutes of the match against Bradford City in a
collision with Dean Saunders. By the end of that game, Bywater had set an
unlikely record, becoming the first Premier League goalkeeper to concede
four goals on his debut and yet still end up on the winning side. It was the
memorable 5-4 victory over Bradford City, a game which featured Joe Cole's
first league goal at Upton Park and a ball wrestling match between Paolo
Di Canio and Frank Lampard for the right to take a penalty. Bywater didn't
become a regular in the first team until 2004, but the following year he won
a Championship play off final winners medal for West Ham, again coming
on as a sub, this time for the injured Jimmy Walker. He left for Derby County
the following season, winning a Championship play off medal with them in
2007, and chalking up over 150 appearances.

In his time at West Ham, Bywater was trained by the late and great Les
Sealey, whose mantra could have been 'Why use two syllables when one
will do?' such was his dexterity with the sharp end of English vernacular.
This may have rubbed off on an impressionable Bywater once he got to
Derby, where he managed, quite literally, to spell out the C word during

an interview with Claire Tomlinson on Sky Sports' Goals on Sunday in 2007, leading to her taking an unscheduled extended sabbatical, for not apologising (don't they train these interviewers?). He then managed to offend his neighbours by erecting a piece of 'erotic art' in his garden featuring a blow-up doll, a mattress and a 'vandalised horse box' which he refused to take down until the press got hold of the story and forced him to remove it. And they say you have to be mad to be a goalkeeper? It's perhaps not unsurprising that he has an unenviable record of loan placements.

He wasn't given a squad number at Derby this season, and has finally been given a contract at Hillsbrough after his extended loan spell, by Wednesday manager Gary Megson. He has endured eight career loan spells at Cardiff, Coventry, Derby, Hull, Ipswich, Sheffield Wednesday, Wolves and Wycombe Wanderers. Perhaps this move to Wednesday, and faith shown him by the Wednesday manager, will be the opportunity to get his career back on track. T-R-A-C-K.

As for Gary Megson, he won't need reminding of his FA Cup quarter-final appearance here as a player for Wednesday against West Ham in 1985-86, when they put the Hammers out 2-1 despite a brilliant second half opportunistic goal from Tony Cottee. In the semi-final they lost 2-1 to Everton who lost 3-1 to Liverpool in the all Merseyside final. The other two teams who spoiled West Ham's season that year.

The story of this FA Cup tie, a quarter of a century later, ends with a late goal, plundered by Wednesday's Chris O'Grady from a right wing run, which Hammers' occasional keeper Ruud Boffin allows to slip under his belated dive. As for this season, it's a no matter match, so the result spares Allardyce's team the extra fixtures with the potential injuries and skewed focus. The draw reveals West Ham might have ended up playing Blackpool if they'd got through...

In terms of no matter matches, there is always the what if suggestion if John Lyall, in his hunt for promotion to the top division back in January 1980, had decided to put out a second string side against West Brom in the Third Round of the FA Cup. The conclusion would probably have been that West Ham would not then have won the FA Cup in 1980, the last team from outside the top division to do so. And then what about the West Ham fans who trekked up to Yorkshire on the Sunday to spend their hard-earned watching Brian Montenegro play his only career twelve minutes for the club?

West Ham: 31 Boffin, 2 Reid, 3 McCartney, 17 O'Brien, 48 Potts, 10 Collison, 19 Sears (46 Hall 72), 22 Lansbury, 32 O'Neil (26 Montenegro 78), 7 Baldock, 11 Carew (24 Nouble 65)

FA Youth Cup Fourth Round 2011-12, Upton Park
Wednesday 11th January 2012 (1,306)
Referee: Jake Hillier (Surrey)

West Ham United U18s 4	**Brighton & Hove Albion U18s 1**
Lee 16	Cumming-Bart 80 (pen)
Hall 40, 63	
Fanimo 78	

Greg Demetriou has been in place as Head of Media for four years at the club, an effortlessly efficient professional who eschewed publicity in everything he did. My thoughts are that he is likely to be replaced by Paul Stringer who was 'let go' in February 2010 in the austerity cull at the club as the last in. He had been making progress in his role, advancing the club's internet and website profile. He is a local boy through and through, from the last two generations of his family, and has been attending matches as a fan in the interim. He is the kind of man the club needs to facilitate continuity.

There is no official announcement, but Paul rings me early in the week to ask if I'd be up for taking the commentary mike for Tony Carr's U18s FA Youth Cup Fourth Round tie against Brighton at Upton Park on Wednesday. Back to the land of commentary. I have done live games as audio stream feeds on the internet, with Tony Cottee as summariser, under Greg, but Paul wants this one to be a 'with pictures' broadcast, a first for the club, though it's just a one camera feed with no replays or summariser. Even so, I won't need asking twice.

The youth team aren't as familiar to me as they would have been if we were still filming their games at Chadwell Heath, but I'm primed by club programme editor Rob Pritchard, and prepare my match notes a couple of hours before the game.

The form of the youth side is impressive, starting the season with five successive victories, and Elliot Lee, son of Robert, managed to hit two hat-tricks in the first two games to complement his other on the final day of last season. Three threes in three! He is top sorer for the team going into tonight's game. Dan Potts and Rob Hall are now getting first team action, but are still allowed to appear for the U18s, and won't miss this high profile opportunity. The wonderfully named Pelly Ruddock is cup-tied, having appeared for Borehamwood in the competition earlier in the season. The rules are just as strict at U18 level.

Tony Carr is now an MBE and has been in his job in charge of the academy for an impressive 39 years, taking four West Ham U18 sides to the FA Youth Cup final, famously winning in 1999 with the Bywater – Cole – Carrick team. Recently the academy has produced current first teamers Jack Collison, Mark Noble, Freddie Sears and James Tomkins. Carr coaches the U18s along with Nick Haycock.

This evening there is only ever one team in the tie, and West Ham run out 4-1 winners, scoring through Elliot Lee with two from Robert Hall and a final nail from Matthias Fanimo twelve minutes from the end.

West Ham U18s: 1 Jake Larkins, 2 Jake Young, 3 Dan Potts (captain), 4 Taylor Miles, 5 Kenzer Lee, 6 Leo Chambers, 7 Blair Turgott, 8 Jack Powell, 9 Elliot Lee, 10 Robert Hall, 11 Matthias Fanimo.

Game 26: nPower Championship, 2011-12, Fratton Park
Saturday January 14th 2012 (18,492)
Referee: Kevin Friend (Leicestershire)

Portsmouth 0   **West Ham United 1**
                         Noble 24 (pen)

(West Ham: 2nd in the table, 50 points from 78)

West Ham's defensive record in the Championship is lauded in the Portsmouth match programme, having conceded just eleven goals on their travels in fourteen games. This is another defensive success, made easier by the dismissal of Portsmouth's David Norris just after the break for a foul on Winston Reid. Reid has already been fouled in the first half when Tal Ben-Haim brought him down in the area. Mark Noble, back in the side, slotted the penalty away to give West Ham the lead on 24 minutes.

Portsmouth are unbeaten in seven home games, but are unable to put away any of the chances they create thanks to a combination of their profligacy and Rob Green's determined defensive performance. One particular fingertip save from a powerful effort by Liam Lawrence is especially worth a mention. West Ham end the day at the top with Southampton, but again second due to an inferior goal difference.

West Ham: 1 Green, 2 Reid, 3 McCartney, 5 Tomkin, 17 O'Brie, 18 Faubert (22 Lansbury 84), 4 Nolan, 10 Collison, 16 Noble, 21 Diop, 9 Cole

January has been a good month for West Ham's battling cup teams over the years, including last season's journey to the semi-final of the League Cup where they faced Birmingham City. Thirty-one years previously they had faced another midlands team Coventry City at the same stage of the competition, and nine years before that another in Stoke City. Still a two-legged tie, the 1972 clash with Stoke had taken two replays to decide before a 3-2 defeat at Old Trafford in a second replay. Nine years later they lost to Coventry City 3-2 in the first leg but went through to the final after winning the second 2-0 at home. Despite an excellent performance in the 1-1 Wembley final against Liverpool as second division underdogs, they lost the Villa Park replay the following month 2-1.

Last year's third midland semi must have possessed a mouth-watering appeal to the new directorial triumvirate of Brady, Gold and Sullivan, having recently moved their investments from Birmingham to West Ham. The optimism many felt before the tie should have been rewarded with something better than the rather feeble capitulation to three late Birmingham goals, especially as Hammers had at one stage led the tie 3-1 on aggregate. Birmingham went on to beat Arsenal in the final but, like West Ham, were relegated at the end of the season.

Game 27: nPower Championship, 2011-12, Upton Park
Saturday January 21st 2012 (31,718)
Referee: Tony Bates (Staffordshire)

West Ham United 2   **Nottingham Forest 1**
Noble 45 (+3, pen), 64 (pen)   McGugan 90 (+1)

(West Ham: 1st in the table, 53 points from 81)
If West Ham can get something from this game, they will be top at teatime

tonight. Southampton don't play until Monday. Opposition Forest are five points off the bottom of the table, above Doncaster Rovers and Coventry City, just one place behind our next Upton Park visitors, the lovely Millwall. But Forest have won four games on their travels, something even Southampton can't currently better. The story today is the return to Upton Park of the Forest and West Ham favourite Marlon Harewood. He was a player who scored twice here for Forest in an FA Cup 3rd Round tie in January 2003, a game that was to prove West Ham's first home win that season after 13 failed attempts. The first home league win came later that month against Blackburn Rovers.

Forest's home form isn't so good; they've only won three games there this season. I'm doubly confident because this afternoon I have Jim Goddard with me, a running mate in the athletic and not political sense. West Ham generally win when he's here.

James Tomkins has just signed a new long term contract with West Ham, a fact that is announced by Jeremy Nicholas before the teams emerge, to great cheers. There would have been a stunned silence if this had been announced after the 1-3 home defeat v Wolves in 2009-10, but with purported recent interest from Alan Pardew and Newcastle United, it represents a decent portion of confidence-lifting news before the game. Chris Akabusi has been drafted in to cheer on the side from the technical area. He yells out 'West Ham United's Claret and Blue Army!' over the faint strains of 'Bubbles', but it helps to raise the spirits prior to kick-off. I wonder whose idea that was? And why are we kicking off at 3.05pm?

Forest fans have taken half of the Trevor Brooking lower, well supported on their travels as always, with nearly 2,000 travelling hopefuls. Forest are wearing a black strip with green shoulders and green-topped socks, looking like the TA on tour in Guernsey. Marlon Harewood is given a standing ovation from the West Ham fans. Signed by Alan Pardew in November 2003 from Forest for just £500,000, he was top scorer for the club in the 2004-05 promotion season with 23 goals. In his career at West Ham from 2003-07, he scored 57 goals in over 150 appearances for the club. My favourite two are the brilliant FA Cup semi-final winner in 2006 against Middlesbrough at Villa Park, and, possibly best of all, the 89th minute winner at Upton Park against Arsenal the following November, that led to a delightful contretemps between Alan Pardew and an aggrieved (surely not!) Arsène Wenger. Harewood scored two more goals for the club, but fittingly the Arsenal winner was his last at Upton Park.

Harewood has been given the number 18 shirt. I struggle to remember which number he first took at West Ham. Wes Morgan is called into defensive duty action early on to shield the ball from Sam Baldock, and Faubert gets through wide on the right, but his cross is blocked. Come on. Cole is booked for an innocent-looking aerial challenge on the half-way line, right in front of the technical area. Allardyce resists the temptation to vent spleen. Marcus Tudgay fires over after being picked out by a vicious inswinging corner. McCartney fires in a powerful low left foot cross, but no-one can get a boot on it. Lewis McGugan now shoots over for Forest when it seemed impossible to lift the ball from so close in.

The game is quarter of an hour old and Forest look untroubled, though Harewood has yet to make an impression. Greg Cunningham looks handy in defence and is making life difficult for Julien Faubert down the right. Forest miss a corking opportunity, Tudgay placing the ball high from a right wing cross when he only needed to breathe on it to score. So long as they're missing the chances... If only West Ham could create a few...

Cole stoops under Wes Morgan as the next cross comes in and the crowd cry 'Penalty!' It would've been wrong. Three successive corners produce nothing. Greg Cunningham, on loan from Manchester City, now leaves the pitch on 23 minutes after a knock, to be replaced by Paul Anderson, a winger. Apparently, Forest have no defenders in their squad today, other than those that took to the field twenty-five minutes ago. That's a bit of a stupid plan. Barely a Plan A.

Bouba Diop gives the ball away with a misjudged pass, the incident timed perfectly with a volley of praise I have delivered to the Forest reporter on my left about his recent performances. End to end stuff now, mostly fuelled by goalkeeping clearances. Faubert, liberated from his tussles with the recently departed Cunningham, gets in a penetrating cross that Collison dummies but Baldock slots wide. Now the best chance of the match so far. Forest break down the right and as the cross comes in, sub Paul Anderson has a simple tap in. Faubert appears late on the goal line however to block the effort after Green is beaten, a truly miraculous escape. Unlike the Forest defence, West Ham are having a torrid time of it, with Winston Reid twice losing the ball in the centre circle, but Faubert tidies up and launches an attack. The corner that results, however, like all the West Ham corners before, is wasted. It's waste, but you can't recycle it, not even as entertainment.

Collison hits a decent volley as the ball drops to him in the area, his shot turned neatly round the post by Lee Camp, Forest's goalkeeping captain. Further wasted corners time. A few minutes later Papa Bouba Diop, untroubled by the attentions of anyone, even from his own side, collapses on the ball clutching his right calf. The Hammers coach looks at the team sheet. Faye seems the obvious choice, but Lansbury is Allardyce's selection, just a few seconds before the two added minutes of first half time are announced.

Baldock and Cole earn an injury time corner. Faubert gets the cross in and Moussi handles from two yards. A penalty seems somewhat harsh, but for the second time in a week Noble scores to give West Ham a half-time lead that has seemed unlikely throughout the half. The Forest protests continue until they are halted by the referee's half-time whistle.

Is my memory messing me around here? I'm not convinced that Hammers are playing the kind of football that might merit first place in the Championship, but they're top, at least for the moment, in the 'as it is happening' league table. Colin Benson reminds me at half-time about the West Ham v Forest game in 1987, famous for Tony Cottee's acrobatic overhead goal (in today's match programme), a visit from the King of Norway, three goals in the first ten minutes and the army dropping into the ground on rope ladders from three helicopters before the game. Benno's mate turned up a quarter of an hour late for the game and asked him if he'd missed anything.

The second half begins with the Forest players, still clearly unable to believe that they're behind. They must be reflecting on their record of 16 points from 51 under manager Steve Cotterill. The manager would have been sacked but for the fact that Forest don't have the reported £500,000 it would cost to pay him off (they are currently £76m in the red). Delicious.

Forest have been mighty unlucky this afternoon, and the poor luck continues. Substitute Paul Anderson is through with just Green to beat, Green's parry hits him on the knee and the rebound trickles wide with both men watching in helpless impotence. Two minutes later Forest force a corner which drops over Green's head and comes back into play off the far post. The Forest fans sing, *Come on you Reds!* to their black and green heroes. Another substitute for Forest, Dexter Blackstock, sounding like a comedian from the 90s, comes on. The next chance falls to West Ham, with Collison weaving in and out of the path of defenders until he pulls the trigger back... and blasts over. Three minutes later it's Lansbury with a similar opportunity which he keeps down, but Lee Camp acrobatically turns it over. A minute later Camp rushes off his line and, misjudging the bounce, Gunter handles, and a second penalty is awarded by referee Tony Bates. Noble neatly slots into the same right hand corner as before - this time all along the ground - on 62 minutes. It's at times like these when I feel making Mark Noble the captain would be the right move by Allardyce. I'm not sure what Kevin Nolan has done in the game, despite rating him as West Ham's 2012 Mr Motivator. As if to emphasise the point, Noble bursts through from the right, on a hat-trick, but his powerful shot goes across Camp's goal just past the upright.

Almost a year ago came the Premier League game that probably decided West Ham's fate last season. Facing Manchester United, the then league leaders, West Ham were enjoying an astonishing four match unbeaten run of form. The previous weekend, a brave and pugnacious 0-0 draw at free-scoring Tottenham had temporarily lifted them out of the bottom three. Inside the first half an hour they were 2-0 up against the champions, thanks to two penalties, both put away by Mark Noble. United had never conceded two penalties in the Premier League in the same game, let alone had them both converted. The fearless referee for the record (and this record still stands as I write this) was Lee Mason. Unfortunately, West Ham conceded four second half goals, including three from Wayne Rooney, and dropped back into the relegation zone. Worse still, they lost the following six league games and plummeted embarrassingly out of sight into the Championship. Note well all you Mark Noble critics that this man knows how to put away penalties. If only he could have taken all five in the 2006 FA Cup final.

The Bobby Moore Lower are singing, *Marlon, Marlon, give us a wave!* but the disappointed Forest striker is down the other end of the pitch and perhaps pretends not to hear. The crowd boo gently in mock disappointment. Then the poignant moment. Harewood is substituted on 72 minutes, and the crowd rise to applaud him from all sides. He raises his arms above his head and applauds to all four sides of the ground. *There's only one Marlon Harewood!* the crowd sing in unison, and I can hear my garbled ecstatic commentary describing that final Upton Park Harewood goal against Arsenal.

Now Collison surely makes it 3-0 with the goal gaping after Lee Camp has beaten out Baldock's effort. Nope. He screws it wide, much like the cramp-laden Harewood did with his half-chance in extra time during the 2006 FA Cup Final. Green is fouled as he punches under pressure from a Forest corner.

Now we see Rob Hall, number 46 and star of the U18s recent FA Cup 4th round 4-1 victory over Brighton comes on for twelve minutes with another chance to show the Upton Park crowd his tricks and skill. He replaces

Sam Baldock who has had another disappointing afternoon after such a promising start to his career a few months back. I am coming to a conclusion about Baldock, that he may well have served his purpose. His last goal was scored over two and a half months ago, away at Hull City, when his season record was five goals from six starts. Since then he's doubled the starts with no further goal.

Hall turns his man brilliantly, and is floored. Welcome to the Championship Robert! Carlton Cole steps off in the 85th minute before the free kick can be taken, to be replaced by Freddie Piquionne. Hall takes the kick himself with immense power, but it flicks off a Forest defender's head, dropping over the bar and into the top of the netting. The sponsors pick James Tomkins as man of the match. I guess it had to be a defender after that performance.

Jim and I are contemplating the walk to Plaistow as three minutes of injury time are announced. Forest have the last input on the match with a stunning twenty-five yard arrow of a shot from Lewis McGugan that is in the back of Rob Green's net before you can say, 'At least they scored the only goal from open play in the match.'

So West Ham are top of the league, if only for forty-eight hours. Wasn't that where we came in?

West Ham: 1 Green, 2 Reid, 3 McCartney, 4 Nolan, 5 Tomkins, 7 Baldock (46 Hall 79), 9 Cole (30 Piquionne 85), 10 Collison, 16 Noble, 18 Faubert, 21 Bouba Diop (22 Lansbury 45)

One of the benefits of exiting the FA Cup at the first hurdle is the free Round 4 weekend at the end of January. Being a cup side (ie form too sporadic for a decent league finish) West Ham don't always have this weekend free, but this time they do. I've had a little think about what each of the side that started today's game might be recommended as an activity for the day.

1) Rob Green – A kick boxing class with Fabio Capello and Clint Dempsey (Martin Jol would have to give Dempsey the day off from the Everton game, which he has probably earned because of the hat-trick he scored in the third round against Charlton at the Cottage).

2) Winston Reid – Plays for New Zealand, but has a bit of a history in Denmark, playing in the Danish league, and representing Denmark at U19, U20 and

U21 levels. I'll buy him the box set of 'The Bridge', the Scandinavian drama set in Denmark and Sweden, featuring an Asperger's Syndrome Swedish cop who struggles to make successful relationships because of her condition. With ten sixty minute episodes, that should keep him busy.

3) George McCartney – I'd hire a music room in Islington I know, often used by songwriters, and as he's only likely to be substitute for Spurs' Watford cup game, invite Aaron Lennon to join McCartney to pen a 'Lennon-McCartney' belated Christmas single. It was the one thing that the Beatles failed to do in their illustrious career – organise a cynical money-grabbing exploit, based on nothing more than a desire to make as much cash as possible. And it'd be perfectly in keeping with the whole Premier League ethos.

4) Kevin Nolan – 'Kevin will be on song for us once the rest of the Nolans are with him' was the headline for Sam Allardyce's Evening Standard article on Friday 30th September 2011. To that effect, then, I would suggest that we organise a few seats on the next Ryanair flight over from Dublin, and book in the Nolans (reformed in 2009) for a fortnight's stay in the hotel at Upton Park. Kevin could have a personal audience on the Saturday with the sisters Maureen, Anne, Bernie, Coleen, Linda, Denise, Amy and Julia (whom I seem to recall are all Catholic). They would perform their three greatest hits *I'm In The Mood For Dancing*, *Gotta Pull Myself Together* and *Attention To Me*. These three hits were from their most successful period, 1979-81, the year before Kevin was born, so he would need to consult 'Survivors: Our Story' the seminal work on the group. This was released a couple of months ago, possibly as a marketing opportunity response to Sam Allardyce's original article.

5) James Tomkins – Has formed an excellent partnership in the centre of defence this season with Winston Reid, so he should spend the day at his place, watching The Bridge with him.

6) Shirt retired

7) Sam Baldock – See you at Chadwell Heath for some penalty practice!

9) Carlton Cole - A day at the Benetton Outlet in Cheshire Oaks, Ellesmere Port; one of my favourite stories was at the beginning of the 2006-07 season, when we were targeting players to interview to put on the West Ham site – this was when it was run by Danny Francis in the very early days, before Greg D arrived. We had requested slots with Nigel Reo-Coker and Carlton Cole after training. Reo-Coker was the first there, barely fifteen minutes after finishing the session. He responded very seriously in his answers, almost piously at times, but we thought that was just him on the day. Carlton Cole (then newly signed by Alan Pardew from Chelsea) came for his interview about half an hour later, wearing the same seventies flowery tank top that Reo-Coker had worn. It was hard to conduct the interview in all seriousness with all these colours bouncing up and down on the screen. When we finished the interview we had to give Danny the tape of the two featured players wearing the same jumper, which of course Reo-Coker had 'borrowed' to wear while Cole was in the shower. You can imagine the fans' reaction to the interviews on the site later in the day.

10) Jack Collison – After Jack's difficulty with keeping calm after being allegedly wound up by Reading players, a problem that led to his red card early in December, I would offer Jack a morning at a two hour anger management counselling session run in Croydon. The distance he'd have to travel would further test his temper and help ensure this was the last such incident to impede further progress in a very promising young career.

16) Mark Noble – Once Fabio Capello is finished with his kick boxing class, I'd invite him to spend the afternoon at Chadwell Heath with Mark Noble. He could watch him practise a few tricks and demonstrate his long distant shooting, free kicks and penalty taking (he can work with Sam Baldock on this). This would give him a chance to add a full England cap to the 47 U16, U17, U18, U19, U20 and U21 caps he already has.

18) Julien Faubert – I would book Julien a morning down at the Olympic Pool in Stratford, filling it with smelling salts beforehand and have him do a couple of lengths. This would ensure he remained wide awake for the rest of the season in case he was ever required to sit out the first half of a game as a substitute.

21) Papa Bouba Diop – As the oldest player in the team, 'Papa' should spend the day on the internet, checking out the best pension plans available for footballers. As we all know public sector workers have better pensions than private sector employees, he might even consider a job as a PE teacher in an Inner London School. Can't imagine the kids messing around with the wardrobe!

The last day of the month is memorable for many reasons. The first is that on a whim I have decided I ought to join the early morning queue at the National Gallery for the chance to catch a glimpse of the Leonardo exhibition. Tickets for the exhibition, which finishes at the end of the week, were sold out back in October when they went on sale, but 800 are kept back for selling at 10am when the gallery opens. It's staying open for extra viewings until 10pm in its last week. I had a check on the net and confirmed that, so long as you get there by 6.15, you should be able to secure admission for sometime later in the day. Why would I even do that? Well, why not?

The various Da Vinci wonders on show at this exhibition have not lived in the same room together since the 1490s, and some are being brought together for the first time ever. As the site describes it, 'the natural and the divine' are blended together in exquisite proximity for the humble art punter. These lovelies alone have lent out their Da Vincis at great insurance expense: Musée du Louvre (Paris), State Hermitage Museum (St Petersburg) and the Pinacoteca Vaticana (Rome); g-d, even Cameron came here with his missus last week.

I get the first train from home at 5.34 which gets into Waterloo at 6.09. The stroll to the National Gallery takes a little over ten minutes, and I pass no-one on a dark but not too cold morning. When I find the queue, which is hidden round the corner to the entrance, I count 200 people already there, so I think my ticket should be safe. Then I discover that anyone queuing is entitled to four tickets. Oops, might be a bit tighter than I thought. Remarkably, the gallery is staffing the queue, and the yellow-jacketed stewards ask each person in the queue how many tickets they're buying, and calculate whereabouts the cut off point will be. How civilized. When I'm asked I say 'four', because by this time I have rung Jeff and Catherine and my mum to check that they're interested. Jules, sadly, has a karate night and will miss it.

My mum arrives at eight o'clock with a flask of hot soup, coffee and croissants which I share with the woman I've started chatting to. She stayed in a hotel overnight having come up yesterday on the train from Penzance. There's a guy in front of us who's travelled over from Portugal, a couple from Los Angeles and two students from some Bavarian town. This exhibition isn't on tour – it's the result of a five year project and it's only showing for twelve weeks. A world exclusive that will probably never be repeated for a century of more, and yet still easier to get into than a cup final. Work that one out. Yes... no corporates.

The exhibits aren't everything Da Vinci did – not even close. There's no Mona Lisa, for example, but it does cover what's available from his time as a painter and artist at the Court of Milan. It even features a recently restored painting showing for the first time, The Virgin and Child with Saint Anne. The warmth and brittle emotion behind the depiction of the religious figures and events are beyond my limited powers of description, but my eyes feel soothed in their presence. Jeff and Catherine and my mum feel the same. We were lucky to have been there. If you were at Wembley on 10th May 1980, you'll know what I mean.

Game 28: nPower Championship, 2011-12, Portman Road
Tuesday January 31st 2012 (22,185)
Referee: Fred Graham (Stanford-Le-Hope, Essex)

Ipswich Town 5	**West Ham United 1**
Chopra 3	Collison 45
Murphy 44	
Martin 45 (+ 3, pen)	
Emmanuel-Thomas 64, 90 (+ 4)	

(West Ham: 1st in the table, 53 points from 84)

West Ham are top of the Championship – finally – and tonight they have the chance to extend the month to a full hand of wins to consolidate their position. Their opponents? The Tractor Boys, who may have won at Upton Park in September with a late goal, but home form of five wins out of thirteen and seven defeats at the hands of Doncaster Rovers, Crystal Palace, Hull City, Southampton, Reading, Watford and even Nottingham Forest could mean only one thing, right? To a West Ham fan, right?

How many times has a manager in his first game in charge of a new team ended up with a win? You're right, it very rarely happens. Certainly not to West Ham managers (though Alan Curbishley recorded a rare victory in his first game in charge against Manchester United in December 2006. He didn't win again for eleven games, and was gone just 19 months later after only one full season). It does happen to new managers who are fortunate enough to find their team has a game against West Ham. Or for Paul Jewell, just any old game against West Ham will do.

Michael Chopra, brought in by Jewell, scores his first goal in eight games after just three minutes, reversing the kind of form that has besieged Sam Baldock. The thrashing on the horizon looks anything but with Carlton Cole hitting the post three minutes later and Tomkins heading over after a good West Ham build up. Then, a minute before half time, Daryl Murphy heads a second to put Ipswich 2-0 up, but even then Jack Collison pulls a goal back on the stroke of half time with a well-taken headed goal. Sam Allardyce might have been given the chance to inject optimism into his half-time team talk had Ipswich not gone straight up the other end and nabbed a third from Lee Martin's penalty after George McCartney had chopped Chopra in the area.

Baldock is on for Noble at the start of the second half. Will this be the game he shows a return to striking form? No. Instead it's Jay Emmanuel-Thomas, twenty minutes into the second half, who hits a skidding shot home from long distance. He then hits a second and Ipswich's fifth with a shot from inside the area four minutes into injury time. West Ham have five efforts on target to Ipswich's seven, but five of Ipswich's seven end up in the back of the net. How's that for stats for you?

West Ham: 1 Green, 2 Reid, 3 McCartney, 5 Tomkins, 18 Faubert, 4 Nolan, 10 Collison, 14 Taylor (46 Hall 69), 16 Noble (7 Baldock 46), 22 Lansbury, 9 Cole (24 Nouble 69)

It's said afterwards that Sam's mind may have been elsewhere what with this game coinciding with transfer Deadline Day. Indeed in his post match conference, Allardyce complained about having a full programme of matches on such a key date in the football calendar.

Despite the 5-1 reverse at Portman Road, West Ham finish January looking down the Championship table at the other twenty-three sides. It's been a strange month, with three wins, a cup exit and a slaughtering, but it still represents a good start to 2012. Harry Redknapp, however, is on trial at Southwark Crown Court for two charges of tax evasion. If found guilty, he could face imprisonment. I am one of his fans, though I appreciate that there are plenty of West Ham followers who think differently, especially since he became manager of Tottenham, and *double espresso* especially since he's signed Scott Parker, got them playing good football, scoring goals regularly, and in a Champions League qualifying place for next season. So what will happen if he's found guilty?

Chapter 9

Stuff and Nonsense

February 2012

Wednesday is a working from home day, so I spend the first one in February with my hands held together in prayer. Have West Ham and Sam signed anyone from anywhere on Transfer Deadline Day to keep us permanently at the top of the Championship until the end of the season?

I tap at my iPhone stairwell to BBC Online for the sports page. And there it is. Sam has signed three strikers to do the job his namesake has stopped doing. Two of them have already appeared at Upton Park this season: Ricardo Vaz Te (Barnsley) and Nicky Maynard (Bristol City). Vaz Te is a bit of a gamble, but has good form with Sam from some shared time at Bolton. Maynard is a wily stick insect of a player, but has scored 81 goals in 197 appearances, and getting them for Crewe and Bristol City can't have been easy. Then there's the long shot, Ravel Morrison. A character who proved too flash even for Sir Alex to tame. This looks like Allardyce's 'Di Canio' style gamble. Can he tame the raw talent? Don't hold your breath.

Game 29: nPower Championship, 2011-12, Upton Park
Saturday February 4th 2012 (27,774)
Referee: Mick Jones (Cheshire)

(West Ham: 1st in the table, 56 points from 87)

West Ham United 2	**Millwall 1**
Cole 45	Trotter 66
Reid 68	

I'm watching this one from the comfort of a couple of duck feather filled sofa cushions. Why travel and freeze and have to wait for two hours after the game while the tube stations re-open. Or putting it more plainly: it's a Millwall game live on telly. Easy decision.

Apparently it's the ninety-ninth meeting between these two. Millwall grab an early corner which is headed just wide. The first thing you notice is... Who ate all the crowd? Millwall fans can be heard screaming and chanting, but the away end looks no fuller than it was at the FA Youth Cup game against Brighton a couple of weeks ago. The cheering of the crowd on the few occasions Millwall are on the attack seems to have been sellotaped on.

Ernie Gregory, a giant of a keeper for West Ham in every sense, has died, aged 90, and as this is the first game at Upton Park since his death, Jeremy Nicholas talks about him before the game under a photograph on the big screens. Gregory was associated with the club for over fifty years, as a goalkeeper from 1944-58 and subsequently on the coaching staff. What a shame they can't have a minute's silence in respect for the club's longest-ever serving employee, rather than take a chance on the Millwall fans spoiling it.

My first two seasons working at West Ham were often spent, when I wasn't commentating, in the directors' box alongside Ernie's wife, who told me several stories about Ernie and what he'd got up to at the club over the years. This was a colourful cockney character whose career spanned the years from the end of the second world war to the club's promotion to the first division under Ted Fenton in 1957-58. When I finally met Ernie, I told him that his wife had told me all about him. 'Oh dear,' he replied, before bursting into spontaneous laughter. A West Ham man throughout his life. A lovely man.

Hammers earn a couple of quick corners. The first Cole sends over the bar with a looping header, and the second Faubert volleys over after a goalmouth melee. It looks a more open game than the usual soulless draw that traditionally characterises these fixtures.

Sam Allardyce's column in the match programme is headed 'It is important that we do not allow our feelings to boil over.' Eight minutes into the game, Hammers' captain Kevin Nolan dives two-footed into a tackle on Jack Smith, brother of QPR's Tommy. Referee Mike Jones emotionlessly raises his red card. Five players have already seen the red of Jones' cards this season, and Nolan takes the devil's number. Few people away from Upton Park are aware that Nolan's contribution to the side's performances this season, apart from the goals, has been vocal and spiritual - he can continue that from the stands, as I see it, so am I bothered? His West Ham obituary, when it's due, may read 'he inspired rather than perspired'.

Sixteen minutes in and ten-man Hammers have a free kick which Noble takes. Curled towards the far post, Tomkins gets a major slab of nut on it, but straight at the keeper. Millwall's new signing, journeyman striker Andy Keogh, has been busy and looks keen. Nine of West Ham's thirteen fixtures at Upton Park have been decided by the odd goal, and Millwall aren't scoring for fun on the road, so one hit in the back of the Millwall net may well do the trick.

I've just worked out where the Millwall fans are. They're occupying the upper tier of the Sir Trevor Brooking Stand - all of it! The lower east stand is sporadically populated by the early risers amongst the Hammers' faithful - getting up early and putting up with this, that's dedication for you. Complacency may well be Millwall's undoing today, with the early numerical advantage, and the Sky stats confirm that West Ham are now ruling the penalty area. Faubert and Cole team up in the air to send a header straight at the Millwall keeper, former West Ham reserve, David Forde. Joey O'Brien has returned to the right back position after more injury misery, and Abdoulaye Faye has also started, making a couple of vital interceptions to thwart Millwall breakaways. Feeney gets a shot in a couple of minutes later, but Rob Green gets completely behind it and holds on.

Nicky Maynard is on the bench, and will almost certainly get the last twenty minutes to show if he might be the goalscoring striker we've been looking for since the premature retirement of Dean Ashton. Green is in action again, dashing off his line as Millwall break, his clearance setting up Joey O'Brien for a hit from just outside the area that rises and dips just over the bar. 'A very watchable game so far,' says the Sky commentator on the half hour. Not quite sure what else you're supposed to do with a game as a commentator, but it fills a space in the play and has the virtue of sounding earnest.

The sides are evenly balanced. Hammers look as though they have eleven on the pitch. Noble's free kick seeks out Tomkins but is cleared by Dunne. Hard to believe Mark Noble is still only twenty-four. With seven years of playing experience for West Ham, he is the longest serving professional at the club, which adds power to my continuing suggestion throughout this narrative that he should be captain.

They're already calling Nolan's tackle a 'reckless challenge', the two words sticking to each other as if bound by a pat of industrial cement. The commentator describes Kenny Jackett, the current Millwall manager, as 'one of the most underrated managers in the Championship'. No danger of anyone overrating him the way the Hated Ones have been playing this season. Four defeats in the last five augurs well for West Ham as the fortieth minute approaches. Millwall's only win at the Boleyn was in 1987 in the Full Members Cup, which I have the footage of, somewhere. In competitive and serious fixtures though, Upton Park remains a permanent no win venue for Millwall.

Noble is on the ball as the half-time break approaches. Perhaps he feels the responsibility as a West Ham fan, understanding the significance of the fixture. To knock Millwall back towards the relegation zone as well as securing the three points, with Southampton at Birmingham in the 17.20 fixture, is what is called for. Two minutes of injury time are added, and as they elapse, Noble hits another free kick towards the centre of the Millwall goal. Winston Reid makes mischief and Cole extends his neck muscles back up to reach the loose ball, steering it powerfully over the Millwall keeper into the back of the net! GOAL! Millwall barely have the time to kick off before the half time whistle sounds.

During the break it's cheering to see, in extended replays, Julien Faubert barging malevolently into Jack Smith after the red has been shown to Kevin Nolan, suggesting Smith had contrived the tackle to get the Hammers' captain sent off. The brilliant duplicity of football.

Matt Taylor is on for Jack Collison, who was having a bit of a shocker by his high standards. Taylor will offer a bit more width, an expression I would never be disappointed to hear associated with me, though not of course in a footballing context. As has already been established, this isn't a Full Members Cup fixture.

At half-time Sam Allardyce has told Sky Sports that the sending off decision was the 'correct one', whilst simultaneously lamenting the departure of the days of the good old-fashioned 'leg breaking' challenge. Oh dear.

George McCartney, in the first genuine piece of goalmouth action of the second 45, hits a long cross towards the centre of the goal. Julien Faubert rises brilliantly on the six yard box edge to lever the ball over the keeper, onto the underside of the crossbar and out to safety; unlucky not to make it 2-0. There's a player who has improved fourfold under Sam Allardyce - a Frenchman improving under an Englishman - that's the New Europe for you.

The pitchside advertising boards under the Millwall crowd scream out 'Cash Paid For Scrap Metals!' It's one industry that surveillance seems to have failed to police. Still, if anything goes missing from the structure of the Sir Trevor Brooking stand, the local constabulary will know which dockers' jackets to look under to find it.

Stand up if you hate Millwall! the West Ham fans sing raucously.

Millwall! Millwall! Millwall! the Hated Ones reply.

Going down! Going down! Going down! West Ham fans sing.

Down with the Redknapp! the Millwaulians reply, *You're going down with the Redknapp!* Now there's an inventive use of the definite article.

Darius Henderson rescues the ball that Faye is shepherding out of play. His return pass is hit from outside the area with a dipping volley by Liam Trotter over Green and into the back of the net for a heart-stoppingly unexpected equaliser. Of course, it had to be the 66th minute. West Ham always seem to concede after inventive sloganing from opposition fans!

Less than two minutes later, the genius of Julian Faubert plays a huge part in the restoration of West Ham's lead. A giant punt towards David Forde looks harmless until Faubert leaps with the keeper, causing him to spill punch it only to the edge of his area. Winston Reid gratefully slaps it into the back of the unguarded net, 2-1! Replays indicate a clear infringement from the French One, which perversely makes the goal even more delicious.

Hammers' fans now go with the more traditional, *You're Not Singing Any More!* A couple of minutes later, this gestates to the inappropriate *Go Back To Your Caravans! Go Back To Your Caravans!* There is no reply.

In the magical 76th minute, it's Millwall who create something. A twenty-five yarder leaves Rob Green watching the darkening sky as the ball skids just wide of his right hand post. It does seem as though all the bad luck and misery of last season has somehow generated a welter of good fortune and refereeing blindness to West Ham infringements throughout this season, both blatant and subtle, barring Nolan's red card. Faubert slams a shot just over before being substituted for Gary O'Neil with ten minutes left, the volume of applause indicating the high esteem in which today's crowd hold him.

Just a few minutes to hang on. But why exactly are we hanging on against these strugglers? Abdoulaye Faye takes one for the team, getting a yellow card for a late challenge that spares Rob Green after his feeble goal clearance. The free kick is thankfully wasted by Kane, on loan from Spurs, unAbel to do anything productive in the circumstances. Never mind about the opposition's poor record here, if Hammers can hold on it will be the first time they've beaten Millwall at Upton Park for twenty-one years. These matches always seem to end up in a draw.

Millwall right back Alan Dunne suddenly finds himself in space on the edge of the six yard box, but Rob Green grabs gratefully at his schizophrenic effort, half shot, half cross. The match flips. Now it's all Millwall. Why should West Ham ever have things their own way? Gary O'Neil throws himself at Millwall's sixth corner and somehow manages to head it over his own bar when he's trying to clear it away from the goal. I am reminded of the heading versatility of the great Iain Dowie.

Carlton Cole is substituted with 90 seconds to go for one of the new boys, Portugeezer Ricardo Vaz Te, to make his debut. Playing well this season for Barnsley, this is a player who made his debut as a sixteen year old for Bolton under Sam Allardyce, and who has journeyed back to him in East London. He has the chance to shoot in the first of the five additional minutes, and although he beats Forde with his effort, it's a little on the puny side, and skittles a good yard and a half wide.

O'Neil then links with Vaz Te, looking for an opening, but he's shepherded away to a position in the area from which his shot is no more likely to challenge the Millwall keeper than it is to open a current account at a local branch of the Royal Bank of Scotland. Millwall manage one last corner, in the very last minute. Faye heads it away to great cheers from the Hammers fans. As the ball drops out of play, great cheers again. Ten men have beaten eleven man Millwall at Upton Park, with a justifiably hotly-contested winning goal, for the first time in twenty-one years. As Mark Noble subsequently reports in an interview on the pitch, 'The Boys Worked Their Nuts Off.'

West Ham: 1 Green, 2 Reid, 3 McCartney, 4 Nolan, 5 Tomkins, 9 Cole (12 Vaz Te 89), 10 Collison (14 Taylor 46), 15 Faye, 16 Noble, 17 O'Brien, 18 Faubert (32 O'Neil 80)

Sam Allardyce, once a player at Millwall, later calls this, 'the greatest win of my career.' Maybe calm down a bit, Sam.

On Wednesday, after an eight million pound, five year slog, the Harry Redknapp trial finally concludes just before midday at Southwark Crown Court. The jury's unanimous verdict is not guilty. The case, which was over an alleged £189,000 tax fraud, has only managed to highlight an error of stupendous proportions by a misguided CPS and a typically over-zealous Revenue department. It's the romantic celebrity-chasing notion of success and the kind of grotesque hubris that was also found wanting in the Revenue's waiving of £8bn in tax allegedly owed to the UK by Vodafone. To the uninitiated, Harry may occasionally come across as football's equivalent of Arthur Daley, but as someone who has had the pleasure of working with him over the years, I would stake my limited reputation on the fact that he is no criminal. Thankfully, the jury have also managed to recognise this. If it had been twelve unforgiving Hammers' supporters (the type who were singing about caravans at the last game), the result might have been different.

Within two hours and with the synchronicity that such news days often possess, Fabio Capello resigns as England manager. Or is sacked. Or jumps before he is pushed. The rather long and drawn out reason for all this lies behind the fact that John Terry has been stripped (why do they use that word?) of the England captaincy for a second time, and this time for an act difficult to connect, even obliquely, to the term 'stripped'. The FA have taken the decision that the media focus on the captain of a national team at a major European tournament might prove difficult if said captain is subsequently found guilty of calling one of his opponents a 'fucking black cunt'. Now I'm no lip reader, but I've seen the footage on one of the many You Tube videos, along with at least 282,147 others, and, despite his protestations that he is only repeating Ferdinand's alleged words back to the ex-Hammer, the people's court have decided unanimously, *he guilty*. However, as Capello still can't speak English, and Terry did not repeat the comment in Italian, this fact passed the England manager by. He got the hump (not sure what that is in Italian) and said in some interview with an Italian journalist that he wouldn't have 'striped' (bad translation) Terry of the captaincy if it had been down to him. Unfortunately for Capello, the FA employ an Italian speaking department just for such occasions, originally called in to lip read and comprehend just what previous England manager Sven Goran Eriksson was whispering about them to his Italian girlfriend at the time, Nancy Dell'Olio. This department is on a retainer so large that the FA have had to find something for them to do other than manage the U17 team. So, they have measured the scorn and disrespect of Capello and have taken 'appropriate action'. It would be a beautiful story on any day, but coming, as it does, on the heels of the 'Harry Walks Free' headlines, the two premises now fashion a delicious conclusion.

The press have unanimously given this morning's two news stories the punchline *Harry for England*. Yes, I think, it is your time. Arise Sir Harry. England is waiting. That film with Laurence Olivier brandishing his sword at the head of the English army. I'd have given the story the headline 'On

The Heels of Redknapp' were it not for the cameo role played by Harry's beloved canine Rosie in his recent trial (the password to get into his Monaco bank account was Rosie47, the name of his beloved dog and the year he was born). The only thing in the trial to challenge Redknapp's honesty is his confession that he lied to a News of the World journalist about the money. With the Leveson Enquiry in full swing, no one's going to blame him for that. The same morning I find myself at our accountant's in Wrecclesham. Maybe Frankie58 would be a good password for our Internet account…

Back in February 2006, five years ago, my brother and I decided that we might pool our financial resources and set up a Media and IT Company. I had acquired commentary and filming work and he had got a consultancy job at the Food Standards Agency that required him to have a company to be paid his salary. We took advice, put a website together, got an accountant, and off we went.

It's said you should never to go into business with family, and what with my brother's 'softly softly' approach and my 'Bull in a China shop' game plan, the saying has a lot to commend it. It sometimes feels as though my brother is actually one of those South Bank statuesque silver-sprayed characters. Tall, elegant, majestic, but ultimately they never move (unless you try to nick their hat full of money). But he has a kid now, so he must have moved a bit. I'm the opposite, unable to endure the tedium of waiting, time poor, hating to waste anything, especially time. Bit of a chancer. Hate PCs, Love Macs, hate manãna, love now, hate aimless, love direction. A bad candidate for the demands of a West Ham supporter, you could say.

Within a couple of years of forming the company I cut my teaching down from four days to two and began to train as a film editor to widen the scope for work. 'Train' here is perhaps best defined in its loosest sense of simply ringing Neil up every time I came upon something I couldn't do. It must have driven him mad. Green screening, colour correction, aspect ratio, the unforgiving randomness of digital formats, codecs, which field to lead with, DV Pal or DVC-Pro… I could go on, and I had to. I often deliberately took jobs I had no idea how to complete, forcing myself to learn how if I wanted to be paid. I suppose, unlike my brother, I love the pressure. I mean *really* love it. I could have been a West Ham manager in another life. Is that a job for a chancer? Imagine being Glenn Roeder at the beginning of the 2003-04 season, still in a job that you should have been sacked from. Unsure when the axe might fall… Or the beginning of the 2002-03 season, full of promise, over-confident, with a squad filled with overpaid internationals... What would you do differently if you'd been in his place? 'Just about everything,' is probably the correct answer.

Not Game 30: nPower Championship, 2011-12, London Road Stadium
Saturday February 11th 2012 (Postponed)
Referee: Chris Sarginson (Staffordshire)

Peterborough United P   West Ham United P

The Peterborough game is postponed because of a frozen pitch. I struggle with my normally sound football memory. When was West Ham's last postponed match because of the weather? The Aldershot Town FC game was put back because of the riots, but the weather? Posh and West Ham fans both spend the early part of the day attempting to clear snow off the pitch, but even when they do, the surface underneath is still unplayably rock solid.

Whitney Houston has been found dead in a hotel bath on Sunday. She is just 48. Why do these things shock us? I didn't know the woman, I don't have any of her albums. Still, it's... shocking. Horrible way to die. To be found like that. There'll be the usual Bobby Brown this, her sexuality that, so much rubbish for her family to endure. My memory of her is from 26 years ago on that Michel Drucker live French chat show in 1986 as a nervous twenty-two year old with Serge Gainsbourg, the controversial but brilliant singer songwriter. He is, unsurprisingly, completely pissed and puffing on a gauloise, openly propositioning her in English from the other side of the set. Neither she nor Drucker knew how to stop it, which made Gainsbourg's slurred smiling utterances all the more outrageous.

I have an exhilarating run that morning in Richmond Park, clocking just under an hour and 25 minutes. This is somewhat undermined when editing on Monday as I stretch to grab a firewire cable on the desktop and trap a nerve in my back. It will take two weeks before I am back to normal. Maybe I overdid it yesterday.

I'm editing a film for Newsnight freelance journalist Paul Martin for the BBC about an online friendship between an Israeli and an IT worker from Gaza that he has spent a lot of the last three years putting together. He has been out to Gaza and Israel to film both the men, and has got into a lot of trouble as a result of his endeavours. I'm sitting in the editor's seat at his studio in

Kentish Town, only having to travel a few stops on the train and press a few keys. Paul, the intrepid journalist, has travelled all over the Middle East to bring this breathtaking footage back. He is in demand on the political lecture circuit to describe tales of his exploits. A long way from Upton Park, you can be sure.

On the way to West Ham from Paul Martin's the next day, Paul King rings me, a voice from the past whom I haven't seen since our friend and fellow runner Colin Wilkie's funeral back in March 2008. Paul has written a book about growing up in a children's home, and is looking for me to help him find a publisher. This is farcically good timing, even spooky, with Belinda and me putting the e-books operation together just a couple of months ago. I promise to read his book when he sends it, and suggest we go out for a run in Richmond Park next Sunday, unlikely though that may be. I am certain that his book will be a no-holds-barred account, and one that won't be reading matter for the squeamish. I know a lot of the details of what happened to him in his life, and writing this will probably have been pretty good therapy for him. What kind of experience reading it might be like is another story altogether.

Actual Game 30: nPower Championship, 2011-12, Upton Park
Tuesday February 14th 2012 (34,936)
Referee: Lee Probert (Wiltshire)

(West Ham: 1st in the table, 57 points from 90)

West Ham United 1	**Southampton 1**
Noble 21 (pen)	Hooiveld 75

As my mate Alan Jones said when he studied the fixture list, 'Only West Ham could organise a game on Valentine's Day'. He wasn't quite right, as there is a full programme of Championship games this evening. He is also forgetting the St Valentine's Day Massacre back in 1990 when Oldham Athletic turned Lou Macari's West Ham side around 6-0 in the first leg of the League Cup Semi-Final. I'd prefer to call it the Plastic Pitch Pants Performance. In the final analysis, I say take the missus out and forget the football.

This evening, however, I am at the match. As you'll see, I may have made the wrong decision. Vaz Te has a scoring chance from the edge of the six yard box with just forty seconds on my stopwatch, which Kelvin Davis athletically gets down to and turns round the post. A quick glance over my shoulder shows Iain Dowie reporting on the match live for Sky, and called into action after just 58 seconds. That is impressively fast work, boys.

Southampton have filled nearly two-thirds of the Sir Trev Lower tonight, and most are in full voice. What with the cancelled Peterborough game from Saturday and the Saints winning their game, a victor tonight is guaranteed top spot. I've made a stupid prediction of 4-2 to West Ham. Stupid, because Joey O'Brien has already skied one on seven minutes from about three yards from under the posts. Southampton have a free kick. And now a corner. It's crumbled away to safety, or 'scrambled' if you don't have a cliché corrector on your computer. Rickie Lambert misses out on the far post for Southampton; this is fast and furious stuff with just ten minutes gone.

I've still got this trapped nerve in my back. Every time I stand up or try to bend down it's like a thousand volts shooting up my spine. I only mention that in case I come across a little less than my usual upbeat joyous self in this particular recording of events. I got here, anyway, so that's something. Palace are 1-0 up at Bristol City. See if I care. But you can always think of someone who will be enjoying such a revelation. Every score brings a smile. In this case it'll be my old mate Tom Cross.

Hammers have a penalty for handball. In his effort to grab the ball, Taylor loses his cool and lashes out at Billy Sharp, who won't release it. Taylor is sent off. Ludicrous. Now the ref is having a close and personal chat with his assistant below the Press Box. Noble takes the penalty and scores. Jack Collison is immediately sacrificed, substituted by George McCartney. So we've got to survive a second successive home game with ten men and we're not even halfway through the first half. In this absurdly important match! That strange screaming duet behind me is the Mud Mouth twins giving the referee hell. Well at least we have a lead to defend.

It looks as though Billy Sharp is going to need a police escort home this evening. Delightful to see that the booing appears to be trashing his game, forcing three errors in as many minutes, including an impressive lack of control in front of his manager with no Hammers' player within twenty yards of him.

Coventry 1 Leeds 0. Nope. Can't think of anyone smiling there. Brighton 0 Millwall 1. Again. More people miserable at that news, I suppose. Forget that earlier theory. Faubert is having another brilliant game, filling the Schemmel / Repka role of the attacking and determinedly pugnacious right back. Cole is floored in the area after a punch from the keeper. *You're not fit to referee!* the Bobby Moore lower lets out. Cole is led off for treatment.

Leeds have equalised against Coventry.

Still haven't really had time to work out that Collison off / McCartney on substitution. Looks sensibly defensive I suppose. Taylor leftie off for McCartney leftie on? Collison now has a good reason to join in the chanting at the referee. Green makes a stunning save from Do Prado when the goal is yawning at him like Cleopatra's Aunt. I confess to being on the delighted side as a fan that Rob Green has remained at Upton Park. My Arsenal mate Richard O'Dwyer was doing his best to drag him to the Emirates, spending most days in the close season on ancestry.com, looking for a distant French aunt called Verte.

Hammers remain on the attack as they have been for most of the half. The missing player hasn't made much of a difference. Cardiff 1 Peterborough 0. Actually, that really is a stupid theory.

Adam Lallana, wearing number 20 for Southampton, looks like a modern day Danny Wallace. I'm suddenly remembering a terrible Hammers' performance here under Glenn Roeder against Southampton, for whom James Beattie scored a 109th minute winner. *Who's the wanker in the black?* rises from the Bobby Moore Lower, as Faubert gets pulled up for a perfectly reasonable three-footed tackle from behind on Rickie Lambert. The striker takes the resulting free kick himself, bending it round the West Ham wall and wide of Green's right hand post. Just.

My back is aching.

Four wins on the trot at home for West Ham is another contribution to that guaranteed promotion place in April. Five will have me reaching for the John Helliar Bible. Oh yeah, Mick McCarthy has been sacked by Wolves; losing 1-5 at home to their arch nemeses the Baggies wasn't exactly avoiding one of the February P45s that hit the footballing world all too often. From his days managing Millwall to fake Irishman status rants from angry fans, Mick has been the Yorkshire management king of the last twenty years. He only has to manage Leeds now and achieve the impossible. Make them a team everyone loves. Guly Do Prado is booked for having a stupid, unpronounceable name. The ref is also going to need a police escort home tonight, even if it is a fashion hair police escort. He blows for half-time after four minutes of further discord.

Nobody during the break can throw any further light on the penalty incident, and even the half-time highlights unaccountably omit the incident.

After the break Joey O'Brien earns a first minute corner, followed by another. Hammers are looking well worth their place in the league against their nearest rivals. Southampton's yellow tops and blue shorts are a reminder of days when this was the de rigeur seventies' away kit. Looking around the ground, Upton Park is full tonight, and even the atmosphere seems a little more charged.

I still can't believe that I didn't have a single Whitney Houston track on my iPod. Not even the one with that note she holds for thirteen seconds. There was a story about this woman who'd been jilted by her boyfriend and used to play *I Will Always Love You* on repeat throughout the night, at full volume, much to the chagrin of her neighbours. They got together to arrange the first ever social restriction order against someone for the repeated playing of a piece of music. The court even went on to legislate just how many successive plays might constitute the term 'unreasonable'. The added problem was that she used to accompany Whitney on the chorus with backing vocals that did not merit the term 'harmonious' other than, perhaps, in sentiment. I have never been able to hear that song without a mental picture of her bawling along to it in the dead of the night.

The Southampton fans are warming up, but the Hammers' faithful belt out Bubbles into the cold East London night air to raise the spirits of their ten man heroes. Vaz Te steps over a through ball, breaking up a promising move, and Lambert's chip at the end does not bother Green. West Ham endure a couple more scrambles in the penalty area, ending with a deflected shot that Green can only watch float by. From the corner, the penalty area, packed with yellow shirts, watch in slow motion, fascinated, as the spinning ball eludes all of them.

Carlton Cole comes off to rapturous applause to be replaced by debutant Nicky Maynard on 64 minutes. Meanwhile David Connolly, aka the 'Angry Ant', sits on the Saints' bench, awaiting another appearance on the ground he made his own for a few months, prompting Glenn Roeder's single creative managerial moment.

Abdoulaye Faye is having another strong game in defence, and Hammers have settled again. Frazier Richardson lifts another cross into the West Ham box, but Green claims confidently. Another Hammers' substitution on 71 mins as Vaz Te comes off to be replaced by Gary O'Neil. The boos from Saints' fans show they remember his career at Portsmouth, and cannot forgive.

Another Southampton corner, for which all yellow shirts go forward. Lambert rises above all others, but his header is thankfully inept. Quarter of an hour to go. The guy two seats to my left looks like a 1978 version of Elvis Costello. Just as I'm fathoming the grey matter for that clever line in *This Year's Girl* (something to do with the girl having 'double vision' when you want her 'double jointed'), Southampton equalise. It's a 76th minute goal gone the wrong way, and it's Jos Hooiveld, the scorer from their win in October, who pokes the ball home to finish off another goalmouth mudfest. I thought we didn't get mud at grounds anymore. Only Mud Mouth twins. I haven't heard them this half, so we must have been playing well.

It's a tough thirteen minutes to get through to save a game and preserve the top place, but the ten men hang on and Hammers end the 90 on top. Saturday's Blackpool away fixture has been put back until Tuesday as the tangerines are still in the FA Cup. With Derby at home, Southampton will most likely be back on top by Saturday evening.

West Ham: 1 Green, 2 Reid, 5 Tomkins, 9 Cole, 10 Collison, 12 Vaz Te, 14 Taylor, 15 Faye, 16 Noble (capt.), 17 O'Brien, 18 Faubert

Belinda, my business partner of a couple of months at mardibooks, has the ability to push my buttons. These are buttons marked 'annoy'. You might ask why I'd form a company with someone who can do that, and it's a reasonable question. Our mission is to push new writers' work out into the kindle world by publishing ebooks on Amazon, the social marketing required to generate movement and interest is profound and labour intensive. She is driven and she has energy, two traits that can make me tired just thinking of them. Over the last few weeks I have found myself agreeing to unreasonable requests in an effort to keep up and feel like I'm 50% of the enterprise, too. Her latest stunt is to persuade Frank Bruno to read one of her poems so we can put it on the website. If you're thinking 'there's no way she can make that happen', think again. She's got me driving up to some school in Hertfordshire to film it.

It's school half-term, so the building is empty. But Belinda has found a few volunteers to be the class, and Frank is to be the teacher, pointing at them as he delivers the lines of the poem. It's hilarious. Frank is told to play it straight, which he does. The outtakes are magic, and I put them at the end of the piece when we edit it for the website and You Tube as 'Frank does Mrs Godbothers'. Bruno has lost a lot of weight, but he is as quick-witted as ever, and a genuinely good guy. He'd have to be to agree to all that.

I am able to grab one of Belinda's volunteers, Sam Foster, to take back with me to Perform Sports Media, in west London, where I'm putting commentary on the Chelsea v West Ham FA Youth Cup Round 5 tie played just down the road at Staines FC. The game is fed out from BT Tower and will go out on Chelsea's cable channel, but we are taking a clean feed of the match ('Clean', of course, means without Chelsea's commentators all over it) and putting it out live on West Ham TV on the club site. Sam is vital as researcher for the game. He is bright, lightning on the laptop, and loves football, so will be an enormous help.

Chelsea's U18s play at Staines FC, but unlike the Hammers, who let their U18s play their cup fixtures at Upton Park, Chelsea prefer to keep their kids on the kid pitch. Good attitude. West Ham U18s won here 3-2 last month in the league, so they must be in with a chance. For those who say competing in the Premier League without expensive foreign players is impossible, West Ham's U18 squad for tonight's tie features only English players and one Irish player in Kieran Sadlier. Chelsea's U18 squad features Nathan Ake, a Dutch international bought from Feyenoord, Amin Affane and Anjur Osmanovic, an U17 international, both signed from Sweden's Angereds and Lucas Piazón, a Brazilian U17 international signed from Coritiba. If Chelsea had a proper football academy, they could have nurtured just as effective a squad as West Ham's, instead of shelling out a conservatively estimated £20million plus for other teams' kids. The obscenity of that amount of cash is that most clubs in the Championship don't even have that for their first team... not even for the total running of their club. West Ham can match them, even beat them, with home grown talent. I'll leave you to make your own conclusions here, whilst reminding you that John Terry started his career at West Ham as a ten year old, only to be poached by Chelsea four years later. (I actually think that one worked out okay, though)

FA Youth Cup Fifth Round 2011-12, Wheatsheaf Park
Wednesday 15th February 2012 (1,588)

Chelsea U18s 3*	West Ham United U18s 3
Barker 11	Miles 41
Feruz 64	Turgott 76
Chalobah 90 (+ 5)	Lee 90 (+ 4)

* AET; Chelsea win 5-4 on penalties

I link up with Paul Stringer at the game over the phone, and he hands me over to one of the Chelsea commentary team, before the sides come out, to get the sp on their starting line-up. Should I be less than surprised when the Chelsea man says, 'Sorry mate, ain't got time to talk to you now'? Good old Chelsea, obliging even at U18 level. But then when you've got that much money, I guess you can dispense with luxuries like courtesy.

What follows over the next ninety minutes proves to be one of the games of the season. I can only hope Perform are streaming it successfully over the Net.

West Ham's number one striker, scorer of two in the last round and first team squad member Rob Hall is injured and will miss the game. It's a squad that plays deep so time for others to do their bit.

Goalkeeper David Wooton is in action several times in the first ten minutes as Chelsea break quickly and look a determined and well organised side. They take the lead in the eleventh minute as Baker taps home after an excellent run by John Swift, looking like one to watch. Hammers come back strongly and after Potts has gone close, Hammers equalise four minutes before half time with a bomb of a 25 yard shot from Taylor Miles. They then rely on Wooton for another couple of good saves to go in level at half-time.

In the second half Islam Feruz is put through by John Swift on 64 minutes and finishes well to restore Chelsea's lead. West Ham don't panic and begin to take control of the game, equalising for a second time when the brilliant Blair Turgott slots home from just inside the area after a neat interplay of passes, in the 76th minute, of course. I'm still quite reserved on the mic, but I can't help raising my voice in excitement when Elliott Lee puts West Ham ahead for the first time in the match in the 93rd minute, surely winning the tie? Incredibly, from the kick-off, Chelsea break as one and after Feruz's effort has come back off the post, the Blues' captain Nathaniel Chalobah is on the line to hit an unlikely equaliser. My reaction is silence. Stunned.

After a goalless extra time, it goes to penalties. Elliott Lee, taking second, has his penalty smothered by Chelsea keeper Blackburn. Chelsea's Feruz, kicking last of the initial 5, blasts his effort over the bar. 4-4, so sudden death. Substitute Dominic Vose, who has been an inspiration in extra time, goes for the over-confident, disarming subtle chip, which turns into a silly short sausage and the Chelsea keeper Blackburn anticipates to save easily. How awful that kind of trick looks when it goes wrong. Todd Kane, Chelsea's number two, slots home the winning pen, and Chelsea are through. I can hardly speak, choked by the way West Ham have lost this tie, and with a voice worn out by two hours of growling hopeful comments behind my Coles' microphone.

West Ham: 1 David Wooton, 2 Jake Young, 3 Dan Potts (capt.), 4 Taylor Miles, 5 Kenzer Lee, 6 Leo Chambers, 7 Kieran Sadlier, 8 Jack Powell, 9 Elliott Lee, 10 Blair Turgott, 11 Matthias Fanimo. Subs: 14. Dominic Vose, 15. Frazer Shaw

Thursday is my last day working on the Paul Martin film edit. Most of it is dominated by a backdrop provided by Paul's discovery that he knows Whitney Houston's 'real' bodyguard. Once he's contacted the poor man and got his permission, he attempts to sell the story to The Mail on Sunday's hack who arrives halfway through the afternoon. All of this provides unintentional hilarity and makes completing the edit on time a difficult task.

On Friday Belinda arrives with her willing assistant Claire to complete the edit of the Bruno video. I have to try to get her husband's mate a ticket for the Hull City game. It's a regular ask from those who are up for a chance to see the Hammers. Perhaps this isn't quite the deluge it would be if it was Arsenal or Manchester United. Nevertheless, when West Ham got to the FA Cup final in 2006, my email inbox shook at the hinges like a queue for Saturday morning Lottery tickets at Tesco's. Belinda's hubby has almost given the secret birthday present away, but birthday boy's wife intervenes just in time before he gets a sniff of the information trail.

On Saturday I read Paul King's book, half of it anyway, before sleeping. It's preferable to ITV's FA Cup coverage of the fifth round games, which is the worst I've ever seen. It seems hard to believe that they've just paid £90m for this, a few England internationals and some live FA Youth Cup games. I guess from the quality of the 'coverage' that their budget has already been spent.

Sunday – I don't go running as my back is fudged.

Tuesday – go into school for Child Protection training. Don't even ask. Come back and go for a run. Then on to AOP (Adventures of Parsley) rehearsal from where I'm texting Jason updates from the Blackpool game while I try to sing, too.

Game 31: nPower Championship, 2011-12, Bloomfield Road
Tuesday February 21st 2012 (13,043)
Referee: Oliver Langford (West Midlands)

(West Ham: 1st in the table, 60 points from 93)

Blackpool 1
Phillips 45

West Ham United 4
Tomkins 28
Maynard 32
O'Neil 74
Vaz Te 90

I'm rehearsing on the night of this Blackpool game for an AOP gig on Wednesday March 7th. The gig is straight after (actually some of it is *during*) the home game v Watford next month, so if I'm going to get to sing in it I'm going to have to get my skates on and possibly miss the last part of the match.

The band, who bang out TV Themes from the 60s and 70s, haven't played together for a while, though we have been together for nearly twenty years. We performed a live set on Mark Radcliffe's Radio One show in June 1995, and have three album releases and a few single releases out there that you occasionally see on eBay for inexplicably inflated prices. We do need rehearsals, though, as we have a little cluster of forthcoming gigs including a live set at the Twelve Bar club in Denmark Street next month.

As usual on such occasions, my phone is serving as prompt for (forgotten) lyrics in addition to providing me with updates from the game at Bloomfield Road. I've promised Jason, who can't get near a radio tonight, that I'll keep him up to date with goal flashes.

Blackpool haven't been beaten for seven games, so with the reverse psychology in action, West Ham must fancy their chances, especially on the road. This proves to be an accurate mindset, but despite two early goals from Tomkins and new boy Maynard, things don't go their way for long. In first half injury time, Blackpool pull one back through Kevin Phillips, with a deliberate low angled header. It seems like the first time Rob Green has handled the ball as he picks it out of the back of the net.

Unfortunately, for the third game in a row, West Ham will complete the ninety minutes with just ten men. Tonight it's Rob Green, nine minutes into the second half, who is trapped in the mist after a so-called 'professional foul' on Roman Bednar, with the score at 1-2. Somehow, unexpectedly now with Henri Lansbury between the sticks (Sam has no sub keeper on the bench and, anyway, he once played in goal for the England U21s), West Ham withstand Blackpool's expectant onslaught before hitting the Seasiders twice with attacks of their own. Gary O'Neil makes it 3-1 with a low shot from the edge of the area on 74 minutes, and the other new boy Vaz Te hits a fourth in injury time to confound the statisticians. Three games finished with ten players, yet seven points won out of a possible nine. And we're still top!

West Ham: 1 Green, 2 Reid, 3 McCartney, 5 Tomkins, 8 Maynard (9 Cole 82), 10 Collison, 12 Vaz Te, 15 Faye (32 O'Neil 66), 16 Noble, 17 O'Brien, 18 Faubert (22 Lansbury 54)

Game 32: nPower Championship, 2011-12, Upton Park
Saturday February 25th 2012 (34,900)
Referee: Graham Salisbury (Lancashire)

(West Ham: 2nd in the table, 61 points from 96)

West Ham United 0   Crystal Palace 0

The Palace team this afternoon look like a bunch of bananas in their all yellow strip, but they are unbeaten in four games and are taking on a side who have trembled at the knees on more than one occasion at home this season.

I'm in the company of seasoned Palace aficionado Tom Cross for the return Palace fixture, and I'm expecting a draw.

Mark Noble continues as captain in the absence of suspended Kevin Nolan, not a bad thing in the penalty-taking department, at least. Hammers have become the Manchester United of the Championship, with a shipload of penalties accumulated and put away in the main (except, thankfully, Baldock's miss in the FA Cup against Sheffield Wednesday last month)

Darren Ambrose finds himself with a glorious opportunity on the break to beat Green, but fires wide. Twenty seconds later George McCartney chips a through ball over Julian Speroni, but wide of the far post. Superb start. Jermaine Easter's effort is neatly blocked by Abdoulaye Faye's well-timed challenge. The pace of the game after five minutes belies the pre-match hype about a tough defensive ten-men-behind-the-ball Palace approach. I've already been up early and done the weekly shop at Tesco's (other supermarket brands are available) and got here in plenty of time, so I feel more awake than usual for a Saturday lunchtime kick off. Long distance shot straight at Green from Kagisho Dikgacoi, a copywriter's nightmare and South African international who made his way to Palace from Fugging Fulham. He will no doubt be remembered by West Ham fans as receiving his marching orders from Philip Dowd at Upton Park on debut for Fulham back in 2009, for elbowing Scott Parker in a midfield bust-up.

Tomkins is down after a mid-air collision with Mile Jedinak's shoulder. Jedinak is not a Serbian rebel, but an Australian international who came to Palace on a free from Galatasaray. Tomkins goes off after five minutes of poleaxe, but returns to generous applause after treatment off the pitch. West Ham get the first corner of the match after eighteen minutes, but to little effect - Palace look very well-organised. I'm trying not to think the phrase 'this is their cup final', but no doubt someone will soon be saying it.

At the other end, Wilfried Zaha wins a free-kick for Palace. This the younger brother of Serge Zaha who was in court earlier in the month for allegedly robbing a disabled driver who subsequently ran him over in Thornton Heath. The different ways two lives within one family can lead are rarely so effectively evidenced. Green is tested by loanee Norwich striker Chris Martin from twenty-five yards, beating his shot out and then gathering it at the second attempt. Palace are having most of the play, but it's Hammers who are winning the corners, and wasting them... Collison needs to go on a few corner kicking contest weekends to learn how to provide a few of those Hanging Gardens of Babylon moments for the big boys to get on the end of.

They're calling it, 'the game we don't talk about'. Exactly what happened for Hammers to have crashed 5-1 at Ipswich Town? And why bring that up in the middle of a Saturday lunchtime fixture against Crystal Palace?

Palace have three excellent opportunities to take the lead in barely a minute. First Easter's shot is beaten out by Green and then a deflected cross from Zaha off Tomkins' shoulder is spectacularly turned over the bar by the Hammers' keeper. From the corner, Paddy McCarthy somehow manages to put a free header over the bar.

Ricardo Vaz Te looks very polished in possession, but his Duraglit invariably loses its sheen on the final ball, a justified criticism of a lot of skilful Hammers' players over the last few seasons. Jonathan Parr, the Palace left back, is competing in his 62nd fixture without a season break, having come to Palace straight from a Norwegian side, whose season leaves off when ours commences.

West Ham force another corner. Noble takes this one, which proves to be a dangler, but Speroni is adjudged to have been fouled in the six yard box melee that follows. At the other end Ambrose blasts an excellent free kick opportunity into the West Ham wall, punctuated by the announcement that there are a further five minutes to be added to the half. And another corner. Wasted.

Palace have a small patch below the neck of the back of their shirts that says, simply, 'Jelly'. This makes Chris Martin's shirt read 'Jelly Martin'. I am keen to write the world 'Roll' between these two words at half-time, but it's a bit of a schlep down to the changing rooms. Jeremy 'Irons' Nicholas reveals that both the Belgian and the Scandanavian Irons have made the journey across the North Sea to catch this afternoon's game.

Sam brings Carlton Cole on for Julien Faubert, recognising perhaps that a little height in the Palace area might eventually put away one of those goalmouth opportunities. Quite who is going to provide the chances this half is a point for discussion. Winston Reid has moved across to centre back and Tomkins is now playing in front of the back four, as Cole takes up a loose ball and switches direction to hammer a shot just wide of Speroni's left hand post.

After ten minutes of the second half it becomes clear that the Palace supporters in the Trevor Brooking stand have seen most of the goalmouth action. That is until 'Jelly' Easter (children's party performer) is straight through, his run only arrested by a perfectly-timed tackle from Faye. At the other end, a low direct shot from Vaz Te is well fielded by Speroni. Now Vaz Te goes off for Gary O'Neil, or as Jeremy Nicholas puts it, 'replacing Vaz is Gaz...'

Nicky Maynard is starting to assert himself this half, and I've only just noticed him. He powers in a great shot from the edge of the area, just over, and looks very comfortable on the ball, a quality sadly lacking in many so-called 'ball players' at the club over the last few seasons. Darren Ambrose, crocked, now leaves the field for Palace to be replaced by Sean Scannel, the dreadlocked academy player. Tomkins arrives perfectly at the far post for a curling cross, but heads over. How long can this goallessness continue?

Maynard could end up playing in two goalless draws for two different sides at Upton Park in the same season. Another potential first for the stattos. Gary O'Neil is booked for an unkempt off the pitch tackle in front of the cameramen. Everyone is back for a rare Palace corner. Whatever happened to those days when the centre-forward used to spend such moments standing on the halfway line?

Baldock is now on for Maynard, and immediately has a goal scoring opportunity on the break down the left hand channel, which the keeper turns away. Barely a minute later he has another chance from a brilliant flick by Cole, but again Speroni saves, this time with his legs. A minute later he is through again, but gets tackled as he pulls back the trigger. With Southampton at Watford later this afternoon, this is obviously a game that West Ham badly need to win.

Two corners in quick succession, but still nothing. On a rare break West Ham are relieved to see the assistant referee's flag held aloft as Dikgacoi gets behind the defence in a superb scoring position. Final substitution is Palace's as Chris Martin leaves to be replaced by ex-Ipswich centre-midfielder Owen Garvan.

Carlton Cole has looked only half-present, and only Noble has really performed today in the claret and blue shirt. Wilfried Zaha has been sublime for Palace, and manages a great cross under pressure that Green grabs close to his chest with relief.

Mark Noble is announced over the tannoy as sponsor's man of the match, which is right, for a change. Palace have a free kick just outside the area in the last scheduled minute of the game. Green grabs easily. One final attack? Nope. What a disappointment to get just a point here after such a brilliant win at Blackpool in the week. Four minutes of injury time. Palace fans spend most of them singing, *Top of the League? You're having a laugh!*

When the whistle sounds, the capacity crowd deliver a groaning of low boos at the performance they have just witnessed, and for the first time in four matches, 11 players - not 10 – finish, only to lurch off to those sounds with their heads bowed. They have already conceded top place mentally to Southampton, and the disappointment manifests itself in everyone connected with claret and blue wishing for a personal transporter moment.

Hammers will be top for another two and a half hours, but the difference is that they can now be caught.

West Ham: 1 Green, 2 Reid, 3 McCartney, 5 Tomkins, 8 Maynard (7 Baldock 73), 10 Collison, 12 Vaz Te (32 O'Neil 58), 15 Faye, 16 Noble, 17 O'Brien, 18 Faubert (9 Cole 46)

Chapter 10

We Play On The Floor

March 2012

I have finally got round to watching a five part documentary about London's tube network. It's a series that has remained stubbornly on my Sky+ hard drive since it was recorded last month. Having begun watching it, I can confess that it has changed my attitude to the hard-working and incessantly cheerful employees I come into contact with daily. They cope with people being sick, trying to kill themselves, cheating their fares and even urinating at the far end of platforms. But then I have always been fascinated by human behaviour on public transport.

Lately, on my way to work, I have found myself sharing the carriage with the same young people on their way to a Drama college up in town. I'll spare you the name. It is impossible to avoid their conversation, wherever I find myself placed in the carriage. They speak loudly as if trying out material on a hostile audience in a huge theatre. I'm not remotely concerned about the prosaic nature of their subject matter. It's just that they upspeak. Incessantly. This is where the last word or part of the phrase they utter shoots upward in tone, as if they have been suddenly poked with a stick, to turn their statement into a question. The odd thing is, the more banal the topic, the more pronounced the upspeak. It's as if the device itself is of greater interest than any meaning in what's being said. How annoying is that? It's even got into our writing for g-d's sake, with question marks left at the end of sentences (usually in texts or brief emails) like abandoned sheepdogs on a cricket pitch?

Game 33, nPower Championship, 2011-12, Cardiff City Stadium
Sunday March 4th 2012 (23,872)
Referee: Chris Foy (Lancashire)

Cardiff City 0

West Ham United 2
Nolan 41
McCartney 76

(West Ham: 2nd in the table, 64 points from 99)

West Ham at Cardiff is live on BBC1. I have started my Sunday already with a nine miler three parks run, cutting through Osterley Park, the Grand Union Canal (from Norwood Green to Brentford) and finally through Syon Park. I am disappointed to find a time of over ninety-seven minutes when I thought I was getting faster. *Can* you get faster at 54?

The earnest and occasional London Marathon runner Jonathan Bloke is behind the lip mike this afternoon for the Beeb, ably supported by summariser Mark Bright. I red button the 'choose audio' instruction, and after several further taps I am offered the additional choices of BBC London Radio or BBC Wales. The hoped-for 'no irritating commentaries' is not an option. I return to hear Bloke saying, 'Whittingham... Gifted player.' Would you put anyone in your side who wasn't gifted? Perhaps Bloke is peed off at having to slum it in the Championship after the hospitality of Manchester City yesterday. 'The quality of passing has been very poor,' he says. It's the fucking Championship, mate, get used to it.

I look at my watch and discard yesterday's paper. More variety, yes, but still very little to entertain. It's hard to believe that the half is almost up, with very few opportunities created. Cardiff are knackered from their efforts in last Sunday's League Cup Final penalty shoot out final defeat against Liverpool, and West Ham are pissed off that Southampton took all three points from Leeds United at Elland Road, with a goal from their only attack.   Now Faye is saying Vuckic elbowed him in the face, which replays indicate he has, but it's obvious it was not deliberate. Collison misses the best chance of the half with a volleying opportunity just inside the area that he twats kilometres over the bar.

Then the goal. Vaz Te picks the ball up on the edge of the area and slips a pass through to Nolan, coming in on the left. He hits the ball right-footed with just enough pace to beat the Cardiff keeper's dive. Hammers take the lead on forty-one minutes. How does this guy manage to score so many important goals? I'm not really asking that question. I could care less about the answer, so long as he keeps converting the chances. It's half-time already in this non-match. Thank g-d my only journey at full time will be upstairs for a hot bath rather than that long drawn out M4 trek back to London.

'It's nine matches without a clean sheet for David James,' says the Championship round-up man. His summary of yesterday's games concludes with Bristol City's 3-0 defeat at Ipswich Town. James' embarrassment is complete with the knowledge that he was beaten by Chopra after a midweek 'drinking incident'. Even drunks can beat the Oldie from twenty yards. What will James do when he finally retires? My suggestion is 'I'm a Celebrity Surrey resident, Get me out of Shere'.

'What an astute signing Nolan was for Sam Allardyce,' says Jonathan Bloke, clearly reading from his list of 25 lines with which to punctuate lapses in play - problem is that's number 23, and he ignored his own parenthesised question mark in voicing it. He now speaks the dreaded phrase 'the departing Scott Parker', qualifying it with the suggestion that bringing Nolan and Faye in somehow assuages the situation. Just commentate on the action, mate. Forget the poorly prepared notes. Just do the verbal wallpaper.

We're seeing a lot more of Maynard this afternoon, and in one goalmouth melée he has two golden opportunities to widen the lead over Cardiff. The first is blocked, and the second he stabs inches wide. Newcastle have equalised against Sunderland in the second minute of injury time at St James' Park. Black and white striped riot. Maynard is now presented with a one on one with the keeper following an ill-judged back pass, but wastes the opportunity. Twenty seconds later and he's in there for a second time, and still fails to convert. Then it's Cardiff's turn. 'What a mistake again. Whittingham this time,' says Bloke. The gifted one, as I remember.

Vaz Te is now in with a chance, but skies it. Cardiff are terrible. This is the side, remember, who could easily have beaten Liverpool at Wembley last weekend but for a couple of lousy penalties. Carlton Cole is warming up, and if he'd been on the pitch during the last fifteen minutes, Hammers would surely be three or four-nil up. Maynard is off and Cole, 'Taller, stronger, better threat in the air,' as summarizer Mark Bright subtly puts it, is on.

Mark Hudson has a heading opportunity from a Cardiff corner, but his contact sends the ball just over. 25 minutes to go. West Ham have Watford on Wednesday, so a win today would give them the chance to keep on the heels of Southampton. Whittingham substantiates Bloke's fulsome praise with a quite brilliant free kick that beats Green's flailing left hand. It comes back off the inside of the post, across the goal line and away to safety.

Now the chat has turned to the fate of Portsmouth, and how, if they end up dissolved before the end of the season, all Championship results against them will be expunged. The important 4-3 home victory that I missed as I was working for MUTV. 'Pyramid Hygiene' it says on one of the stand hoardings. What might that mean?

Cometh the hour, cometh the 76th minute. George McCartney, having run 35 yards down the left and banged in a cross, finds the ball returning to him off a defender and, cool as you or I might like, strokes it into the far corner of the net with his right foot. Touch of the Christian Dailly's (ibid.) How amazing is that? Even Jonathan Bloke seems unsure about when his last goal was, eventually sticking with a West Ham pot against Bolton in November 2007, also with his right foot.

Bright now explains how well-organised West Ham are defensively, and how this is their game plan. Oh, if it were all as simple as that! At least there is an attempt to explain the 1-5 reverse at Ipswich, blamed as it is today on the logistics of making something out of the last minutes of the nightmare transfer window. Is that the same transfer window that currently appears to have offered us very little in the way of season-changing signings? I guess on that topic that if José Mourinho is the special one, then AVB, newly-sacked Chelsea manager, must be the special needs one.

The Cardiff fans are leaving the stadium in droves. And what exactly are droves? Misspelled doves. Or the irregular past tense of 'drive'? Jonathan Bloke desperately suggests, in the first of two injury time minutes, that a goal from Cardiff might set up a dramatic finish. Yeah, right. Remember - West Ham have that defensive thing bottled. So what will we do when Reading come to Upton Park? That's for later. Kenny Miller, who hit a late winner for Cardiff at Upton Park on the opening day of the season, now hits the crossbar with a header for the last action of the game, the replay of which reveals it to be a brilliant save from Rob Green.

Jonathan Bloke redeems himself in his wrap with a brilliant quip about McCartney's Long and Winding Goal, that Mark Bright does not get. This is unexpectedly capped by the revelation that John Terry is now 10-1 to be appointed manager of Chelsea.

When David James suggested Terry was in the frame for the England job after Capello departed, the BBC summariser responds brilliantly, 'A certain logistic could have caused problems there.'

West Ham: 1 Green, 3 McCartney, 4 Nolan, 5 Tomkins, 8 Maynard (9 Cole 63), 10 Collison, 12 Vaz Te, 15 Faye, 16 Noble, 17 O'Brien, 22 Lansbury (32 O'Neil 75)

West Ham appear quite secure in that second automatic promotion place. Three of the next four matches look like relatively safe home bankers. I should be thrilled. But this is March. Beware the sides of March.

This afternoon I am at West Middlesex Hospital for tests. My INR (international normalised ratio) was 2.3 this afternoon, which means I could be in a fight to keep my cardio version procedure going ahead on Monday 19th March. But, a natural optimist, I think I can persuade those at St Mary's that I am clotless. Cardio version has, as a procedure, been alternatively entitled 'Three Irons On My Chest' to preserve my football mania while I am undergoing the necessary electric shocks to get myself back in sinus rhythm. If none of this paragraph makes any sense, then I'll take it that you and your family have never had heart problems.

Tonight, thanks to a late goal from Ipswich's Jason Scotland, West Ham have the opportunity to return to the top of the Championship if they can beat Watford at home. Leading scorer with 9 goals, Carlton Cole, starts, along with the returning Matt Taylor. Baldock, Lansbury (2 goals for England U-21 last week) and Vaz Te are the goal scoring (we hope) substitutes.

Game Thirty-Four: nPower Championship, 2011-12, Upton Park
Wednesday March 7th 2012 (31,674)
Referee: Keith Stroud (Dorset)

West Ham 1	**Watford 1**
Vaz Te 87	Murray 68

(West Ham: 2nd in the table, 65 points from 102)

The referee blows for kick-off and then blows again for a false start. I don't think I've seen one of those before. Why? I've been to enough matches. No, I mean why haven't I seen one before?

The actual start is brilliant. Matt Taylor arrogantly tries his luck from thirty yards. His effort beats Tomasz Kuszczak but springs up into the air off the crossbar and behind for a goal kick. This Watford side has conceded 24 goals in their 16 away fixtures, and Hammers have already been good enough to put four past them at Vicarage Road earlier in the season. My favourite Watford West Ham game is the 2-0 victory at Vicarage Road, coming towards the end of the 1985-86 season. West Ham played seventeen games in a week and came within a gnat's pubic hair of winning the league.

Hammers have had some season on the road. They've already notching up ten wins to the nine they have managed at home. The last time they managed ten away wins was 1992-93, with Julian Dicks whacking them in from all angles and distances. Billy Bonds' second promotion in three years. That was the first season they did away with the back pass, should you care.

Back live, Matt Taylor has come close to putting Cole in for a chance, which he can't quite reach. If I were a gambling man I might have a few bob on him scoring a goal or three tonight. Julien Faubert fails to connect with a great Taylor cross at the far post after twelve minutes. He has been converted into a pacey attacking right back by Allardyce, and it's good to see him back after missing the Cardiff game. A poor attempted headed clearance by Nolan is converted into a decent clearance by Taylor and those nervous members of the Lower Bobby Moore can breathe again.

One look at Watford might suggest that this is not a top level English footballing side, but in 1982-83 under Graham Tayor they finished runners-up in the old first division, something West Ham United have yet to do. Now a skidding low brute of a shot from Kacaniklic beats Green but is a good three feet wide of his dive and left hand post, so only worth mentioning to exercise my footballer's surname spellcheck.

Tonight I am performing with the Adventures of Parsley at the Twelve Bar Club in Denmark Street, just a gobbet of spit away from the Two I's coffee house where Cliff Richard and the Drifters were discovered back in early 1958. We are on at 9.30, but the first half of our set is made up of instrumentals, and I am cautiously optimistic that I will make it there by the requisite time of 9.45. If I make it I will be wrapping my vocal corduroys around such gems as *You Only Live Twice*, *Avenues and Alleyways* and, naturally, our classic Billy Childish single-released rendition of *Magpie*. This rather sadly means I will have to leave tonight's game halfway through the second half. Several years ago I'd have been taken for an imbecile to be abandoning the sacred turf at such a ludicrously early hour. These days, even with a team almost at the top of the Championship, people understand, even if they might wonder just what that tambourine sound is rattling from the inside of my bag.

What's happening in the match? I can almost hear you cry. Not very much is the answer. A crash of approach plays from Sam's boys but with little to show for them, and already 25 minutes of the game have passed. A throw upfield alongside the old Chicken Run comes to nothing. Cole can't turn, but Faubert can, though his cross is smothered by an inelegant formation of eight Watford defenders. In a rare advancement, the Hornets give their travelling 1500 fans something to shout about. Green punches the curling free kick out for a throw. West Ham have to notch a goal to open the game up, or the next hour will follow a predictably dismal pattern, one we've seen all too regularly at Upton Park this season. Half an hour gone. I'm already looking nervously at my watch.

On Saturday West Ham play struggling Doncaster, but it's a game I may miss as I've been asked to help my neighbour David Freeman film the video of his mates miming, X-Factor style, to a compendium of 80s hits in time for a forthcoming stag night. This is actually the pre-stag stag night. And we are potentially filming the pre-stag pre-stag stag night. Admit it, it sounds potentially more fun than watching West Ham struggle to beat Doncaster 1-0. I may have to eat my words there, I realise, but it's hardly an act of wild speculation.

A radio reporter calls in his summary of the first thirty-six minutes of this game, and I am impressed at his professional and clipped enthusiastic musings on the night's events. The second his report is concluded, Noble advances on the left wing, and puts in a brilliant curling left foot shot that the Watford keeper acrobatically palms over the bar. Best chance of the game so far. Not saying much. Then again, if every Watford right-footed hoiked clearance had somehow been converted into West Ham goals, I could move off to the gig now, assured of the three points.

A minute before half-time Watford have a free kick just on the edge of the West Ham penalty area, but even before I can finish the sentence, they've wasted it. At the other end a curling lifting shot from Matt Taylor raises the odd ooh and aah. The media area behind me is empty. They know. West Ham have a corner. Two minutes of injury time. The crowd raise the decibels. Kuszczak punches the ball clear with a leaden fist. McCartney loses the ball from a Watford break-away but chases furiously after Troy Deeney and blocks the cross to give a corner away. Green punches it to safety, and that's your lot for the first 45. It wasn't much, I think, as I hear the radio reporter's half-time summary, which unexpectedly includes the phrase 'West Ham in control'.

As they start the second half, I have just worked out that it's now nearly 220 minutes since West Ham scored a goal at Upton Park and even longer since they scored one from open play. All I'm currently thinking about is how long before I must leave. There's bound to be a late goal tonight... I only hope West Ham can score it. I'm on stage in fifty minutes and the tube journey (my Tube Exit App tells me) is twenty-six minutes, including a cross-platform change at Mile End. Two quick corners and from the second Tomkins heads into the turf and the ball bounces over the bar. The temperature has dropped a good seven or eight degrees since kick off and my fingers are going numb. O'Brien's shot comes back off a defender's outstretched foot. A Watford player is down in the area and a stretcher is called for. Two stretchers are called for. Looks as though two defenders have collided. Hardly surprising with how tightly they've been packing the penalty area. A third stretcher comes out. Are they requiring a fitting?

A long delay ensues. Time to slip away perhaps? It will be soon. There is almost a football team of 'pitch rescue' officials in the Watford penalty area, crowded round the injured players. It is beginning to look quite serious. The crowd have gone quiet to the extent that the Watford fans can be heard singing over in the other corner of the ground. I've counted the outfield Watford players. Eight. There are definitely two players down there under all the pitch rescue professionals. Two neck braces suggest neither is going to play any further part in the game. In the end, it's just one who leaves, to a generous round of applause from all corners of the ground. The departing player, we are informed, is Dale Bennett, who is replaced by Martin Taylor - almost a commentator. Clearly even if there are any goals in this game, I'm going to miss them. An hour gone, but with a mountain of injury time to follow, I might even be on stage before this one is over.

I've barely got to the station when a buzzing on my phone confirms my concerns that the small cheer I just heard was Watford scoring. Whatever happened to innocent days when this miserable piece of trivial information might have lain undiscovered until I was home two hours later? The goal is scored by Sean Murray with a low shot from the edge of the area past Green. This much I can ascertain before the train heads underground. In the 60s, if you went 'underground', it would put you in touch with things you were unlikely to encounter in ordinary everyday life. Psychedelic people, hippy times, narcotic substances and music to 'let your hair down' to. Today, of course, if you go underground you are blocked from finding out anything about anything. A wall of Internet silence, where you can't send texts (though perversely you sometimes receive them). You can't find anything out underground, even if you've got a Blackberry with the fastest web access, hi-definition display and a phone that answers rude questions.

I get out at Tottenham Court Road and check my watch. 21.45. Just enough time to get to Denmark Street for the second half of the set. The game has still not finished because of the eleven minutes' delay following the Watford defenders' clash of heads, but I notice with relief on the live match details that Ricardo Vaz Te has ended a four hour home goal drought with an 87th minute equaliser, prodding home after a frenzied goalmouth melée.

Within a breath I am on stage grabbing my Captain Scarlet hat and jacket, and launching into *What's New Pussycat*, the Tom Jones' 60s' hit from the Woody Allen film of the same name. We are so tight for time that there is little opportunity for banter, the songs crunching into an orgiastic medley. The stage is almost four feet off the dance floor in the tiny club's main room, and I have to climb up to get onto it. There is a balcony of about thirty-five people at tables over the dance floor beneath, and to my left as I thrust my vocal chords round *You Only Live Twice* (film and TV themes, remember?) there is a gathering of dancing girls, one with a Purdie blonde bob over dyed black roots and a cute smiling face, to whom I direct the song.

I dedicate the next one, *Avenues and Alleyways*, to Ricardo Vaz Te, prophetically on the cover of that evening's programme, for his timely equaliser, now the news has reached me that the game is over. It's another point, so we're still in the automatic promotion places, and I knock off the final three songs in a strange stunned relief.

The Adventures of Parsley all wear costumes depicting specific characters from Gerry Anderson television programmes. Guitarist Bruce is Steve Zodiac from 'Fireball XL5', his silver suit with red and gold epaulets a snazzy outfit. Sean, the bassist, is Scott Tracy from Thunderbirds, the poor bugger having to wear a bright sky blue uniform with a light blue hat that has a black badge with IR on it (that's International Rescue, not international ratio). Drummer Ravi wears the shiny grey uniform of Troy Tempest from Stingray, and Andy, on keyboards, wears a spaceman outfit, from UFO. I complete the set with the flashy red festooned gold zipped Captain Scarlet top. We're quite interesting, visually, whatever you think about the sound.

West Ham: 1 Green, 3 McCartney, 4 Nolan, 5 Tomkins, 8 Maynard (7 Baldock 62), 9 Cole, 14 Taylor (12 Vaz Te 74), 15 Faye, 16 Noble, 17 O'Brien (22 Lansbury 74), 18 Faubert

I hear on the grapevine, a couple of days later, that West Ham have signed a defender from Stoke City on loan. I tear upstairs to the internet to see whether or not it's the return of Matthew Upson, in contrition for all the money he took off the club in wages in his time here. He and Lucas Neil remain for me the two most overpaid footballers, in terms of their respective efforts and levels of performance, in the history of the sport. Yes, even more than Freddie Ljungberg and Kieron Dyer (the latter on £85k per week and Saturdays off). With a sigh of relief, however, I realise it is not Upton, but Danny Collins, the Welsh central defender. Ex of Sunderland, he will join up with previous teammate George McCartney and provide cover for James Tomkins, Winston Reid and former Stoke captain Abdoulaye Faye, one of several current pretenders to the title of Hammer of the Year 2012.

If you've ever found yourself dulled up at home through one of life's little kickings, you might have momentarily strayed into the world of daytime television. The corridors of this enterprise feature some of the more eccentric areas of British life, and often showcase its fifteen minutes of fame-hunters propped up on panel games. One of these is BBC2's 'Eggheads', a quiz programme where pub and sports teams take on the intellectual might of the host brainbox regulars in pursuit of a sum of cash which grows each week by £1000 for every time they aren't beaten.

My running club put a team up at the end of 2007, and we passed the audition to compete in an episode filmed a few weeks later. It was eventually broadcast on 10th March 2008, when the rolling prize money totalled £19,000. My only concern, having taken the subject area of Arts and Books, is that, as an ex-Head of English, I should not fail miserably at the challenge. The subjects areas are Damien Hirst, Shakespeare and C.S.Lewis, and I manage to get all three answers right. Through the early rounds and past the group stage, we proceed to the sudden death. With one right and one wrong, the same as the host team, we get to within one question of beating the strange crew. Our earlier answers are edited out in the final programme, and the quotation 'But I being poor, have only my dreams...' proves our undoing. It had to be a question about dreams, didn't it? Well, these fade and die, and our guess 'Robert Browning', proves wrong. It is W.B.Yeats. They have enough material from our valiant efforts to make a seventy minute programme, so when the half hour edit is shown, we are all a bit disappointed. Nevertheless, we've given the eggheads a running club for their money, and in the true spirit of the English eccentric and double entendre, have held our own. Rather bizarrely, the programme is repeated two years later.

Game Thirty-Five: nPower Championship, Upton Park
Saturday March 10th 2012 (34,650)
Referee: Andy D'Urso (Billericay)

West Ham 1   **Doncaster Rovers 1**
Nolan 9   Coppinger 73

(West Ham: 2nd in the table, 66 points from 105)

My decision, keeping me from the game this afternoon, has been to take up the offer of employment behind the camera lens, filming a song miming routine for a local guy's stag night. Why, you will be asking yourselves, would I turn down the chance to see Hammers facing one of the weaker teams in the division, with the chance to go to the top of the league and stack up a mountain of goals to up the old positive goal difference tally? The difficulty is that I can see and hear this game coming like a train from the back of a deep tunnel, and I know the three points are not nearly the neatly packaged gift that results thus far this season suggest they should be. Yes, I'd rather have a few bob and the relief of knowing that, just over a week from my fourth cardio version, I am giving my heart and my wallet the respect those two imposters deserve.

As for the game, West Ham face a Doncaster Rovers side in this division for the first time at Upton Park since their promotion season of 1957-58. West Ham finished champions then, while Doncaster Rovers finished bottom, and were therefore relegated. That season Hammers won 2-1 at Doncaster but were held to a 1-1 draw at home. If I were a gambling man, I can see a pattern here that I would be acting on. In the event, Dean Saunders' side repeat the achievements of their footballing ancestors from 55 years ago. They aren't permitted to play their loan striker Frederic Piquionne, but they have the notorious El Hadji Djouf on their books, himself a West Ham triallist for seven days back in October (he didn't play, thank goodness, not even on the training ground).

West Ham look to have taken the lead when Vaz Te fires home after a great run down the left channel, but no goal is given due to a (negligible) infringement. At an officially timed 8.7 seconds, it would have been the fastest goal ever scored at Upton Park, eclipsing Jim Melrose who scored for Charlton here against West Ham in October 1986 after just 9 seconds, following a through ball by Hammer-to-be Robert Lee. Ken Bainbridge remains, at the time of writing, the fastest Hammer to score, after just 11 seconds, against Barnsley in 1949.

Following Vaz Te's disappointment, Cole hits the bar, before Nolan stabs the ball over the line six minutes later after Tomkins and Cole look to perform an 'after you, no, after you' sequence. Doncaster come close through James Coppinger's shot. They finally equalise late in the second half, the goal coming from Coppinger after a right wing cross from Djouf. Djouf then prompts the save of the match from Green just before the end after his powerful low shot is palmed away by the keeper's agile dive.

West Ham: 1 Green, 3 McCartney, 5 Tomkins, 15 Faye, 4 Nolan (25 Collins 80), 10 Collison, 14 Taylor, 16 Noble, 22 Lansbury (32 O'Neil 57), 9 Cole, 12 Vaz Te (7 Baldock 25)

On the Wednesday of the following week I am at the David Lloyd Sports' Centre, in south-west London, to meet up with Fulham, Queens Park Rangers and Manchester City goalscoring legend Rodney Marsh. He is introducing our new collection of ten ITV Big Match DVDs, and I have a stash of typed prompts for him to work through, recording two for each DVD.

For those who don't know, Marsh was a talented and flamboyant footballer who played in the 60s and 70s, but who, ultimately, was an individual with brilliant skills, whose style of play did not always suit sides who preferred the team ethic. Clubs could choose to build their play around him, as Queens Park Rangers did most successfully from 1966-72, but at Manchester City (1972-75) the going was a little tougher, and his flair was not always deployed to the team's greatest advantage. Many even said his arrival cost the club the First Division title. Marsh won nine England caps from 1971-73 under Sir Alf Ramsey, not the most tolerant of men, and if he'd played in a different era, I think it's generally felt that he'd have won many more.

Marsh has become a controversial TV pundit in recent years, with an uncompromising set of opinions, and is the master of opinionated twittering that goes out into the twittersphere. He is perfect for our DVDs as he has become a spokesman for his era, with a stack of followers who are interested in pretty much anything he gets behind these days. I have brought a pile of old QPR programmes from games he played in for him to sign for the many friends I have who follow the Rs.

We are filming Rodney against a green screen background so we can put anything we want behind him at a later stage. My feeling is that we'll end up with a light brown fabric background and a dodgy-looking 'Big Match' logo. Rodney occasionally takes a moment to ring some hired muscle outside the room we're filming in. 'I had this death threat recently,' he tells me. 'You can't be too careful.'

'It's not one of Francis Lee's mates, is it?' I ask.

'Haven't a clue who it is,' Marsh straight bats his response. 'But you have to take these things seriously.' Amazing. Who on earth would want to threaten Rodney Marsh?

The first hour or so is spent deliberating over whether he will learn the openings or read them in a more traditional Big Match TV style, pre-autocue delivery. Eventually we pick the front desk reading typed script approach and start filming. Marsh gets better across the morning, and we film the first two again at the end to capture his developing ease in front of the camera. One of Rodney's most memorable career pundit moments was to sacrifice his Sky position in pursuit of a 'Toon Army' / 'Tsunami' double entendre while watching a live game with Newcastle going goal crazy. Needless to say, we get creative when it comes to his opening piece on the Newcastle DVD.

We have lunch at the sports centre, and Rodney sends a few twitters out for his followers. By late afternoon they are already asking when the DVDs will be in the shops.

Game Thirty-Six: nPower Championship, Elland Road
Saturday March 17th 2012 (33,366)
Referee: Peter Walton (Northants)

Leeds United 1   **West Ham United 1**
Becchio 83   Collins 90

(West Ham: 2nd in the table, 67 points from 108)

We have just over a month left of this crazy season, and yet it is the first time in 2011-12 that Elland Road has been filled. Sleeping coma giants.

The sight of Ken 'Norman' Bates in the stand and Neil 'We'll sue you for £6 million' Warnock in the dugout is hardly something to inspire the thousands of travelling West Ham fans. Then there is the issue of four successive home draws, three against teams that should have been beaten. This Leeds side is no front runner, and should be dispatched. The Irons record at Elland Road, however, haunts the expectations of such a fate.

The game would be hard enough to bear, had I made the impossible journey up and back, but from the warm depths of my bathtub it is perversely even worse. Phil Commentator is doing the honours for BBC London Radio. He's doing his best to create the image that he is simply commentating over a one camera feed on an ISDN box from his bedroom in Surrey Docks. This does stretch the imagination on the role of the summariser, but at least it offers a crumb of inspiration to the otherwise unedifying verbal painting of a frustrating ninety minutes, only interrupted by updates from the Barnet game.

In the end we have to be satisfied with a point having looked, after Becchio's unexpected late goal, as if we were about to surrender all three. Loan boy gets a debut goal heading home Noble's corner, but even though there are only ten games left in the season, we have still yet to see a player hit a double figure goal tally.

The result extends Sam's unbeaten run to eight, but more ground has now been lost on the top two, both of whom have won away this afternoon, Reading winning their ninth in the last ten games. A horrible threatening shadow is beginning to cast itself across the words 'automatic' and 'promotion'.

West Ham: 1 Green, 3 McCartney, 5 Tomkins (32 O'Neil 46), 15 Faye, 17 O'Brien, 25 Collins, 4 Nolan, 10 Collison (23 Morrison 81), 14 Taylor, 16 Noble, 8 Maynard (9 Cole 56)

One of the irritating things about my mother is that she was born halfway through March. It isn't anything she can be blamed for, but it does mean that in the Clinton and Hallmark world, two cards and two presents are demanded in a very short space of time. As someone whose birthday is just twelve days after Christmas, I am more than over-familiar with the well-meant expression, 'We got you something for Christmas and your birthday. Is that okay?' Why ever would it be? And so I can hardly offer my mother the same thing for her birthday and for Mother's day.

In the end, I drop off her first present on the morning of Mothering Sunday, but despite it not being until the Monday, I refrain from delivering her birthday present at the same time, though it's unlikely she'll get her hands on it for at least another week. I come a very poor second after my brother in terms of visits to mum's house. Like the cat in the cradle, other events seem to always make a pretty good conspiratorial job of keeping me away.

The job keeping me away this birthday, however, might prove my last. In April 2008, cycling to my mother's, I came off my bike at some speed trying to avoid a stationary refuse truck, which was wedged halfway up a narrow alley alongside the entrance to the London Apprentice pub. I soon found myself in hospital being diagnosed with atrial fibrillation. To the uninitiated, this is an irregular heartbeat, caused by a mischievous signal sent alongside all the good ones to the heart. The heart gets confused and like an alcoholic Ringo, loses the beat. The condition itself remains undiagnosed, apparently, in more than half the people who have it (how do they know that?), accounting for deaths from resultant strokes in hospital of hundreds of people under forty. If your heart isn't beating right, it doesn't pump the blood efficiently around your body, and clots can build up in the extended lulls between beats. It's probably the most efficient regulator we currently have in this country for population control, but it's also something that a national awareness campaign might well eradicate. Poor old NHS. They'd have to pay a shitload of money to raise public awareness just so a shitload of people would be saved from an early death. No wonder governments feel compromised in these austerity-obsessed days.

I was profoundly lucky to have had the condition discovered. Of course I didn't feel it at the time, covered in blood, my arms and chin badly bruised, and being informed that I wasn't 'in sinus rhythm'. The ECG (electrocardiogram – measurer of rhythm and electrical heart activity) printout looked like a chart of the last twenty West Ham seasons. Up and down, up and down, with no diagnosable pattern or visible cause.

A regime of warfarin and beta blockers became my new way of life, the crazy heptahedral names of the drugs tripping off my tongue like newly signed foreign players. I underwent three cardio version procedures, a neat little event where your heart is artificially stopped and then shocked back into rhythm by three electric terminals. It's a process I have since fondly nicknamed 'Three Irons on my Chest'.

The patient has to have a general anaesthetic for this procedure, something I had never previously experienced. The process is best described as having half a pint of cold liquid shot up a catheter into your arm until the room around you surrenders its brightness to the stealthy sedative in your veins. Awaking to a perfect heartbeat, these procedures demonstrated that maybe my irregular beat condition wasn't permanent. Unfortunately I usually drifted back into slipbeat a few weeks after the procedure. Then I was offered something called a catheter ablation. Three of them, in fact. Well worth a quick surf on the internet to check out. If you want the brief version, they slip a tiny piece of catheter tubing, less than a millimeter wide, with a camera and a laser in it, up into your heart from your groin area. They then find the errant ventricle that is sending the wrong information to your heart, and burn it away with the laser so the remaining well-behaved ventricles can do their intended job properly, undisturbed.

Fast forward four years and various courses of drugs that also might have helped control it, but didn't, and here I am, still in atrial fibrillation. The first two ablations worked for a few months, but then gave up. The third one only worked for one night. Now they have agreed to give me an (as they first term it) unprecedented fourth cardio version, a year after my third ablation, mainly because I did my homework, showed that I ran twenty miles a week, and argued that the guy in the bed next to me last time had been given six ablations.

They only do these cardio versions on a Monday, so here I am at 8am in the basement of this west London hospital, on the morning of my mother's 75th birthday. I didn't mention, either, that these are all potentially dangerous procedures. I signed more waivers that morning than Avram Grunt must have before he took the West Ham job.

I wake up barely an hour after the procedure, and my heart is beating beautifully. Really beautifully. It feels different this time, though I can't exactly explain how. And it isn't the anaesthetic, either. I ask for a spare printout of the ECG, which the nurse gives me. If you've ever been in this situation, you'll know how wonderful it is to see that glorious symmetry on the chart. Like running your finger down the fixture list of the last eleven matches or so of the 1985-86 season and seeing win after win after win, home and away.

I text my mum once they've disconnected all the wires and leads. Happy birthday, mum. In perfect sinus rhythm. See you later x

Game Thirty-Seven: nPower Championship, Upton Park
Tuesday March 20th 2012 (27,250)
Referee: Scott Mathieson (Cheshire)

West Ham United 1   **Middlesbrough 1**
Faye 67   Ogbeche 84

(West Ham: 3rd in the table, 68 points from 111)

The next day I am off to Upton Park with my perfect beating heart to see if West Ham can return to their own metaphorical sinus rhythm. And you'd have to conclude that there is no room for failure tonight. A game in hand on Reading and three points behind them, these unnecessary dropped points at home must finally stop for Sam's Shams. West Ham must turn Upton Park back into some kind of fortress before it's too late and the season turns towards the lottery of the play-offs.

Sky have nabbed the game at the last minute, so it becomes a rare live 19.45 kick-off that is within the ambit of their schedules. There is a minute's applause for Patrice Muamba, the Bolton player, who appears to be getting better after suffering a cardiac arrest on Saturday. The fact that he was kept alive with a defibrillator makes me focus again on my good fortune, and his. This game, I soon calculate, is the first I have attended with a correctly beating heart since Gianfranco Zola's last game in charge at Upton Park, a 1-1 draw against Manchester City on 9th May 2010. Unfortunately, as I will realise in about an hour and a half, this one will finish with an identical scoreline.

Middlesbrough grab a quick corner in the first few minutes but encouragingly waste it spectacularly. So what is the mystery about winning at home? Hammers have drawn four successive games here whilst managing three wins out of four on the road, just one victory away from a new club record of eleven. It's good to see Carlton Cole start - the sooner he gets into double figures the better. Maynard has also been targeted by Allardyce for improvement. Marvin Emnes looks tricky on the ball and shows a good first touch. Cole at the other end forces a West Ham corner, and Mark Noble is busy and industrious, but it's still not happening.

Adam Hammill hits a sweet right foot curled shot from about twenty-five yards that, with a couple of feet more bend on it might have troubled Green. I've spent most of this afternoon with my new found sinus rhythm flicking through West Ham's season so far. It hasn't been a lack of opportunities, possibly just that they're not scoring anything spectacular or even speculative. Middlesbrough are playing with one striker, of course, which means no room for error. Another Noble corner. Faye and Taylor are the ones I'd call the 'unpredictables', but no-one up front can carry that adjectival phrase with any confidence. To think I'm travelling up to Burnley to watch this lot next week. I fancy it'll prove one of those reverse fixtures that you lose at home and win away. I'm hoping that isn't what tonight's fixture will prove.

Matt Taylor manages the first genuine shot on goal from wide on the left, which Jason Steele saves with his feet. It wakes a few up in the Sir Trev Lower.

Cole's touch seems to have deserted him. Is this waning confidence because automatic first team selection is no longer assured? A second Boro corner is wasted. There is a lot of chasing back and blocking and very few opportunities for penetration for Middlesbrough. I suppose it's just a matter of scoring and holding on, like West Ham failed so spectacularly to do against Doncaster. Now Maynard tries something from close distance, but it's straight at Steele. Middlesbrough are clearly happy to hang on for a point. Something has got to give. Hasn't it?

O'Brien finally gets round the back, but his cross is beaten away by the keeper for a corner. Noble, who is playing quite brilliantly, fires in a twenty-five yarder that just clears the crossbar. The long ball game would be fine if it yielded goals, but this isn't even that. West Ham seem to have the defensive side of their game zipped up, with Danny Collins looking like an astute loan.

Cole makes himself a toe end of space and curls a shot just over. A controversial moment is replayed on the tiny tellies from the Sky feed suggesting a handball on the corner of the six yard box by Matthew Bates. Off the shoulder and down the arm. 'Inconclusive,' says Alan to my left. It's his favourite word. It's a rugby word, though, not one that a footballer or manager would use. Joey O'Brien is getting stuck in. The way he does.

George McCartney and Matt Taylor are having a barney over who should be marking whom. Luckily the ensuing free kick from the error is well cleared by Faye, but that kind of personalised dispute can only inspire the Boro forwards. A Thomson-Hines sandwich on Maynard leads to a free-kick which Noble thumps into a three-man wall. A crafted and deep outswinging cross from Taylor is given the respect normally afforded to the eight day old contents of a South London park's waste bin.

Jeremy Nicholas interviews Frank McAvennie on the pitch at half time. Frank says the crowd have to get behind the team if they are going to beat Middlesbrough. His announcement is met by enthusiastic applause by all who aren't gorging on pies. Then the announcement, 'Let's have a look at the highlights from the first half,' is met by howls of derisive laughter. I look the wrong way for a couple of seconds and miss it all.

Cole is through early in the second half with just the keeper to beat, but chips when he should have blasted. 'What the fuck is that, Cole?' the first of the Mud Mouth twins shouts out. Haven't heard either of them for a while. It's a bad sign.

The Sky cameraman is picking out dispirited and surly faces in the crowd for his story. More of a story than he'll get following any of the 'action' on the pitch. Faye finds Cole after taking on and beating two Boro midfielders, but Cole's reverse pass is horribly underhit and Middlesbrough break up the move.

Just where is this goal coming from?

Middlesbrough almost answer the question with a far post heading opportunity that is thankfully wasted as fulsomely as anything West Ham have binned. The fans are beginning to sing *West Ham's Claret and Blue Army*, but not very convincingly. I start to feel sorry for the ref.

This really is terrible. The footballing equivalent of Mao's great leap forward.

Stirring at the back of the Bobby Moore Lower is something urgent. Matt Taylor whacks in a shot that cannons away for a throw. It is like all out there are on drugs and have forgotten everything they ever learned about playing football. But Hammers have a corner. And here comes the goal, and what a pervy goal it is. An aerial ball hit hopefully towards the far post which Faye heads hopefully back across the goal, rather higher than he intended. Steele looks in horror as the ball drops over his head and into the top corner. If anyone deserved a goal other than the referee, it is Abdoulaye Faye. Sky later decide it is an own goal by the defender who challenged Faye for the header, Joe Bennett, robbing Faye of his first and only 'goal' for the club.

Allardyce takes Cole and Maynard off and brings Collison and Carew on. Now Middlesbrough will have to score, so the game should open up, and he'll want someone creative there to provide opportunities for West Ham's hungry strike force. Hopefully that will be Collison setting up and Cole finishing.

Tony Mowbray, the Middlesbrough manager, is 49 years of age. I mention this in the hope that you have a picture of him nearby and can share my surprise. He looks a lot older. After Tomkins' header is tipped onto the bar by an agile Steele, Mowbray brings on the interestingly named Marouane Zemmama, adorned with an Amy Winehouse beehive of hair. Noble unaccountably loses the ball in midfield and thankfully Adam Hammill's shot on the run whistles just wide.

Mowbray manages another two substitutions, but like a piece of Ikea furniture without an assembly instructions booklet, I can't work out what the hell he is planning. Maybe it's a ruse.

The fans seem in a good mood now. It's proof that anything can be forgiven when you're in front in this spaced out league. Why oh why didn't Mowbray play three up front to start with and take the game to West Ham? They'd have been comfortably in front by half-time.

Now the second goal, Middlesbrough's this time. A twenty yard drilled shot across the area from substitute Bart Ogbeche, that beats Green and finishes up just inside the far post. According to Sam, it's a 'wonder' goal. The impossibility of a fifth successive home draw is now anything but. That will surely be a record somewhere, somehow... if it happens. Noble is taken off for Baldock. It's too late Sam, I hear myself mumbling, it's too late...

The crowd is just 27,250, which makes sense. I hear Reading are losing 3-1 at Peterborough. What a chance missed this might be. McCartney heads off the line with Green beaten. Yes, it could have been worse. It's like pinball out there now with four minutes of injury time to run, but the fate has been sketched out for printing. Another home draw. Southampton, Crystal Palace, Watford, Doncaster and now Middlesbrough. Five in a row looks like a record to me, with Reading next up at the end of the month. Worse, somehow, is the revelation that West Ham haven't won a home game under the floodlights on a Tuesday night since beating Stoke City 2-0 in October 2004. But that was a season that ended with promotion.

West Ham: 1 Green, 3 McCartney, 4 Nolan, 5 Tomkins, 8 Maynard (10 Collison 71), 9 Cole (11 Carew 71), 14 Taylor, 15 Faye, 16 Noble (7 Baldock 87), 17 O'Brien, 25 Collins

On the Friday night before the Burnley game I am in Preston to celebrate the 38th birthday of Jamie McGee, the editor of all my West Ham end of season

DVDs since December 1998. Jamie was just out of college when I met him, but is now the proud father of two, and senior editor at the company he works for. Paul McMullan, another film editor, is with us for the evening, and we all have an excellent few beers and a curry to celebrate our shared history.

Game Thirty-Eight: nPower Championship, Turf Moor
Saturday March 24th 2012 (15,246)
Referee: Mark Haywood (West Yorkshire)

Burnley 2	**West Ham United 2**
Bartley 25	Nolan 68
Paterson 36	Tomkins 70

(West Ham: 3rd in the table, 69 points from 114)

After a hearty breakfast on the Saturday, I get the train east across Lancashire to Burnley, for my first game at Turf Moor. My friend from the college I work at, Shaun Kelly (namesake of the bassist from AOP), is from Burnley, and we have been planning getting along to this game since West Ham were relegated at the end of last season. Shaun has got us a couple of passes into the supporters bar at the club and he meets me at the station to take me there via a short tour of the town.

My own journey to the station has been spent in a carriage filled with regular West Ham away fans and their booty of lager, more lager and yet more lager.

Shaun takes me to the ground past the library, where an exhibition of the club's successes and heritage is being held. Burnley is a town with an interesting history, one of Lancashire's most successful mill towns during the Industrial Revolution, and it subsequently became a centre of engineering. After recent years of stagnation, the town has a new economy of electronics and computers, a sports university and, I am told, has a future it couldn't have imagined just twenty years ago.

The build up is traditional and edifying, and we move to our seats at the Burnley end in good spirits for the kick off. The game has all the appearance of another away win for the first twenty minutes. Burnley then surprise the visitors with two goals in ten minutes from Marvin Bartley and Martin Paterson, and West Ham find themselves facing a half time grilling from

Sam. It's a little unsettling seeing the side in claret and blue score twice, especially with programme cover star and ex-Hammer Junior Stanislas on the bench, wearing their number 11.

The second half is a different story, with Sam bringing on his two young strikers Baldock and Maynard for Cole and Taylor. Whether Burnley think their two goal lead will be enough or whether they simply haven't the ability to get the ball out of their own half, West Ham are soon on top. Nolan finally turns the pressure into a goal on 68 minutes and Tomkins scores two minutes later. His goal comes in the 70th minute but it's going to be at least another few days before West Ham hit the majestical total of 70 points, as they cannot quite grab a winner. Shaun is satisfied with the result, and being with him momentarily has me accept the point as won, rather than two lost. I make my way on the long walk back to the station, and it's then that I begin to feel a gnawing at my stomach once I check the scores and realise that Reading have beaten Blackpool 3-1, and Southampton have overturned Doncaster 2-0. At Preston I meet up with Lloyd Bishop and Paul Stringer from West Ham's media team, and we share thoughts on the match.

West Ham: 1 Green, 3 McCartney, 5 Tomkins, 17 O'Brien, 25 Collins, 4 Nolan, 10 Collison (11 Carew 82), 14 Taylor (8 Maynard 46), 16 Noble, 32 O'Neil, 9 Cole (7 Baldock 46)

Game Thirty-Nine: nPower Championship, London Road
Tuesday March 27th 2012 (13,517)
Referee: Chris Sarginson (Staffordshire)

Peterborough United 0   West Ham United 2
                           Vaz Te 52
                           O'Neil 58

(West Ham: 3rd in the table, 72 points from 117)

It's no use saying things like 'this is a game West Ham cannot afford not to win' and not just because it's a double negative. When sports journalists say something like that, whoever they are referring to will lose, or draw, or whatever you don't want them to do. And if it's West Ham, and you have to listen to the commentary on BBC London bloody Radio, then the torture will be complete.

This midweek game, rescheduled from the February 11th postponement, follows a run of FIVE successive draws. Watford, Doncaster Rovers, Leeds United, Middlesbrough, Burnley. Five successive draws or, to put it another way, ten dropped points. You don't have to be a West Ham fan to work out what that might mean at the end of the season. It also happened in 2003-04 between the temporary reign of Trevor Brooking and the arrival of Alan Pardew, but that was much earlier in the season.

West Ham are four points behind Reading, so a win tonight will do much to put the automatic promotion target back in the frame. Winning will equal promotion if we can make it a habit again. And in the modern game, winning is all. Look at Sam Allardyce, a man who became the manager of Bolton Wanderers in 1999-2000, and stayed at the club for seven years. He was put on a ten year contract from which he said he would see through and then walk away from football. Some commitment.

Sam Allardyce's sides have been tarnished with the brush of long ballism. Whether this is true, and the stats are inconclusive, no-one will complain if the side are winning every game. Once the wins start becoming elusive, they are replaced by excuses and complaints rather than genuine analysis. Sam has been looking for a goalscorer like Southampton's Rickie Lambert or Barnsley's Ricardo Vaz Te. Well, one out of two ain't bad.

Tonight the travelling fans are tetchy, and the tactics for the game, playing just Cole up as a lone striker in the first half, especially on the back of five disappointments, are a bit of a worry. After just twelve minutes Peterborough's Paul Taylor curls in an exquisite effort which Green just manages to tip onto the bar, only for Lee Frecklington to follow-up weakly, straight at the keeper.

The Posh begin to take control with some neat football, and build up promisingly only for Taylor to waste an opportunity, shooting straight at Green when finding himself in yards of space. He has an even better chance five minutes later, darting into the area, but shoots straight at Green again. Three minutes' later Ferguson's side have an excellent shout for a penalty when Tommy Rowe goes down in the box, but it's thankfully ignored by referee Chris Sarginson. Peterborough are then forced back into their own half, but on a breakaway George Boyd looks to put Peterborough ahead, but for a well-timed block from Tomkins that closes down his effort. The Posh then miss another couple of clear cut chances that few teams would have squandered at any level. Having played over-careful tactics for most of the first half, West Ham are lucky to go in still in it at 0-0.

At the beginning of the second half there is the odd sight of Hammers' fans behind the goal standing on the terraces, but sitting, slightly melancholy, on the side by the dug-out. Collins and Faubert are on for Faye and O'Brien, and the team now have a sense of urgency about them. Sam has spoken. Before the fans can even mutter 'about time', the game shifts towards a magnificent eleventh away win, equalling the club record. Ricardo Vaz Te and Gary O'Neil notch up two memorable goals in six magnificent minutes. Vaz Te starts things with a far post header from a well-targeted Matt Taylor cross. O'Neil then makes it two after dispossessing Grant McCann in midfield and hitting a beautifully curved shot on the run from 25 yards that catches the keeper dreaming of a career at a bigger club. This just two minutes after Kevin Nolan has hit a crisp effort from just inside the box, which goes wide of the post by less than a foot. Nolan then hits the bar with a brilliant back-heeled effort after a set of on the floor passes that puts any criticism of long balls to bed for the rest of the game.

The 5000 West Ham fans now break into voice, singing, *We Play On The Floor, We Play On The Floor, We're West Ham United, We Play On The Floor!* celebrating the shift in approach and it's heady consequence. Even the players are stirred into action by the power of the song. The seated set of West Ham fans sing, *East side, East side, give us a song!* to which the East side respond, *You only sing when you're winning!* That's a song we haven't heard since the beginning of the month, I'm thinking. They then chorus back with, *We forgot that you were here!*

Carlton Cole, who has only scored one goal in the whole of 2012 but has accrued three yellow cards, misses two chances in the penalty box that he might have put away on a better day.

One of the more enjoyable aspects of the game is to have Ferguson, Darren Ferguson of Ferguson & Son, moaning about a penalty that they didn't get as the justification for their failure to win. The stats tell the tale about West Ham's second half dominance, taking the overall possession in the match to 66%. Hard to imagine what it must have been in the second half after the disappointment of the first.

West Ham's record 11 away wins
13 Aug: Doncaster Rovers 1-0
16 Aug: Watford 4-0

28 Aug: Nottingham Forest 4-1
24 Oct: Brighton & Hove Albion 1-0
05 Nov: Hull City 2-0
19 Nov: Coventry City 2-1
29 Nov: Middlesbrough 2-0
14 Jan: Portsmouth 1-0
21 Feb: Blackpool 4-1
04 Mar: Cardiff City 2-0
27 Mar: Peterborough 2-0

(also achieved in 1922/23 and 1957/58, both promotion seasons)

Though it might seem odd to say it, this may well be the moment Sam Allardyce starts winning over the fans. The jury has been out so long on him that they might well be staying in the West Ham hotel all season. Now I think the critical mass moment has been reached. Allardyce has had a tough night, but his side deserved to win at Burnley the previous Saturday and played some superb football in the second half in that game. Tonight they have also played better in the second half, but more importantly, the game has been won. The fans made him the scapegoat for a poor and uninspired first half display, and resurrected much of the long ball game fears that Allardyce's time at Bolton was plagued by. The truth is that for much of this season Allardyce's side have played spells of inspired and intelligent football, but without the goals and winning that is needed to occupy an unassailable position in this league. Eventually some of the measures have been questioned. Tonight, however, has featured, either side of half time, the best and the worst of the team's football. Before half time, excruciating; beyond it, sublime. A song that was begun by the fans as a criticism, ended up as a celebration.

A critical moment from the previous season was when Avram Grant threw his scarf into the crowd after a 3-0 home thrashing by Arsenal. Though Grant remained in the job, and denied he had 'thrown in the towel', his gesture was seen as surrender to the pressures he was under and an admission of failure to get any kind of results and performances that would keep the club safe. Grant denied it soon afterwards, but the damage had been done, and the smell of relegation got stronger by the week until the eventuality revealed itself in the miserable 3-2 reverse at Wigan on 15th May 2011.

After the game, Sam declares himself 'sick of all that rubbish', when he is aggressively questioned by journalists about the so-called 'long ball' tactics of the first half. He responds with righteous indignation, and calls their suggestions 'deluded', for which he is misrepresented and misquoted by many newspapers the following morning. His anger demonstrates a passion that many are surprised by. The papers are all too keen to portray it the next day as arrogance, but those who were there know different. This is a man who is beginning to connect with the club, and whose side are going to be playing it on the floor for a while yet.

West Ham: 1 Green, 3 McCartney, 5 Tomkins, 15 Faye (25 Collins 46), 17 O'Brien (18 Faubert 46), 4 Nolan, 14 Taylor, 16 Noble, 32 O'Neil (8 Maynard 88), 9 Cole, 12 Vaz Te

The delight to be savoured from the result is that West Ham are now in a position where they can wrestle the second automatic promotion place back from form team Reading, whom they face on Saturday. This, of course, if you'll pardon the double negative, is a game that they *cannot* afford not to win.

Game Forty: nPower Championship, Upton Park
Saturday March 31st 2012 (33,350)
Referee: Chris Foy (St Helens)

West Ham United 2	**Reading 4**
Cole 8	Gorkss 44
Vaz Te 77	Hunt 45
	Harte 59 (pen)
	Leigertwood 84

(West Ham: 3rd in the table, 72 points from 120)

The last game of the month has become the most important game of the season.

Reading have won 6 of the 10 meetings between the two clubs, West Ham just 3. It's the kind of stat that experience voices loudly over vain hope. Mark Bright is a couple of rows in front, waxing lyrical into his Coles' lip mike over what might be about to happen out there today. His accomplice is a blonde female commentator, with chiselled features that would make Richard Keyes quake in his permanent gardening leave boots.

'We must never be silent,' Jeremy Nicholas says in his Churchillian pre-match crowd warm-up, and he's right. The only team who don't currently enjoy playing here is West Ham United. It's the opposite of a fortress mentality - what might we call that?

The last time West Ham beat Reading was in a 1-0 victory in August 2004, in the last promotion season, where an 81st minute Teddy Sheringham goal saw off the Royals. Today Reading are captained by Jobi McAnuff, a player Alan Pardew brought to Upton Park but eventually sold despite some promising cameo appearances.

Ricardo Vaz Te and Gary O'Neil complete the feel of a full-strength side which Allardyce continues to find a place in for Carlton Cole, and striker and club captain, Kevin Nolan. As the sentence leaves my digits West Ham score a brilliant eighth minute team goal. Matt Taylor collects a ball wide on the left and hits in a sharp low cross which Nolan somehow reaches at the corner of the six yard box, sending a deft header against the post and out to Carlton Cole who swivels to hit it skilfully past Adam Federici. Great start!

Reading have brought an Olympic Stadium load of supporters who are very vocal, but their team's early efforts aren't particularly threatening. Hammers seem very strong in defence. Jimmy Kebe is getting a serious crescendo of boos from the crowd, for his sock pulling antics at the Madjeski, earlier in the season. Mark Bright is yapping excitedly in front of me at the expectation that he's currently watching two of next year's Premier League clubs in the making.

Now Reading finally begin to string a few passes together. This leads to an excellent chance for Noel Hunt which he bangs in towards the far post, only for James Tomkins to head it clear, virtually off the line, with Green beaten. At the other end Vaz Te's intricate ball skills set up the chance for Carlton Cole's cheeky back heel which Federici drops down well to save.

The great sheet of Upton Park winless misery seems to have been lifted. Jason Roberts is booked for elbowing Carlton Cole as they challenge for a high ball. I remember just how many times that guy has played in sides winning at Upton Park against the odds over the years. He's only been at Reading since January, but is very much a part of their fantastic winning run, and he is looking dangerous.

The BBC, for whom Roberts is a pundit, are here with a full Outside

Broadcast unit, and the screens offer replays of the first half hour's action, which is more than we've seen in the last five home games put together. Abdoulaye Faye slices Ian Harte's poor low free kick out of play for an unnecessary corner, but it comes to nothing.

Now Vaz Te leaps to connect with another Matt Taylor cross, but Federici catches the ball underneath the crossbar. Kevin Nolan is having a magical game today, with intricate and intelligent touches inside the area, quite possibly his best for the Hammers this season.

Abdoulaye Faye stretches out a leg to stop an aerial pass reaching Hunt, just a few yards beyond him. Seconds later Tomkins heads brilliantly out to clear a dangerous attack. Now Gary O'Neil goes down as Roberts beats him and hits a shot across goal that Green is glad to see pass wide of his right hand post.

Another Tomkins interception gives Reading a corner, from which they score. Harte's inswinger is met powerfully at the near post by the bearded Kaspars Gorkss who heads it both past Green and the man on the line. Two minutes later, in first half injury time, they're in front. In his attempt to intercept a pass in the area, Faubert merely provides an assist to Noel Hunt who gleefully smacks the loose ball into the net. The game has been turned round in just ninety seconds.

The interval view around the Press and Media Area is that only West Ham could surrender such a comfortable position. Although it was a smash and grab effort against the run of play, I don't believe it should signal a home defeat and, perhaps stupidly, remain optimistic as the second half begins. There is just one substitution from Big Sam, with Danny Collins on for Mark Noble. For some reason, this worries me.

West Ham start well and force a couple of corners, which are unfortunately wasted. Jason Roberts then runs clear of the defence, but is thankfully flagged offside. Matt Taylor finds himself with a little latitude but wastes the chance, hitting a long shot well wide from outside the area. Reading have some tough games before the end of the season, but they'll fear nothing if they win today.

James Tomkins controls the ball with his head before firing in a low shot that has the Reading keeper stretching to keep out. Uh oh. Reading have a penalty. The rarely erring Abdoulaye Faye connects with Noel Hunt, and not the ball, and the referee blows for the penalty, just a second before the loose ball is volleyed into the net. The advantage is missed but Ian Harte still coolly steers the ball in, to give Reading a 3-1 lead on the hour. What's a claret and blue to do? We have been on top pretty much throughout the game, but are now behind by two goals. The home crowd has been silenced. Big Sam brings on Baldock for the limping Taylor.

Another free-kick is wasted... Is there a way back from this now? It would seem not. Nolan breaks free down the left but his cross is banged away for a corner by Ian Harte, chasing back. Just 25 minutes to save the game, but no clear indication of where the two goals might come from. The Reading fans sing, *Sacked in the morning, you're getting sacked in the morning...* There is no effort from the West Ham fans to contradict the message of their song.

The Reading substitute Jay Tabb is now substituted himself by Robson-Kanu, having received a blow to the stomach. Maybe it's that Jason Roberts, I think, clearly an Upton Park Janus where the Hammers are concerned. And was it 24 degrees yesterday? It's about six in the wind now and my fingers are freezing. Looks like Nicky Maynard is about to come on, which he does, for Carlton Cole. Tomkins is booked for remonstrating with the assistant referee for the non-awarding of a corner that the replay indicates should have been given.

Another corner. This one is brilliantly headed home by Ricardo Vaz Te, beating his marker Gorkss, the very Reading player who scored from the same position at the end of the first half. Despite seeing their lead reduced to 3-2, Reading come straight back with a corner, and Ian Harte's inswinger almost finds the back of the net but is punched clear by Green. Jimmy Kebe goes off to more boos and is replaced by a number 51 Benik Afobe.

West Ham, unfortunately, cannot get the ball out of their own half, and it's no surprise when number 8 Mikele Leigertwood strokes home a loose ball after a Reading break. They put the ball in the net again shortly afterwards, but this time it's ruled offside. The game is concluding with a very different look to the one it possessed in the first part of the first half. What will Allardyce do now? Maybe this is playing the West Ham way, but the sieve of a defence has had a terrible second half.

The fourth official has indicated there will be six minutes of perjury time, the news greeted without cheers by those still left in the ground. *And it's super Reading... super Reading FC!* the Royals' fans sing. Sam tucks his shirt in and looks out at the play, lost for words. Jason bloody Roberts, the talismanic Championship stalwart.

We want five! We want five! they sing. Thankfully, the final whistle brings the insane chants to an end.

West Ham: 1 Green, 3 McCartney, 4 Nolan, 5 Tomkins, 9 Cole (8 Maynard 72), 12 Vaz Te, 14 Taylor (7 Baldock 60), 15 Faye, 16 Noble (25 Collins 46), 18 Faubert, 32 O'Neil

What a month. Began well, ended badly, with an agonising middle. I am remembering extracting triumph from the ashes of defeat from another March month, and the superb way West Ham played in a 3-4 home defeat by Spurs in the Premier League back in 2007. Never has a defeat felt more like a victory. Why? Because West Ham played some of their best football of the season. Each and every one of us who was there knew that even though West Ham were rooted at the bottom of the league, some stirrings of hope had been established. Wins at Blackburn and Arsenal and at home to Middlesbrough in the next three games proved the feelings were right. Survival was the target then. Now it's promotion. The mood of the fans at Peterborough in that second half have helped create signs of hope, despite the disappointment of the home defeat by Reading. With six league games to go, that hope remains.

We Play On The Floor! We Play On The Floor!
We're West Ham United! We Play On The Floor!

Chapter 11

Last Feet Backwards

April 2012

I start a new month in sinus rhythm for the first time since August 2010. Let me explain to you what that means. Everything in your life is better. Food, travel, conversation, music, running... and sex. Hypothetically, that is. No, I'm sure it would be, the others all are. It's like putting new duracells in your portable speakers and hearing that dynamic range kick in. It's like finally getting a table at Tayyabs (Punjabi restaurant in Whitechapel) on a busy night after a thirty minute wait, and possessing the rare self-discipline to nibble slowly at the contents of that plate of sweetly spitting paneer tikka. It's like watching Di Canio trying to do something impossible, and succeeding. Those two goals at Stamford Bridge; you couldn't ever forget that game if you were there. Saturday 28th September 2002. *Mamma Mia!*

In just two weeks I have noticed my running times improving and my breathing getting better. I plan things more efficiently and don't make so many miscalculations when getting through the week. My patience in conversations is more measured. I can even tolerate people whom I would ordinarily be mentally slicing into bacon joints whilst listening to their bullshit. I have even found myself philosophical about the way West Ham have managed meekly to surrender what looked like a safe seat to next season's Premier League. Please get this team up, and keep me in sinus rhythm. That is all I ask.

Game Forty-One, nPower Championship, 2011-12, Barnsley
Friday April 6th 2012 (11,151)
Referee: Tony Bates (Staffordshire)

Barnsley 0

West Ham United 4
Nolan 7
Maynard 23
Noble 35
Vaz Te 55

(West Ham: 3rd in the table, 75 points from 123)

For the second month in succession, West Ham start with a convincing away win live on BBC TV. Again it begins with a goal from captain Kevin Nolan. The team look invincible again. Will they need May to secure promotion at the end of this perverse season?

Jason and I have decamped to the back room for this Good Friday romp, armed only with beers and, two generous portions of fish, chips and beans. Defeat against Reading last Saturday still feels like a passport to the play-offs, but the latent optimist lurking in my bile bubbles up to the surface as West Ham speed swiftly into a three-nil lead. Nolan taps in on the goal line before Maynard skilfully slots in his second for West Ham and tenth of the season. Does that make him joint top scorer with Cole, or do only the two he scored for the Hammers count? I should know that sort of stuff, but I find, strangely, that I don't.

The third goal is a result of a poor back pass which the locally booed old boy Vaz Te slides in to intercept. His collision with the keeper leads to the ball running loose to Noble, who chips it expertly back into the empty net.

The second half offers another tap in, this one for Vaz Te. Maynard then hits the crossbar with a breathtaking shot from close distance and Vaz Te has further chances to add to his tally. It is still a satisfying and goal difference inspiring performance that puts West Ham four points behind the top two, with five winnable games making up the last of the April fixtures. Southampton still have to play Reading, a reverse six-pointer that could let Hammers close in on the loser, so the doom and gloom visions are kept at bay, at least until Bank Holiday Monday when Birmingham will be the visitors. Meanwhile, this has certainly been a Good Friday.

West Ham: 1 Green, 2 Reid, 3 McCartney, 4 Nolan, 5 Tomkins, 20 Demel (29 Collins 59), 14 Taylor, 16 Noble (Diop 80), 32 O'Neil (22 Lansbury 70), 8 Maynard, 12 Vaz Te

My cameraman colleague Neil Corbett has introduced me to the most fantastic application for my mobile phone. It is called 'Strada', Italian for the 'street' or, as I prefer it, the 'road'. My running obsession has kept me fit, and running has changed my life since I first ran a mile, voluntarily, in August 1992. This little application might just take things one step further. The only problem is finding something to put the mobile in as I run. Finally I track down a belt pouch that does the trick. It measures the elevation change and pace on your route, as well as the calories burned, average speed and distance travelled.

My Sunday run round the three parks, now in sinus rhythm, clocks up a time of just inside ninety-one minutes for a distance of nine miles. Still slow, yes, but now I have targets and results to work with. I am feeling very positive about the whole running thing now. Maybe I can start 'upping the ante' and improving those times significantly.

Game Forty-Two, nPower Championship, 2011-12, Upton Park
Monday April 9th 2012 (31,045)
Referee: Jonathan Moss (Yorkshire)

West Ham United 3	**Birmingham City 3**
Vaz Te 45, 89 (pen)	Mutch 27
Cole 70	King 30
	Burke 45

(West Ham: 3rd in the table, 76 points from 126)

Bubbles everywhere, but a feeling of gloom in the Upton Park evening air. Southampton have strolled it 2-0 at Crystal Palace, and Reading are at Brighton tomorrow. A loss tonight will leave West Ham looking at the lottery of the play offs again. The only way they go up these days it seems.

Reid is back at right back for the first time at Upton Park since the Crystal Palace goalless draw, and has already added a bit of steel at Barnsley on Friday. Allardyce is still starting with Carlton Cole, Ricardo Vaz Te and Nicky Maynard. Sky cameras are here again, but don't seem to have anywhere near the same fortune-generating power as the BBC, who were at Cardiff and Barnsley.

A good win today will put pressure on Reading tomorrow night. Alan Pardew's Newcastle are closing in on a Champions League place against all the odds, while Alan Curbishley was in the Sky Sports' studio without a care in the world. He left the Boleyn Ground well compensated for his time at the club. He was never given the building period necessary to put his long term plans for the club into action. Then again, Gianfranco Zola did not get too far with his project either.

Birmingham's squad are still a long shot for the play offs, but that could all look very different at half past seven this evening. The fans are in good voice after seven minutes of WHU one way traffic, but the nerves are evident on both sides. Vaz Te tries one from twenty-five yards which clips a defender's head and spoons away for a corner. Control is lax and periods of play drift from one side to the other. The cautious atmosphere is like a cloud of smog hanging pendulously over the ground.

Tomkins mistimes a run and the ball skids off his outstretched head. Then Vaz Te nods clumsily over from McCartney's cross. Maynard is offside for the second time in a row. Suddenly Birmingham put together their first move of the game, a breakaway, with Chris Burke haring down on goal. Green flaps out a left paw at the shot which spins away for a corner. Curtis Davies heads Jordan Mutch's inswinger just wide. I notice the Birmingham fans don't even bother singing, *You're supposed to be at home!* What's happening here these days is no secret.

There is some intelligent approach play from Tomkins and Maynard, and something of a patience that is welcome. Vaz Te cleverly maintains possession, but Noble's rushed cross breaks the move down. The camera catches a nervous Allardyce rubbing his hands like a penniless moneylender.

The crowd seem aware that they have been blamed for the poor home form of 2012, and are clearly reluctant to make any kind of noise today. Cole goes down in the area, but is unlikely to be awarded a penalty for clumsiness. The slow build up starts again. I realise how important the missing Matt Taylor is to the side. Plenty of goal kicking practice for the keepers, but little more.

Then the ball is lost in midfield by Gary O'Neil who remains prostrate. A three man passing move ends with Jordan Mutch slotting the ball home for Birmingham on 28 minutes past a strangely static Rob Green. What now?

Just like the last home game v Reading, Birmingham hit a second in just over a minute, that's what. The recidivist Marlon King finds himself in space on the left, and powers the ball past a helpless Green. Now I member where Gold, Sullivan and Brady came from. They can't be enjoying this.

You're getting sacked in the morning! the Birmingham fans sing.

Stand up, if it's all bollocks! the Hammers' fans sing, just minutes from a poorly scanned but unparalleled moment of crowd harmony.

George McCartney is floored by a collision on the halfway line and is replaced by on loan Danny Collins. Now Birmingham are in charge and have a free kick just outside the area. Green has come a long way off his line and delivers a heart in mouth gawp as the ball drops over his head and just a few feet wide. Next Faye charges down a goal bound shot from King.

Up the other end, Maynard is felled outside the area. O'Neil sends the free kick into the Sir Trevor Brooking Upper. Allardyce is beginning, rather worryingly, to look like Oliver Hardy to Wally Downes's Stan Laurel. Tomkins has gone to right back with Winston Reid in the centre and Collins at left back. I'm already beginning to think about the Hockney exhibition at the Royal Academy where I am heading after this disappointment.

Reid finds Collins before falling over. An unanticipated cluelessness is descending, and the crowd finally give in with an extended and tired session of booing. It is probably the worst first half display I have ever seen from a West Ham side. And still, what now? I look for Carlos Tevez on the bench.

Maynard restores some first half pride with a wonderful chip from the edge of the area. It beats Boaz Myhill but comes back into play off the underside of the crossbar. The rebound finally finds it's way back to Nolan who shoots straight at the keeper. The first genuine chance in the half for West Ham, seconds after which four minutes of injury time are announced by Jeremy Nicholas. The fans cheer the award of a subsequent corner. This one is headed back goalward by Tomkins and deflected into the net by Vaz Te. Before the joy can even begin to sink in, Curtis Davies heads goalwards beyond Rob Green and the despairing outstretched lunge of Abdoulaye Faye to restore Birmingham's two goal advantage. Rob Green has conceded seven goals at home in just two matches.

Over half-time Jeremy Nicholas plays 'The Final Countdown'. I imagine the fans won't forgive Big Sam if he doesn't rescue West Ham from what looks like an impossible position. Henri Lansbury is on as sub. Are we seriously thinking Gooner magic?

A couple of swift Hammer attacks suggest urgency, but can they manage any goals? It seems that the clue is in the attitude, and Hammers have another corner. The attitude is forward forward forward. And another corner. This is better. This from O'Neil. Tomkins gets away from the defence but his cross finds Maynard offside. Why didn't they play like this in the first half? Allardyce and Downes are in the technical area screaming as the cross comes, which Nolan misses by a whisker.

I look on the monitor at Wally Downes' concentrated expression in the dugout. Hard to imagine him as the freckle-faced spikey blond-haired third year at St Clement Danes in 1975 who I used to want to hit every time I saw him. Problem was, I was a sixth former. That kind of behaviour wasn't the done thing. He was quick-witted, though I just found him irritating at the time. I'd been sent home for wearing brown Doc Marten boots to school at the beginning of term, and he'd somehow got wind of this story. Every time he saw me he would ask what happened to my boots, in this whining high-pitched voice. I suppose you had to be there to know what I'm talking about.

When Downes joined Wimbledon many years later he became their first full-time league apprentice. He scored on debut as a 17 year old against Barnsley, and went on to make over 200 appearances for the club. He was part of the side that rose from the Fourth to the First Division in less than ten years, and is even credited as being one of the founding members of The Crazy Gang. I can believe that. Although from what I can see, Downes only has two legs, he somehow managed to suffer four broken legs in his career. That says something about his tenacity, or insanity, you might say.

Downes' greatest achievement for me was being one of the few on the staff to avoid the Avram Cull at the end of last season. Allardyce obviously saw something in him when he took over as manager, and promoted him to first team coach. Downes has previous with ex-West Ham staff, having worked with Alan Pardew at Southampton, after being sacked as Kevin Dillon's coach at Reading. He was later sacked with Pardew at Southampton in August 2010. He then came to West Ham to replace Zeljko Petrovic who was sacked in November 2010. You might say it was a pity Grunt didn't go with him, then. Downes alone might have managed the job better than Grunt did.

The crowd are still screaming for a penalty every time there is the slightest contact in the area. They have finally realised the kind of influence that they can exert. All one-way traffic. Nolan attempts a spectacular overhead in the six yard box but misses. And another corner. Birmingham break away but waste their first opportunity for ten minutes.

Now Lansbury hits a shot across the goal, just wide. And yet another corner. Myhill is bundled over for a free kick as we approach the hour. Lansbury attempts a cheeky chip but it's well wide. They have to win this game. Can they score three goals in twenty-five minutes?

Birmingham have no alternative but to try and soak up the pressure. Their players begin to drop to attract attention from the physio. Fans boo. This is terrible. How would a team so apparently incapable of winning a home game manage in the Premier League?

Cole shapes to shoot in the area and is floored, but referee Moss waves play on. Finally someone the fans can boo at. Birmingham have a free kick and organise a substitution to waste a few more seconds. West Ham scored four against Blackpool back here in October. Now another surge and turning skilfully, Carlton Cole hammers the ball into the back of the net, 2-3! *Come on you Irons!*

Substitute Nikola Zigic is booked for aggressive play, throwing his weight and height around, call it what you like... Birmingham enjoy a little passage of possession which thankfully comes to nothing. It's exasperating. Now the ball drops invitingly to Cole on the edge of the area but he fires over. This is the England international Cole, gaining in confidence, perhaps at the key point in the season... Now Lansbury fires in a great shot from outside the area; again, just over!

The irony in Allardyce's first half passing display effort sending Hammers in 3-1 down is fully switched with the second half panic, all Sam's to the pump, long-ball rubbish turning the tables on Birmingham. The West Ham way, my arsenal.

Marlon King dashes through, one on one, but... he's offside. Hammers have another corner after a brilliant tackle from Noble sets up another attack. The will to win, freshly discovered, has got twelve minutes to work its magic. Myhill comes off his line just in time to stop the advancing Cole. Ten minutes left. King is subbed for Andros Townsend, Andy Townsend's love child.

Every 50-50 ball is now won by the Hammers. Sam Baldock replaces Noble to make it a kind of bizarre 4-2-4. Eight minutes to go. Even a point would be something. And another corner. Nolan does everything he can to turn the ball back, but it drifts away for a goal kick. The fans are beginning to leave as Birmingham break. At least West Ham have played with some spirit this half. They'll need it if they are to make any progress in the play offs. The Birmingham captain Caldwell gives away an unnecessary corner, but there is no turning this one into a goal. Nolan now does brilliantly to win another corner. Now a handball in the area - who will take the penalty kick now Noble is off?

Vaz Te. And he... scores! Two minutes to go! Is it possible to win this? The fourth official puts up his illuminated sign - FOUR minutes! But... no, it isn't possible to win this. Where is Carlos Tevez when you can't afford him?

Like the 2006-07 0-3 reverse at Sheffield United, when it seemed just at the close of the season as if a miracle was around the corner, this performance was not in the script. But a point has been won, and the season is not over.

West Ham: 1 Green, 2 Reid, 3 McCartney (25 Collins 34), 4 Nolan, 5 Tomkins, 8 Maynard (22 Lansbury 46), 9 Cole, 12 Vaz Te, 15 Faye, 16 Noble (7 Baldock 82), 32 O'Neil

Public transport in London has become unpleasantly expensive under Boris Johnson. There's now an added evening rush hour surcharge on tickets and annual above inflation increases. A day in the capital, even if you're not travelling in Zone 1, will cost you the best part of a tenner. It's got to the point where a journey up to see West Ham play is looked at as something I shouldn't waste. This evening I've therefore decided to get along to the David Hockney 'A Bigger Picture' exhibition at the Royal Academy. This is a man whose work in the 60s pop art movement elevated him to the status of a modern great, a subject for the 'newspaper stuff' and speculation (as he put it recently) that he chooses to ignore. He's lived in California for most of his life, but returned to the UK in 2005, and has been working ever since on these massive colourful tree landscapes of East Yorkshire. Some of this work has been created on an iPad. Pretty modern 'stuff' for a seventy-four year old. He's also part of the 'newspaper stuff' with his alleged criticism of Damien Hirst for using other people to help create his works. Hockney's gallery wall displays the line 'All the works here were made by the artist himself, personally' but when pushed, he denies that this is a criticism. I don't know what to think. I'll just see what I think when I see it. When I saw the headline 'Hirst skull to display in Turbine' last November, I thought the controversial artist had died and that this was a rather clever PR idea to front a final exhibition of his work.

Getting to the Hockney show, which only has one more day to run, requires an advanced ticket for a timed entry. As the Birmingham game finishes early evening, I've booked an 8pm viewing. The paintings are huge, and the space given to them is pretty much the whole of the main gallery. I hesitate to use the word, but psychedelic seems a pretty good description of these vast landscapes, with their purples, bright greens and deep blues. As usual, the reactions to the works from people assembled at the exhibition are often as entertaining as what's hanging up in front of them. The preponderance of Yorkshire accents seems almost a cliché, but it provides a perfect backdrop for these wonderful landscapes.

It's the London Mayoral elections in just over two weeks, and Ken Livingstone and Bad Boris are neck and neck in the polls. Johnson has got it on humour, though, and that's more important than anything else these days. He portrays himself as an elegant buffoon, and most voting Londoners will buy that image. Even though his party are behind in the polls nationally, I have the feeling that he will win. Roll on freedom pass. If it still exists.

Game Forty-Three, nPower Championship, 2011-12, Upton Park
Saturday April 14th 2012 (32,339)
Referee: Roger East (Wiltshire)

West Ham United 6	**Brighton and Hove Albion 0**
Vaz Te 3, 8, 62	
Nolan 11	
Cole 64	
Own Goal (Dicker) 78	

(West Ham: 3rd in the table, 79 points from 129)

Yesterday evening Reading beat their closest automatic promotion rivals Southampton and claimed the top place that their current run has been suggesting is theirs for the last two months. This means only Southampton can be realistically caught - their goal difference is better by nine and their run in features a game against Peterborough on Tuesday evening. Peterborough are the only side to have beaten Reading in their last ten, so there is still hope. Today requires a win by three clear goals to set up that possibility (and for Bristol City to win at Birmingham so they are safe from relegation threats by the time we play them on Tuesday...).

Gus Poyet has worked miracles at Brighton, as they target a second successive promotion season in the new Amex Stadium. However, his side are almost a goal down after forty seconds, with Henri Lansbury's shot dipping over Peter Brezovan and off the top of the crossbar. Within three minutes, West Ham are ahead through a fiercely struck effort from Vaz Te from twenty yards, which seems to go straight through the Brighton keeper. The tall Slovakian redeems himself three minutes later with a brilliant far post block from Nolan's effort after Noble's cross. Two minutes later, O'Neil's deeper cross finds Vaz Te whose goal bound header is untidily fielded into his own net by Brezovan. Without irony, the Hammers' fans sing, *How shit must you be; we're winning at home!*

Now Nolan hits a third after just ten minutes as Taylor's free kick is met at the far post by Tomkins, and his header across goal is scooped gleefully into the net by the captain! Brighton finally organise their first attack in the thirteenth minute. Green fields a cross that is hit too close to him. The Press Area is almost empty today, proof, if it were needed, that the real promotion interest is elsewhere. Southampton's goal difference is now 6 better than West Ham's. Plenty more needed, but the attacks keep on coming. O'Neil hits in a powerful shot from outside the area, straight at the keeper. West Ham are playing their most explosive home football since that 4-0 home win against Blackpool... a long time ago.

Brighton's second attack is timed at twenty minutes, and they manage to foul it up with some clumsy approach play and a misguided final ball. Matt Taylor is playing very deep just in front of the back four, but doing enough running around to suggest there are twelve claret and blue shirts on the pitch. Reid is at left back with Demel at right, covering for McCartney's Monday night injury. Vaz Te is back in defence to clear Brighton's next attack, and perhaps it is this extra running back from the front men that is partly responsible for the whirlwind start to this game. I am reminded from another West Ham history book of relatively recent 3-0 first half starts against West Brom and Wimbledon that ended in 3-4 defeats, but I'm not going to dwell on those for the moment. However, Brighton have managed some spectacular wins this season, and deservedly led the Championship for the first three months of the season until they began to get found out in early November.

Brighton have a corner on the half hour. With the posts manned and Green in between, the prodded effort from Inigo Calderon is deflected a good yard wide of the right hand post. I recall saying earlier in the season that the bunch of players Allardyce had assembled were capable of beating any team in the division if they all put in a decent ninety minutes. Today we are seeing the truth of that statement, though the game has quietened down since the lunatic opening ten minutes. One player in particular whose form is good today has been Kevin Nolan, who has urged the side on and raised the confidence of the team.

If West Ham could score another couple then that would really put pressure on Southampton, but as the half draws to a close, they find themselves deeper against an improving Brighton. On forty-one minutes they get a free kick wide on the right side outside the West Ham area. Bridcutt and Vicente threaten, but Nolan heads the cross over his own bar. From the corner, Brighton think they have scored, when captain Gordon Greer's header is scooped from the goal line by the stretching Green. The linesman has a good view but his flag remains down as Greer appeals. From the break away, Vaz Te hits a powerful shot which Brezovan saves well. Brighton, however, improve, and win another free kick in a dangerous edge-of-the-area position. When it's eventually taken, the shot skids just wide of Green's left hand post. Again West Ham respond with a brilliant break away move that generates a positive shooting chance for Gary O'Neil, which he blasts high over the bar with a fourth goal beckoning. Nevertheless, the 3-0 half-time score line has clearly sent everyone off to enjoy a particularly delicious pie. Peterborough are winning 1-0 at Leeds and Bristol City are winning 2-1 at Birmingham, both scores part of the pre-match requirement.

Vicente starts the second half with a bold shot outside the area from twenty-five yards. Matt Taylor's responding corner is headed out from under the bar, but it heralds a spate of West Ham attacks in the hunt for a fourth goal. Cole comes close with a blocked shot from the edge of the six yard box and then Vaz Te's shot from close in tests the keeper's concentration. Poyet brings Lualua and Mackail-Smith on as a double substitution, attacking midfielder and striker, convinced that there is still something in the game for him. Collison is on for O'Neil.

Brighton are defending better this half, and manage to quell the first round of attacks though rarely trouble West Ham's back four. As the hour approaches, the possibility of a drab final thirty minutes hangs in the air. With goal difference likely to be a factor in any West Ham mini revival at this late stage of the season, more will be needed, and there'll never be a better chance than now to get them...

Poyet is in the technical area, pushing his side to get back in the game. West Ham push forward and Lansbury is bundled over in the area. While the shouts for a penalty go unheard, Vaz Te overhead kicks a spectacular finish from inside the box for his hat-trick. One minute later and it's five, as Cole dances into the area and lets fly. His effort spoons over Brezovan via the outstretched running legs of Lansbury. Five-nil will answer the critics, as Julian Dicks, working for BBC Radio London, commented at half time.

Demel in his injury-plagued season now comes off for Danny Collins. Tony Pulis must have had regular appearances for his defender as part of the loan deal with Big Sam.

The referee Roger East seems unable to offer any protection for the West Ham forwards, though, with Vaz Te getting a bashing from Marcos Painter and central defender Adam El-Abd. Calderon's cross is now skewed off Taylor whose deflection sends it just past the post. The hat-trick hero Vaz Te is cheered off and substituted by John Carew. There's a quarter of an hour for the big Norwegian to have his contractual runaround.

Now it's goal number six from Noble's corner, and an own goal from, of course, Gary 'Dick'er. Jeremy Nicholas wisely announces, 'Goal Number Six... Own goal.' I would call that a missed comic opportunity.

John Carew clearly wants to get in on the action, but a couple of heavy first touches let him down. He finally gets a free kick that sends the possibility of a seventh into the minds of the delighted fans. The sponsors' man of the match is, unsurprisingly, Ricardo Vaz Te. A rare yellow card is waved at Carlton Cole after his complaints about having a foul awarded against him. I turn round to check and, yes, the Mud Mouth twins are both there, sitting in silence. If West Ham keep winning, they'll keep silent. Tomkins has moved into the midfield, but it hasn't led to anything. Nolan, however, has his far post effort deflected wide for a very late corner. Taylor's effort is dropped by the keeper, but grabbed at the last second before he suffers a seventh net bulge. Cole is bundled over again, but no whistle. Three added minutes of injury time, as Nolan misses from a yard out, the chance falling to his wobbly left peg.

This has been an excellent display from West Ham, though whether Brighton might have given away their chance of a play off place remains to be seen. This might be a press conference worth witnessing. The fans end the game with a rousing chorus of 'Bubbles' and the first time six goals have been seen for West Ham at Upton Park since January 1998 when a chubby young chap called Frank Lampard Junior scored against Barnsley in the Premier League. Abou, too.

In the Press Room Gus Poyet says that the game has demonstrated to him why – despite all the pundits talking his Brighton side up – they're just not ready for the Premier League. 'If we had to go to Anfield or Old Trafford next season, then I would not go,' he says. 'Gus Poyet would be staying at home!'

West Ham: 1 Green, 2 Reid, 4 Nolan, 5 Tomkins, 9 Cole, 12 Vaz Te (11 Carew 77), 14 Taylor, 16 Noble, 20 Demel (25 Collins 68), 22 Lansbury, 32 O'Neil (10 Collison 55)

eBay has been a revelation for me in the last ten years, I'll confess. Never to sell things, only to buy. The thought that pretty much anything you might be interested in buying can be bought over the internet through this strange site, is a heady concept. I acknowledge that many see collecting things as a futile pursuit, but there are some things I have chosen to collect. You might imagine I would collect football programmes, and I do, but only from games I have attended. My achilles heel is something that hasn't been made in this country for over fifty years, but which is still available, sometimes in abundance. It is the 78rpm record, made out of a brittle shellac-based substance, fortified by the remains of crushed insects and vinylite, a more refined version of Bakelite.

A combination of the ubiquity of eBay and the fact that most collectors from the 40s and 50s are now dead or dying, has led to the market becoming saturated with these items. Although they stopped being produced in the UK in early 1960, their output continued in South Africa until late 1961, and in India until late 1966. This means that there are 78rpm records by the Beatles out there, if you look hard enough. These tend to go for figures in the range of £1000. It's a remarkable sum, bearing in mind how brittle they are. If you buy one, there is still the small matter of awaiting its safe arrival in the post. I've had just as many carefully packaged items arrive in two pieces as discs thrown in a thin cardboard envelope surviving a journey intact from the corner of some obscure town on the outskirts of Glasgow.

The day after West Ham's 6-0 annihilation of Brighton, I am bidding on a 1962 78rpm Indian pressing of Cliff Richard's version of the Jerry Lee Lewis 1957 rock'n'roll classic *It'll Be Me*. I mention this not for the deserved onset of universal ridicule, but because it remains the most I have ever paid for a single item on eBay. It's enough that I tell you what I was bidding for. I'm afraid the final price paid will remain a secret between my record vendor pusher and me. What I will say is that I picked it up from his house in North London, unwilling to take a chance on a postal journey.

Game Forty-Four, nPower Championship, 2011-12, Ashton Gate
Tuesday April 17th 2012 (16,669)

Referee: Craig Pawson (South Yorkshire)

Bristol City 1   **West Ham United 1**
Skuse 30   Tomkins 25

(West Ham: 3rd in the table, 80 points from 132)

With Bristol City needing something from tonight's game for their survival chances, this is going to be a tricky match. Their old man keeper has finally slunk to life on the bench (why doesn't he give up and get a proper job?) and Allardyce is wisely starting with ex-City striker Maynard, hoping he will be buoyed by the West Country boo boys.

It's actually Vaz Te who gets all the early goalscoring opportunities, and squanders them. James Tomkins adds another to his goal tally with a header from Mark Noble's free kick after twenty-five minutes. The lead will need some defending, and it won't surprise anyone who's read this far that Hammers can't do that. Cole Skuse puts Derek McInnes' side level just four minutes later when his 25 yard shot passes through a crowd of man marking mannequin defenders, bobbling beyond Rob Green's late apologetic dive into the back of the goal. Shades of Team USA at the 2010 World Cup.

In the second half Lansbury goes as close as he has all season to adding to his goal total of one when he clips the bar early in the second half. Green makes one decent save from City's Chris Wood before Carew somehow misses not one but three golden late chances at the death to nick all the points. What this means, in the final analysis is almost certainly another month of football to fight for a chance to win that final promotion place at Wembley in May. And despite his efforts over the season, Carew will not play for the club again.

West Ham United: 1 Green, 2 Reid, 5 Tomkins, 20 Demel (18 Faubert 74), 29 Collins (11 Carew 63), 4 Nolan, 14 Taylor, 16 Noble, 22 Lansbury, 8 Maynard (10 Collison 74), 12 Vaz Te

I'd bought myself a ticket to see Ryan Adams at the London Palladium on the Monday night many months before the Leicester City fixture was shifted to Monday, live on Sky. So what do you do? As a Likely Lads' enthusiast, I knew that I would have to censure those who regularly disseminate football facts via their phone to keep their fat fingers to themselves, and I persuaded Jules to join me in the conjugal bed for an 'as live' play of the recorded game from a quarter to eleven that night. Armed with our charity shop Hammers' tops, we sat up, eyes glued to the Bravia, hearts in sedentary mouths.

Game Forty-Five, nPower Championship, 2011-12, Leicester City
Monday April 23rd 2012 (23,172)
Referee: Eddie Ilderton (Tyne and Wear)

Leicester City 1   **West Ham United 2**
Beckford 34   Reid 39
                           Collison 58

(West Ham: 3rd in the table, 83 points from 135)

The points lost at Bristol City took on further significance when Southampton lost to Middlesbrough on Saturday. It was my brother's little girl Phoebe's first birthday, and I imagine that must have been her present to me. Pre-lingual children can do that. They have powers. As a result, if Hammers can beat Leicester this evening and win at home against Hull City on Saturday, Southampton will have to beat already relegated Coventry City to get the other automatic place behind Reading. Let's face it, that's one 'if... then' too many.

However, Jules and I settle down to the game having avoided anything sent by text or e-mail during the evening. Odd, watching a game 'live' so close to midnight. Last time I did that I was in Beijing watching England take on Slovenia in the 2010 World Cup, with the commentator yelling out 'Looney!' every time England mounted an attack and 'Telly!' every time they scrambled backwards in defence.

It's going to be maddeningly frustrating, but it has to be stomached. It would be so easy just to check the score on the Internet. The point is, West Ham fans have to endure a certain amount of frustration and aggravation every season. If I manage somehow to circumvent the latest dose that other Irons have already been through earlier this evening, then I will be out of balance. We can't have that. That would screw everything up. My football chakra would become unbalanced. If that happened... Hammers could end up winning the Premier League. You see where I'm going with this? (What do you mean, 'No!'?)

Leicester City have little to play for, but they take the lead on 34 minutes. An event as predictable as the gossip to come on Prince William and Princess Kate. Ben Marshall crosses to the far post and Jermaine Beckford heads home. He missed an easier chance a few minutes earlier. What is not quite as predictable is West Ham's prompt equaliser, when Reid tucks away Taylor's low cross. That's his third Championship goal, pretty commendable for a central defender.

A quarter of an hour into the second half, Jack Collison finds the back of the net when O'Neil's blocked shot comes out to him and he drills it back in. A magnificent effort that he deserves to twin with a shot two minutes later that Bamba deflects over the bar somewhat flukily. West Ham settle and control the rest of the game until Nolan misses a sitter right at the end. This, of course, is compounded when Morgan's belated header almost grabs Leicester the point that would end West Ham's chance of automatic promotion.

So there it is. It'll go down to the very last game. To recap. West Ham now have to beat Hull by at least four clear goals on Saturday and then hope Southampton fail to beat Coventry City. At home. Who have nothing to play for.

West Ham: 1 Green, 20 Demel (18 Faubert 76), 2 Reid, 5 Tomkins, 14 Taylor, 12 Vaz Te, 16 Noble, 10 Collison (22 Lansbury 88), 32 O'Neill, 4 Nolan, 9 Cole (25 Collins 81).

Paul Martin has come up with a great idea. He has found a box of nine Beta SP tapes that feature some filming he did in Plymouth in 1992 of the newly-elected Falmouth and Camborne Conservative MP Sebastian Coe. Paul's idea is that if he can get me to transfer all this material to the hard drive, we can edit it and produce a film that will make us a lot of money. Why? Because we'll go to the Olympics and do some up to date stuff with Coe to give it the longevity such a programme would need.

You are now perhaps thinking, that sounds great. A couple of days transferring the material onto computer. No real effort. Easy money. And you'd be right. But Paul has a better idea. If we go into this as a 50-50 venture, the pile of cash will be waiting for us at the end. A programme in Olympics' year, in London, about Lord Coe? Has to be a sound investment, no?

No.

Not even if my father was Lord Reith. It isn't going to happen. Ever. But Paul is determined and 'won't hear no'. I set him the task of procuring a Beta SP player, certain that it will prove beyond him. Within an hour, however, he has not only found someone to lend him a machine (how?) but he is bringing it round to me this evening. It would now appear churlish if I were to refuse. So I agree to organise the transfer.

'Are these nine tapes each twenty minutes long?'

'Yes,' he says. 'And I'm bound to have stopped three or four minutes before the end of each one, so it won't take too long to transfer.'

The first tape I put in the machine the following day is filled with content for the full 25 minutes. As is the second. The remaining seven are all 30 minutes long. And I know he will have taped on every single millimetre of tape on them. But halfway through tape three the picture starts breaking up. The tapes are old and dirtying the heads. So I'll have to buy a Beta SP tape cleaner. Have to order it, in fact, over the Net. Once I can find one that will work with this machine. And so the four and a half extra hours of tape transfer will take even longer as I'll have to keep putting the head cleaner in and out of the machine between tapes.

Even when I finish the job I should never have taken on for which I won't-get-paid, there will still be phone calls, meetings, plans and optimistic ideas. These will get more and more desperate until Lord Coe's overworked secretary or PR woman finally summons the frustrated energy to tell Paul that actually, no, Lord Coe isn't prepared to let us travel round with him throughout the Olympics, because there are already five television companies doing that.

You can see why I am already regretting saying yes.

Game Forty-Six, nPower Championship, 2011-12, Upton Park
Saturday April 28th 2012 (35,000)
Referee: Nigel Miller (County Durham)

West Ham United 2 **Hull City 1**
Cole 36, 49   Evans 81

(West Ham: 3rd in the table, 86 points from 138)

Brian Glanville is here. Which could mean anything. But it usually means a story. While you might think the Southampton game is the one to be at, Glanvers has other ideas. He's brought his grandson with him, too. That'll be his son's boy, the son who loves opera and is a Millwall fan.

My guest this afternoon is Peter Masters, who celebrated his 50th on Wednesday. This might be the greatest birthday present ever. Well almost! Chelsea have already proved away to Barcelona last Tuesday that the impossible is achievable. West Ham just have somehow to contrive to make it happen at two venues, somewhat limiting the odds.

Hammers are starting the game with the same curious formation Big Sam deployed on Monday night at Leicester. This includes playing Matt Taylor as an overlapping left back / winger and completing the back four with Reid, Demel and Tomkins. Nolan, Noble, O'Neil and Lansbury will play behind the front two of Vaz Te and Cole, this is how he imagines we might stack the goals up against Hull City. BBC are showing the Southampton game live, understandably, and it's on the screen over my right shoulder. Where to look?

Sam has gambled on Lansbury as the on pitch reserve keeper, and the Gooner has already demonstrated at Blackpool that he is up to the task. Reid has suffered from a head bang after two minutes and is being led off for the moment, but is soon back on. Vaz Te then seems to only have to blow on Lansbury's far post cross to put Hammers ahead, but he doesn't manage any meaningful contact and the ball floats just wide of the far post.

Noble is controlling the midfield at this point, with the Hammer of the Year vote extending inexplicably beyond the last game of the season - cock-up or play off conspiracy? The £250 a seat Hammer of the Year Ball that the awards were focused on looks a tad previous, sandwiched as it now is between the end of season and lead up to the play offs West Ham now find themselves in.

Nolan's characteristic boisterousness sees him launch into a few optimistic challenges early on, as ever but the referee looks like he's not looking to up his card averages this afternoon. It's been raining steadily since the kick-off, light rain, but leaving the top greasy. Eleven minutes and no goals at St Mary's. The atmosphere here is magnificent, no need to gee anyone up, the stadium is full, the buzz everywhere.

The referee is completely bald, reminiscent of the greatest ref ever, Pierre Luigi Colina. This makes me feel irrationally secure about any decisions to come over the ninety minutes. Lambert has just scored for Southampton, I notice over my shoulder, a flaky deflected effort that the Coventry City keeper otherwise had covered. Southampton now have a second, to go with their second place, and it's a neat diving header into the ground that bounces up and over the keeper.

Que sera sera, whatever will be will be, we're going to Wembley, que sera sera! the West Ham fans start to sing. I can't think that far ahead. Noble takes another corner, but the referee blows for climbing. Southampton back in the Premier League. The cameras chose the right game.

Lansbury is put in from Nolan's flick but he skies it horribly. I'm already thinking, will it be Cardiff or Middlesbrough? To think our Championship season could begin and end with a home fixture against Cardiff City. Hull City's Joshua King misses the chance to set up his fellow striker, so Hull stay goalless after their two efforts. Nolan and Vaz Te are involved in move after move of short passing attacks that have yet to yield anything close to a goal. Hull are beginning to believe that they just might get something out of this game. They have ex-Hammer and injury specialist Richard Garcia who, I am reliably informed, is out of contract soon, so is enjoying his last Hull game back at his old club. Garcia only managed 16 appearances for West Ham, one of those unwittingly as a substitute, brought on by Glenn Roeder, in a game that denied Steve Potts his four hundredth league appearance.

Matt Taylor's deep left wing cross clears the keeper Mannone, comes back off the bar and is scooped away for a corner. Mark Noble's corner is headed home by Carlton Cole for a thirty-sixth minute opener. Are we the form team going into the play-offs? Vaz Te is put through by Cole but, steadying himself, he fires wide of the far post with the fans raising their arms in anticipation. Hull have ten men behind the ball, or in front of it, depending on where you are in the ground.

That whole issue about the team finishing third in the Championship never getting promoted seems to have more to do with a run of form rather than a placement. The third team are often an early runner who dropped off towards the end. West Ham have actually only lost a few games this season, but have never really been out and out promotion certainties. That third position issue might not be a problem.

Rob Green is running round and jumping up and down outside his area to keep warm. O'Neil's delicate cross is nervously booted out for a corner by Dawson. The whistle is blown. All we can think of now are play off eventualities. Fixtures and venues will be confirmed depending on Cardiff and Middlesbrough's fortunes at Crystal Palace and Watford.

Graham Gooch is enjoying the hospitality at half-time. As Peter puts it, 'He looks like a bloke who's had a good life.' With a pretty woman on his arm and the hospitality crew on his ear, who could disagree? Cole has soon doubled West Ham's advantage and his personal match tally with a lovely chest down and finish from Lansbury's pinpoint cross, just after the interval. His involvement in the match is over after his goal, when he is replaced by Sam Baldock. 83 points seems a lot not to get a team promoted when 42 took West Ham down in 2002-03. Southampton have a corner when they wanted a penalty, but no matter, they score a third from the goalmouth scramble that follows. Now Ricardo Vaz Te gets a standing ovation as he goes off with twenty goals for the season, to be replaced by Maynard on the hour.

A bad back pass almost lets Baldock in, but the keeper has his wits about him. Southampton now have four and the Wembley calls go round the stadium. Tomkins goes off after a clash, with a juicy black eye, but is back on within a couple of minutes. Now we hear 'Bubbles' grow in volume by the minute. Cardiff are ahead at Crystal Palace, so that's who West Ham will be playing next week. Strange how West Ham's three play offs have all featured Cardiff either as a venue or an opposition.

Nolan has been in a tough clash with Green as the ball breaks loose in the area offering a late opportunity to Hull, but he recovers after some treatment. The few hundred Hull fans over in the corner of the Sir Trevor Lower sing *We're Hull Ci-ty!* with the stress annoyingly on the second syllable. Another free kick is wasted as it gets more and more cold. I don't remember a season ending at Upton Park in the rain, but here's one. Skipper Kevin Nolan is replaced with fifteen minutes to go by George McCartney, whose first task is to end a Hull City attack by clearing for a corner. Green saves well at the near post, blocking a powerful shot from substitute Robbie Brady. Brady has another chance a few minutes later but scuffs his shot wide from outside the area. O'Neil volleys beautifully at the other end only to see his effort turned over by Mannone's spectacular dive.

At the other end Demel has failed to clear and Corry Evans has headed the loose ball over Green into the empty net to give Hull an unexpected late consolation. It's a schoolboy error from the Ivory Coast international. *Nick Barmby, he's one of our own!* the Hull fans sing, this time with the syllables all stressed correctly, as they praise their soon to depart manager. Richard Garcia thinks he has finished beautifully after a superb cross picks him out. It's disallowed, with a delightfully late assistant ref's flag. O'Neil goes down in the Hull area having kicked a bit of the ground and a bit of the ball, neither to any great effect.

The wine has gone a bit flat in these last few minutes. Paul Stringer nips out of the Press Area ready to pick up Sam for his last Saturday Upton Park presser, with three minutes of injury time to be played. Allardyce has said all year that his target was to get two points a game, which would have accumulated 92. The team have ended the season six short with 86. His calculations prove spot on, as 92 would have been enough to top the table and overtake both Reading and Southampton by three clear points.

Brian Glanville watches the last few minutes of the game, bored, as well he might be. 'I've only got four hundred bloody words,' he said before the game. He might be best advised spending most of them celebrating Southampton's promotion. Nigel Adkins' side deserve it.

West Ham: 1 Green, 2 Reid, 4 Nolan (3 McCartney 74), 5 Tomkins, 9 Cole (7 Baldock 52), 12 Vaz Te (8 Maynard 60), 14 Taylor, 16 Noble, 20 Demel, 22 Lansbury, 32 O'Neil

Whatever happens now, there will be one more chapter.

Chapter 12

Final Breath

May 2012

The football season is over for twenty of the twenty-four Championship sides. Predictably, West Ham United, having squandered their dragon's hold on second place with a string of feeble home draws, now face play off lottery land.

Should the recriminations start now, or should we wait until the games are played in the hope that the back door entry into the Premier League stays open long enough for us to squeeze through it? As he led his team out against Preston North End at Cardiff in May 2005, Alan Pardew knew that if West Ham lost the game, his employment was likely to be terminated. Preston were the form team and had finished the season two points ahead of West Ham, doing the double over them by a 2-1 scoreline in both league fixtures. Hammers won two of their last five games that season and Reading, the team immediately below them, had finished just a win away from knocking them out of a play off place on goal difference.

Is it any different for Allardyce? The story goes that Sam has two seasons to get the side up. There are rumours of a £1m bonus on the table, too. With apologies to Alex Ferguson, squeaky buttock time is here again.

I've sat in on several of Sam's post match conferences, and I have found him a lot more fathomable than other managers. He is genial, honest and not over-complicated. He also has less self-doubt than many, and yet this aspect of his character has not blinded him to the randomness of fate in football. He talks to other managers, and isn't past taking their advice, but he's beginning to learn that you have to take the fans with you, whoever you are. Humility is something managers need to show in day-to-day dealings with their public. West Ham managers in the recent past have found such things out to their cost.

May is a month unlike any other in the football calendar. West Ham's three FA Cup wins, their 1965 European Cup-Winners Cup victory and promotion celebrations of 1992-93 and 2004-05 have all occurred in it. On Friday 9th May 2008, however, the month was memorable to West Ham fans for an evening at Upton Park to celebrate the greatest two managers the club has ever known, Ron Greenwood and John Lyall. These were men who, as managers of the club in some of its most successful years, knew all about humility. Lyall's death in April 2006, just a fortnight before West Ham's first appearance in a FA Cup Final since he had led them out against Arsenal at Wembley in 1980, was a great shock. The club had already lost Lyall's mentor Ron Greenwood two months earlier. It was a sad year, and only fitting that the club decided to commemorate these two great men in May 2008 with a gathering of players, staff and fans at the stadium. Hosted by Matthew Lorenzo, the evening was one of the most memorable days of my life. The Guest of Honour was none other than Alex Ferguson, who chartered a private plane for the occasion, with his side still needing to win their last game of the season two days later. Such was his admiration and respect for John Lyall in particular, from whom he claimed to have learned many lessons about football, that he kept his promise to attend the evening. He spoke with humour and passion about the club's games against Manchester United over the years, and about things he remembered about both men. Trevor Brooking spoke about both managers, and the two Tonys, Cottee and Gale provided a perspective from the younger players' point of view. The duty fell to me to provide an edited history of the two manager's achievements, and to film the evening for posterity. It was a great honour, and a little nerve-wracking, too. The Lyall and Greenwood families were in attendance, and spoke movingly of the two men and what they remembered of them from a family's perspective. No one who went to that evening would have any doubt about what it is that makes West Ham fans and their players a very special bunch of people. It was an evening I will never forget.

Coming to the end of the education calendar, like the football calendar, is still relevant for me as an examination tutor and part time Media Studies teacher. These days the final month of the season is also the one where my students submit their films as coursework for their GCSEs. It's remarkable how putting a five minute piece together says a lot about the person you are, and your hopes and dreams. The ten films my students have edited this year are very different from each other, and yet they all say something about the time from which they come. One impressive effort is a five minute compendium of students playing out sophisticated manoeuvres, jumps and twists, on their scooters down the local rec. My favourite is the one where three students have spent an afternoon filming themselves skateboarding in the town hall underpass. They have only been interested in capturing the most crude and disastrous attempts at different jumps and moves, and the result is one of the funniest films you'll ever see. Not that the celebration of failure has ever endeared any manager to the supporters of their club.

The first of the potential three game play off efforts is against Cardiff, a team Hammers beat just a few weeks ago. Despite the adage of lightning and its singular moments of activity, the domination and score-line is all set to be repeated.

Game Forty-Seven, nPower Championship, 2011-12, Cardiff
Play Off Semi Final First Leg
Thursday May 3rd 2012 (23,029)
Referee: Neil Swarbrick (Lancashire)

Cardiff City 0   West Ham United 2
Collison 9, 41

(West Ham: 2-0 advantage)

The last time Neil Swarbrick refereed a West Ham game was the 0-3 defeat at Reading in early December. This was a game from a month with only one win, and a match that featured two West Ham red cards, each preceding a Reading goal from a set play. Cardiff, rolled over alarmingly in this fixture when the teams met in March. They have suffered the ignominy of seeing the rise of their fellow countrymen Swansea into the Premier League. They will not, as another of their countrymen would have it, go gently into that good night. Let's see how much raging the Welsh dragon can do.

I sadly cannot be there. For the second time in just over a week, I am committed for a key Hammers' game. A rehearsal for the Adventures of Parsley gig in Tring cannot be cancelled at this late stage. All potential texters are forewarned and Jules and I go to bed at 10.45 for another 'as live' playback of the game to take us conscious into the small hours of Friday dreaming of Wembley or the unthinkable alternative.

Can there be many times West Ham fans have sung 'God Save The Queen' so vociferously in a football stadium? That lyric always makes me reflect not on its monarchist overtones, but the rare use of the English subjunctive in 'save', as in a silent 'may' God Save The Queen. And, let's face it, up to now, she or he has. Though for what, remains to be seen.

Thursdays are for elections, but rarely for football matches. This one has given us both. It's too close to call between Boris Johnson for Torytown and Ken Livingstone for the Spentforce as they seek to be elected Mayor of London. I fear that Ken is losing the Jewish vote and the waning appeal of his sense of humour may cost him. Is Johnson a clever buffoon or duplicitous schemer? Maybe even time won't tell if he gets in again – we still don't know for sure after his first four years in office.

West Ham's Welsh international Jack Collison is the key to the undoing of Cardiff this evening. He separates the sides after just nine minutes. Vaz Te beats Cardiff's offside trap and though City keeper David Marshall saves his and Collison's subsequent shots, Collison follows up with a header to score. It should've been two a minute or so later, Tomkins missing a not too difficult header close in. Just before half-time Vaz Te is in the thick of the action again when he flicks the ball on from a corner and Collison hits the ball home. His shot takes a debilitating deflection off Cardiff's Liam Lawrence.

Early in the second half Cardiff's best chance evaporates when Turner's header is cleared off the line by Cole. Ten minutes from time Nolan misses a header from ten yards that my mate Mike's pug Danny would have put in, even if she was on her lead. Despite this, a 2-0 victory is a worthy while not perfect lead to take into the home leg. This is next Monday with an afternoon kick off, because it's a Bank Holiday. The floodlights haven't been too kind to West Ham this season, so perhaps the daylight kick off is for the best.

I turn to see if Jules has any comments to add to those of the Sky Sports summariser, but she's asleep. It was asking a bit for her to watch all of the second half as she's been doing karate for most of the early part of this evening. In the space of five years she has become a black belt, second dan, and in the same way that running is my religion, karate is most certainly hers. In short, neither of us likes to lose, so this result will send us both to sleep very happy.

West Ham: 1 Green, 2 Reid, 5 Tomkins, 20 Demel (18 Faubert 75), 4 Nolan, 10 Collison (8 Maynard 86), 14 Taylor, 16 Noble, 32 O'Neil, 9 Cole, 12 Vaz Te (3 McCartney 60)

As predicted, Boris is re-elected when the votes are counted a few more times. He wins 51.5 per cent of the vote to Ken Livingstone's 48.5 in the final 'run-off' between the top two candidates. In his victory speech, Johnson promises, 'I will continue to fight for a good deal for Londoners, a good deal from government.' That sounds to me like a bit of a challenge to Cameron.

Sunday is an important day for me, and my health. Even before that cardio version sent me back into sinus rhythm, I entered the Richmond Half-Marathon. This was a race I once completed in 1:28:40 in 1998. This Sunday I am just hoping to get round inside two hours. Before my cardio version I would have been lucky to come in in under 2 hours 15, but recent improvements since my heart started to beat properly have given me hope. I last did this race on the morning of a commentary game at TWI seven years ago, and came in almost last. Today is different. I feel great throughout the 13.1 mile race, most of which takes place on the Thames towpath to Hampton Court and back. I come in at a sub two hour 1:58.43. It's a fantastic feeling. To have your heart beating properly is the best thing in the world. Never take it for granted.

AFC Wimbledon have finished their first season in the league in a creditable 16th place. Barnet and Dagenham & Redbridge have also managed to stay up, so it's been a good football year for London. Ex-Hammer Chris Powell has taken his Charlton side up to the Championship, too. It's a year that may yet be even better.

Despite their string of seasons in the top division in England, the London Borough of Merton continually failed to help Wimbledon find space for a ground. It's good to hear then that Merton have at last been making noises about helping them return to the borough. It could mean redeveloping the greyhound stadium in Plough Lane near to where their old stadium used to be. It could even be a completely new development. All that's necessary is that they stay in the Football League. Maybe next season they might take a step nearer playing that game against MK Dons, the team that stole their name and status.

Game Forty-Eight, nPower Championship, 2011-12, Upton Park
Play Off Semi Final Second Leg
Monday May 7th 2012 (34,682)
Referee: Mike Dean (The Wirral)

West Ham United 3   **Cardiff City 0**
Nolan 11
Vaz Te 40
Maynard 89

(West Ham: proceed to Championship Play Off Final)

Mark Noble is the Hammer of the Year for 2012, the last local born boy to win the award since Paul Ince, 23 years ago. He is on the cover of today's programme and was presented with the award last week at the London Hilton, Park Lane. Noble was runner-up in 2005, which was also the only other time West Ham achieved promotion to the Premier League through the play offs. He's done it this year without being captain, but his role in the side has been a lot more senior than it was seven years ago. Although Sam brought in his own man to lead the side, most West Ham followers will say Noble has been the captain elect, this season, to take nothing away from Kevin Nolan.

Jeremy Nicholas has idiosyncratically decided to play 'Firestarter' when the fire should be well underway, as a result of the score from the first leg, but then this is West Ham. Fire? Mr Moon can't be far away.

David Sullivan and David Gold have joined forces on the Chairman's page in the match programme. And is that Keira Knightley I can see on the West Ham Hospitality page? The bubbles are everywhere, several splashing on my nose up in the Press Area, and the atmosphere is rocking.

Rob Pritchard's match programme team deserve praise this afternoon for providing an inspiring pre-match read. Most pleasing of all is the innovation of a printed spine that'll do much to improve the storage and accurate retrievability of programmes on those long summer nights of the close season. Odd that such a straightforward development should take so long to arrive.

West Ham's prize for finishing third in the Championship is home advantage in the 2nd leg. This afternoon Jeremy Nicholas is out on the pitch yelling out the team names, the crowd hanging on his every word. If only it had been like this for every game this season, that shoe rack of home draws might have looked a little less tall. Nevertheless, here we are, with a two goal advantage and a fired up crowd. What can possibly go wrong?

I begin considering how many players out there today played in the first game of the season. The West Ham players missing from that afternoon are Joey O'Brien, plus the now-departed quartet of Herita Ilunga, Scott Parker, Freddie Sears and Frederic Piquionne. Those who've made the long journey here across the season are Rob Green, Winston Reid, James Tomkins, Mark Noble, Kevin Nolan and Matt Taylor. Cardiff City are missing just Anthony Gerrard from their August 2011 team sheet. Ben Turner, Liam Lawrence and Stephen McPhail are the new Cardiff starters. Demel and Vaz Te are West Ham's fresh acquisitions from that day, the recovered O'Neil is also a new starter.

The Cardiff fans have woken up a little after their team's first attack. There's been precious little to get excited about so far. Guy Demel hammers in a low cross with enough pace on it to reach the far post only to run wide for a goal kick. At the other end Kenny Miller trips over Demel's foot, but fails to interest the referee, despite the howls of the rapacious Cardiff fans at the other end, who know a Bluebirds' goal will shake an edgy Upton Park to the core. Carlton Cole's continuous tussles with Mark Hudson, Cardiff's number 5 and captain, look like being an interesting sub plot.

First leg hero Collison is playing a blinder, nutmegging defenders and tripping the light fantastic down the right wing. Then there's Nolan on the quarter hour and on the line, pouncing on Cole's flick on to put the Hammers 3-0 up in the tie. How many times has he put West Ham ahead this season? The stadium is alive with noise, and the nerves have steadied. Now O'Neil tries an audacious flick from the edge of the area which beats Marshall but comes back off the crossbar to a ricochet of desperate cries from the fans. Reid heads out well under pressure and Tomkins completes the clearance. Now Liam Lawrence gets bundled into touch at the corner flag by Taylor and Reid and screams at the deaf ears of the assistant referee. Miller, who scored Cardiff's winner back in August, looks the most dangerous of the Cardiff strikers. Thankfully he is generally well marked. Another strange song, *You're not playing, 'cause you're shit!* may well be being directed at Rob Earnshaw, warming up below. I've just seen another replay of the goal on the Press screen and Nolan is almost standing on the line when he heads the ball in. Vaz Te gets to the edge of the area and whacks the ball, full pelt, after skipping past Stephen McPhail, into the upper tier of the Sir Trevor.

Stand up if you love West Ham! the crowd sing. This is the guarantee, the full voice of unadulterated enjoyment. I look behind me. The Mud Mouth twins are unsmilingly silent. Not too many of these moments this season for a promotion year, if that's what it turns out to be. Kenny Miller gets booked for one complaint too many. Do referees have a complaints quota that they work to? Whatever it might be, the Bobby Moore lower, that have had a good view of the yellow card, sportingly deliver, *Miller, Miller, you're a cunt, Miller, you're a cunt!* The close up on the screen of Miller's subsequent exasperated smile is endearing. On a profanity blitz, the fans, having spotted John Terry in the Alpari Stand hospitality box, start singing, *John Terry is a cunt!* and *Stick the blue flag up your arse!* interesting that Spurs no longer seem the hated enemy at the club. It is usually in the purple passages of games that such sea changes are born. It could well be the blue of Cardiff's shorts, but everything in hated football land is now spelt Chelsea. Vaz Te runs forty yards to retrieve an over hit through ball, passing it back to Gary O'Neil. He hits a pile driver that looks bound for the corner of the goal until Marshall turns it brilliantly wide with a two handed full length diving save.

Hammers are playing pretty football now, knocking the ball around with confidence, and Cardiff look jaded. Vaz Te is set free on the right into the area and he hits an unstoppable right footed belter into the top corner of the net. Brilliant goal! Forty-one minutes into the game and here we are, going to Wembley. Vaz Te performs a karaoke mime over the corner flag in goal celebration. Not quite black belt, second dan, but still a decent move. I wonder what song is in his head? Cardiff are soon on the attack up the other end, still keen to trouble the scoresheet. Peter Whittingham's effort is horribly high and off target. At 4-0 on aggregate, this is far more comprehensive than either of the two previous play-off semi-finals of 2004 and 2005. Neither Blackpool nor Birmingham looked particularly dangerous opposition in the other semi on Friday, but Wembley can do strange things to teams.

If West Ham had played like this more often this season, they'd be on their holidays by now.

Collison's earlier shoulder knock sees him substituted three minutes into the second half by Henri Lansbury. Unless he can break into the play off final team, this may well be his last appearance for the Hammers before returning to Arsenal. Vaz Te is floored by Hudson as he turns to break down the left. O'Neil is looking like the man of the match for his hard work and ingenuity. It's as if the team have had some form yoke removed from around their neck and it's released them into the comfort zone. A long throw from Gunnarsson puts the West Ham defence under pressure, but Green handles confidently. Crosses are raining in with pace and accuracy into the Cardiff penalty area, but the ebb and flow continues. Chris Hughton, planning a second leg comeback against Blackpool for his Birmingham team, 0-1 down after the first leg, is at the game watching from the Directors' box.

Cardiff are playing as well as they have done in either leg despite being 4-0 down, but for the first time I can remember this season, West Ham are looking almost invincible in a home game. This is in spite of talented opposition who are clearly used to their bridesmaid play off status by now, already planning to meet their previous boss Dave Jones' newly promoted Sheffield Wednesday side in the Championship next season. Miller now puts Mason through, but he's closed down easily by the West Ham defence. They ooze confidence and sophistication, and the fans finally sing *Sam Allardyce's claret and blue army!* The highest praise. The players and supporters are already celebrating their forthcoming journey to Wembley. Nolan, captain and scorer of the first goal, is substituted for McCartney on 68 minutes, a chance to keep him fresh for the final, and to allow him the pleasure of a stadium applauding him off the pitch. Neat managerial move, Sam.

A rare West Ham attack wins a corner, from which Demel's subsequent cross sees Lansbury penalised for climbing on McNaughton. Another corner and O'Neil catches a clearance full in the face and drops to the ground. Kiss and Cowie, surely a double act from the eighties, replace Miller and McPhail for Cardiff. Quite what Malky MacKay intends with this move only he knows. Cole now puts Taylor through with a delicious flick, but the effort is smothered to prevent what would have been the goal of the game.

Another corner. Taylor's far post effort reaches Tomkins, but he's beaten in the air by a defender who is a good foot shorter than him. At the other end a long shot beats an unsighted Green but also the far post. 'Chris, you're going to need a new Best Man. I'm going to Wembley,' says an inspired sign in the crowd. Now it gets really silly with an inflated plastic shark being punched up above the supporters intermittently replaced by a luminous orange beach ball. Cole gets the second substitution round of applause, replaced by Maynard. In the very last minute of the game, an unselfish through ball from Vaz Te puts Maynard in to score a goal very similar to Cole's earlier effort. Five-nil aggregate score.

The second half shouldn't disguise the fact that this has been one of West Ham's more professional performances of the season. Calm, studied and precise. Allardyce's men have played to their strengths and controlled the game. They have deserved their reward of a third play off final, and it can only be hoped that they produce a similar performance under those two odd silver bendy things.

West Ham: 1 Green, 2 Reid, 4 Nolan (3 McCartney 69), 5 Tomkins, 9 Cole (8 Maynard 86), 10 Collison (22 Lansbury 48), 12 Vaz Te, 14 Taylor, 16 Noble, 20 Demel, 32 O'Neil.

Leaving the issue of how I might get a ticket to the play off final to one side, the journey home is an absolute joy. West Ham have not been to the home of football since 14th March 1981, for a 1-1 League Cup Final draw with Liverpool. *Thirty-one years of hurt.* They were there before that in May and August 1980, beating Arsenal 1-0 in the FA Cup Final, and then losing to Liverpool three months later by the same score in the Charity Shield.

I have been a West Ham fan since the mid-sixties, since I was old enough to think. Despite this dedication, and the fact that West Ham also appeared at Wembley in May 1975 (v Fulham) and in August 1975 (v Derby County), making five Wembley appearances in my supporting lifetime, I have never been to Wembley to see West Ham play.

Let's look at the reasons why that might be. Indulge me for a moment. During the 1974-75 season I went to every single home game, and the majority of the away ones in the southern half of England. My mate Tim Cotsford, the only other boy at my school out of 120 to support the club, went that season to one home game. It was the game against Burnley which, for the record, West Ham won 2-1 with goals from Keith Robson and Alan Taylor, in his first league start for the Hammers. Why did Tim go to that match? The week before, West Ham had beaten Arsenal 2-0 in a mud smattered FA Cup Quarter Final at Highbury. Making his debut that afternoon, and scorer of both goals was Alan Taylor. Tim is a bright spark, and with West Ham in the FA Cup semis, he figured that the next home game might be a significant ticketing moment in the history of the club. How right he was.

Different coloured vouchers were given out at the game: blue, green, pink, red and purple. Mine was ballot card 24 (pink). Tim's was ballot card 28 (purple). We talked at the time about whether one of us should swap with someone who had a similar number to one of us at the game so at least we could either both go together, or both not go, according to the luck of the draw. Tim's better command of stats said keeping our different ballot cards meant there was a better chance of at least one of us going. Or as I put it, a better chance of one or both of us ending up pissed off and ticketless. Even then, a voucher from the Carlisle game from February 1975 offered another chance of a ticket. My voucher number from that game was 38.

West Ham won the Stamford Bridge semi-final replay against Ipswich Town, again with two goals from Alan Taylor, and so reached their first Wembley final for ten years. At the next home game in the league against Coventry City, it was announced that the winning numbers for final tickets were 6, 17, 19, 28, 36 and 37. The lucky Carlisle voucher number was 34. So Tim went to the final. With my luck that season, if we'd swapped, he'd have lost his ticket and would still be telling me the story. I have still got that pink Burnley ballot card.

In 1980 I was at college training to be a teacher, and the programme with the voucher was given out at the home game against Fulham in March before West Ham knew whether their opponents would be Liverpool or Arsenal. For some reason, which I've still to discover, I did not get a voucher, and as we couldn't get programmes once we were in the ground, lost my chance. As West Ham hadn't yet beaten Everton in the semi-final, there was still a chance it wouldn't matter. It did. West Ham were allocated 22,000 tickets for a game with an anticipated attendance of 100,000.

The other three Wembley appearances have just blurred out, probably because none of them were West Ham victories. Fast forward to the three Millennium Stadium appearances in 2004, 2005 and 2006. Working for the club on the end of season DVD for all three of these appearances guaranteed tickets. The first was the disappointing performance against one shot Crystal Palace. The third was the heartbreak of the penalty shoot out against Liverpool after a breathtakingly brilliant 3-3 draw. So to the second. The play off final against Preston North End. Well I wasn't going to miss this one, and checked the dates well in advance before booking my holiday in the States. I was flying on Monday 30th May at 4.00, allowing the full Saturday 28th for the game and Sunday the 29th to film the celebrations back at the club in the event of promotion. You're ahead of me here, I am sure. After the last game win at Watford, the play off dates were announced on the Net. Even then it was a day or two before I realised. I was booked on a plane that would be taking off as Hammers came out for the second half of the play off final at Cardiff. I had no doubt that they would beat Ipswich Town, especially now I'd fucked the dates for the final. I managed to get to both play off semi finals, commentating on the 2-2 home leg against Ipswich Town for the club.

I had to let it go. Maybe as a teenager I'd have dropped the holiday, but this time I couldn't. I decided that I would listen on the radio and find out the score when I got to the other side of the Atlantic Ocean. Goalless at half time, I turned my phone off as I strapped in for the flight. Inspired with a moment's optimism, I stopped one of the cabin crew as she was rounding up people and making sure all seatbelts were fastened.

'Is there any way you could find something out for me during the flight?' I said.

'I'm sorry?' she asked, in a rich American twang. I sighed.

'I didn't hear you,' she said.

'My team,' I said, already using heart. 'My football team are playing an important game this afternoon.

'Football,' she repeated, slowly. What chance? Still, I continued.

'West Ham,' I said. 'English football. If you could find out in an hour or so whether they've won.'

'I'll do my best,' she said, looking across at a man still talking on his mobile. I smiled politely and gave it up. They won? They lost? I'd find out soon enough.

An hour into the journey, by which time I was already hunting the channels for a film worth watching, an announcement came on the tannoy.

'Good afternoon, my name is Captain Tom Williams. Hope you're enjoying the journey.' An unsurprising American accent on an American Airlines' flight. 'Just a brief announcement that next year West Ham United will be playing football in the Premier League. They won 1-0.' I looked across the aisle at the stewardess and smiled. She looked back pleasantly but blankly. Perhaps the pilot was an English football fan. Not that it mattered. We were promoted. And what a great way to find out, for my very own Mile High Club moment.

This time around I have made an application to the Football League accreditation department for a Media Press Pass to the play off final. It's a long and tortuous process, as you'd imagine, and I need to make sure I've jumped through the hoops to get on the club list. Simultaneously my good friend Jim Goddard is pursuing play off final tickets through his contact at the FA, where these items are internally raffled to employees demonstrating an enthusiasm for either of the clubs performing at the game in question.

The weekend before the game I slip out early on Sunday for a seven and a half mile lap of Richmond Park and come in at a breathtaking (for me) time of 1:09:31. My first two miles are timed at eight and a half minutes each. This means that when I am in sinus rhythm I can knock almost two minutes off each mile. These are double edged stats should I drop back into AF (atrial fibrillation) in the months to come, but now all I can think of is the joy of sublime health and what a magic month May is turning out to be...

On the Thursday I have just finished addressing a group of students on the importance of keeping on top of new technology, when a text arrives. This is from the accreditation agents for the Football League, requesting a passport sized photograph attachment by 5pm. Is irony the right word? Coincidence? Whatever the phenomenon, I am able to take a photo on my phone, resize it and email the result over to the right people within minutes. Not a very good photo, aesthetically, but that's not really the point. It looks as though I'm all sorted for Saturday. Barely two minutes later a text arrives from Jim. It looks like he's got a ticket for me, too. Now I just need to nip back in time to the seventeen year old me in May 1975 and hand one of these opportunities over. Would that work?

On the morning of the final I look back at Ken Dyer's article on the day Sam Allardyce got the job. And there's a line about how Sam has 'pledged to continue the club's tradition of playing attractive football at home while making them harder to beat away from Upton Park.' The final Championship table indicates only four defeats away out of twenty-three, Southampton, Reading, Derby County and Ipswich. The home defeats total is also four, Cardiff City, Reading, Burnley and Ipswich. Pardew lost four at home and six away in 2003-04, and six at home and nine away in the promotion season of 2004-05. Sam has used 36 players to get West Ham to the play-off final, the same number Pardew used in 2003-04. He used four fewer the following season. The last thing I look at in the article is Allardyce admitting that he won't be able to prevent Cole, Green or Parker from leaving the club. Just one name wrong from that list, the 'shit Emile Heskey' with the flowery tank top, our beloved Carlton Cole. This is the 28 year old, brought to the club in August 2006 by Alan Pardew, who has, for the fourth season in succession top scored for the club with 14 league goals. It's his highest total yet for the Hammers, and there might even be another one or two waiting this afternoon. Without his goals, West Ham would not be at Wembley today.

I meet up with Jim at Marylebone to get the Chiltern Railways service to

Wembley Stadium. The atmosphere is as exciting as you'd expect, as great as 2004 and 2006, my two previous final day experiences. Third time lucky, perhaps? The opponents Blackpool on the head to head have come out badly against the Hammers, 1-4 at home and 0-4 at Upton Park. They are also featuring in their starting XI the son of a notorious West Ham 'bad boy', Tom Ince. Try as I might, I can't get any feelings about the way this one is going to go.

Jim's mate Bob, a claret and bluer, has been the lucky one to benefit from the unexpected spare play off final ticket. We grab some lunch and sit with the fans on a strip of grass close to the stadiium. I take a few photos of the fans, and a group shot of three from the West Ham Ladies' Team. They play in the Premier League South, whose title has been won by... Portsmouth, a team who only lost three games all season, and a team they completed the double over.

After lunch we make our way to the ground up Olympic Way, taking in more of the atmosphere, checking out the fans with their claret and blue painted faces, and the multitudinous slogans for the day printed on anything from banners to badges. Some chancers will no doubt have printed winners tee-shirts for both sides for the end of the game, preparing to write off half of them in pursuit of big sales. We thrown in our pre-match predictions: 1-2, 2-0 and 4-3, but with the considerable caveat that Hammers must avoid conceding in the first ten minutes of the game and will need to be level at half-time.

Jim and Bob disappear in the direction of the other side of the ground whilst I make my way round to the media area. I put what's left of lunch in the brown leather bag that has been accompanying me to games this season. It has my iPad in it so the report of the game can be written 'live'. I bought the bag in Cairo in December 2006 when we were making a film about Starbucks opening their first outlet there. The man selling it to me demonstrated that it was real leather by trying to set light to it. The hard sell. Some people will do anything to get a sale.

Nonce with a handbag! You're just a nonce with a handbag!
Nonce with a hand-bag! You're just a nonce with a hand-bag!

I glance to my left and realise that about thirty West Ham fans are targeting me with their own version of *Guantanamera*. I look in vain for someone else they might be serenading, but no, it's me. I'm wearing nothing that might identify me as a Hammers' supporter, so I suppose that makes me fair game.

I try to mumble something witty, but they just sing louder. In the end I walk away in the opposite direction. It's a case, not a handbag. Anyone should be able to see that.

The original music to *Guantanamera* was written by by José Fernandez Diaz in 1929, a fact that was only finally established in law in 1993. And you can bet your life he was dead by the time the judgement came through in time to please only his blood-sucking descendants. The musical adaptation was by Pete Seeger and Julian Orbon, both alive when the royalties started to arrive. The original lyric adaptation was by Julian Orbon, and was based on a poem by José Marti.

Thanks for that.

By the time I have walked twice round the ground to locate the Media entrance without having to face my tormentors again, it is nearly quarter past two. I grab a programme and the media pack and slide in with my head down.

Game Forty-Nine, nPower Championship Play Off final, Wembley
Saturday May 19th 2012
Referee: Howard Webb (Yorks)
Attendance, 78,523

West Ham 2	**Blackpool 1**
Cole 34	Ince 47
Vaz Te 87	

The atmosphere inside is a resounding mass of noise and explosions, smoke and cheering, tangerine and claret. West Ham are back at Wembley for the first time since 1981. A lot of claret has flowed under the bridge in that time. A lousy season in the Premier League, a brilliant season on the road, and a manager for whom the jury is still outish. With 2010 World Cup Final referee Howard Webb in charge, it'll be fine. 'The Biggest Game In International Football,' says the stadium announcer.

The last time West Ham were at Wembley, Paul Emerson Carlyle Ince was a cocky thirteen year old from Ilford, and Judas was still just a disciple who betrayed Jesus. A third of a century later, his son Thomas Christopher Ince takes the field for Blackpool against his father's first professional side, West Glam United. Ince the younger originally joined Liverpool in 2008 and made his debut two years later, coming on as a substitute on 22nd September

2010 to be a part of a great Roy Hodgson-led Reds' side who that evening enjoyed a memorable third round defeat at Anfield against the formidable Northampton Town 2-4 on penalties. Ince here was able to emulate his father in the penalty kick stakes... by not taking one.

He's going to get booed.

The Media area is a concrete basement. All bag searches, accreditation and large lifts. After negotiating the labyrinthine corridors, I find myself in the main Media room, ambushed by the smell of fresh pies and a line of fridges filled with bottled lagers of every description. These remain untouched by the majority of journos, the drink of choice turning out to be tea or black coffee as the clicking of laptop keys chatters gently at the back of the growing roar of Wembley. And now I am excited. Throughout the years of good fortune and industry that have seen me follow my team over their last twenty-one years from the inside, few moments can equal this one.

Spending a few days with the team in Romania, interviewing Paolo Di Canio, watching Harry Redknapp put something magical back into West Ham, charting the hope that the Pardew days possessed... none of these moments had taken me to Wembley, the home of football. Today I am here, writing the last chapter of my fifth West Ham United book, still unable to say for certain where the team will be playing next season. All I can be certain of at this point is that they will not be playing Blackpool.

Vegetarian sandwiches, even a meat-free pastie, and a scalding cup of tea, balanced with a china Wembley plate loaded with a slice of banoffee pie drowned in chocolate sauce. I am privy to an embargoed piece of news: the BBC have landed coverage of the Football League for another three years. Whatever bollocks their executives may spout about Football being a 'core' this or a 'major audience' that, no-one disputes the fact that they will make a decent enough job of assembling ragged highlights and shaky-cam clips against a brick-wall-backed studio with that bloke who sounds like a Radio 2 deejay and Steve Claridge. The BBC still has the ability to tempt ambitious and wide-eyed talent into minimum wage employment for the kudos of the state broadcaster as previous employer on their CV.

Despite a brilliant sell-out response to available tickets from the Hammers' fans, the attendance looks to be in the region of 10,000 less than the crowd that saw Swansea beat Reading this time last year. I overhear talk that there were still 5,000 tickets on the Wembley doors this morning for anyone sporting a tangerine scarf. The death of the British seaside town.

I look at my pass. Row 4 Seat 12. It sounds exclusive… unlike Paul Simon Row 635 Seat 1536a, or whatever it was. The stadium looks superb. This is Wembley. They can't fuck it up now, can they? Of course they can. Anything can happen this afternoon. I meet Ken Dyer on the way to the men's room.

'You're not smiling, Ken?' I say. He smiles, but only at the line. Years and years of disappointment may harden the skin, but that irritating quirk of human nature, hope, has a way of peeping through to reveal the vulnerability of a Hammers' follower.

I type out the game header on the pad for the last time this season. It volunteers the cut and paste lie of the Cardiff City 3-0 scoreline. Despite this being the fifty-first game for the tired players in claret and blue, the only scoreline that has repeated in successive games throughout the season is 1-1, four times in March and twice in April. There's your story.

I start my stopwatch as Howard Webb blows his whistle, and the match snaps into action. My choice for player of the season, Matt Taylor, makes a potentially disastrous error almost immediately, slipping as Ince chases him back into the area, but manages to block the booed player's shot and recover to shepherd the spinning ball back to Green. Blackpool have started at a canter. West Ham look a little nervous.

What is immediately apparent is the sea of orange to the left of the halfway line, and the dark claret and blue mix to the right. There are patches of red back seats on the left, but no West Ham seat is empty. I take a moment, like a student five minutes into an exam, to look about me at the other hacks clicking furiously away. Has there been that much to write about so far? The point is, of course, that it's the diatribe of history versus fortune and opportunity versus chance that make this game so great.

We are almost at ten minutes and West Ham have begun to get into gear. Vaz Te breaks on the left, but steers his shot beyond the side netting. There is an eight second delay on the Sky pictures, as if we have stepped slightly into the future. A chance to see your death just before it actually happens.

Thirteen and a half minutes and the first genuine goal opportunity arises. Quick feet at the front and three interchanged passes see Phillips break clear of the West Ham defence, but his hurried finish is weak and straight at Green. Just over a minute later he makes another yard of space for a shot just inside the area but spears it wide of the diving Green, and the post. Two good chances missed inside ninety seconds. Maybe it's going to be the East Londoners' day.

Now a West Ham moment. Approach play from Cole and Nolan to set up

Vaz Te, but again it's into his favoured side netting. Cole now gets his first chance in the air with a cross from Taylor, but is well marked and although he gets the direction right he can't prevent the ball from spooning over. Angel Martinez has decided his shirt will have 'Angel' on the back rather than 'Martinez'. It wouldn't really work with Kevin Nolan, I suppose.

23 minutes into the game and we get the first full-blooded raunchy chorus of 'Bubbles'. Kevin Phillips kills a high ball with breathtaking skill to generate the beginnings of a break for Blackpool, but Winston Reid tidies up from centre of the back four. Reid. How important has he been this season? Martinez has Cole under control at the back with a couple of timely interventions.

Noble's corner, the first of the game after thirty minutes, swings in over Gilks' head, but the Blackpool keeper manages to fist it away for another corner. Taylor and Noble have made the corner kick something creative for West Ham this season.

Who would be West Ham's finest ever corner kick taker? Clyde Best used to take them in the early 1970s. Why? My memory races to Graham Paddon, Pat Holland, even Dudley Tyler. Later architects of the set play were Mark Robson, Mattie Holmes, Kevin Keen, Stuart Slater and Matt Etherington. Di Canio used to take them, too. In the great 1985-86 team the opportunity creator supreme would be the sublime Mark Ward.

Blackpool's captain Ferguson rescues the resulting loose ball to set up Stephen Crainey, but the defender's hopeless lunge drifts up, up into the air and into outer space. Minutes later Taylor breaks away with the ball, and after a stylish one-two with Vaz Te, hits a long pass into the path of Cole, top scorer Cole, who, after a perfect calming first touch, whacks the ball uncompromisingly past Gilks into the roof of the net. Thirty-four minutes gone, and West Ham have something to defend, something they have proved all season they can do well.

Vaz Te minutes later collects a long ball from Nolan but again seems to aim at the side netting with his effort. It doesn't even make it there this time. Sky show West Ham now have 5 efforts to Blackpool's 4. Lies, damned lies and Prozone.

Martinez (Angel) is soon in the action again, juggling the ball acrobatically before volleying it up into row ZZZ. West Ham fans now sing, *Your support is fucking shit!* which seems a little harsh. In the second half West Ham will be attacking their supporters' end, another advantage, perhaps.

Over the half-time break I have another hot cup of tea and more of that banoffee pie. Jamie McGee has texted from ADI Towers up in Preston, where they are editing this live and ready to work on the Champions League final later between Bayern Munich and Chelsea. Whatever he's been seeing today, I've already held for six delicious seconds. The parallel digital universe.

The second half begins in the worst possible fashion. Despite the fact that Reid and Noble seem well placed for a long ball hit towards Ince on the right, they freeze as the number 36 moves confidently forward to steer the ball past Green. How can that be? How can this 20 year old called Ince, Son of Judas, how can he have scored today? The event out on the turf way beyond us seems to only have its madness translated in the Media area as every writer reaches for his metaphors. Even the Hammers' fans are stunned into a religious hush. Ince has silenced his father's tormentors, I keep thinking.

Minutes later it's almost two as put-through Baptiste chips the ball over the advancing Green, only for Taylor, chasing back, to clear off the line. Blackpool's first corner of the game soon offers Dobbie a chance, which is thankfully blocked. Great name, Dobbie. I want to call him 'Dobbin' and start unpacking my cupboard of horse similes. I really want to. This, of course is a man who has been here before. Exactly a year ago he wore the shirt of Swansea City in that well-attended game against Reading that saw his side climb effortlessly, it seemed on the day, into the Premier League.

A forced madness of quick substitutions sees O'Neil and Demel off for McCartney and Faubert. Neither subbed player has been in the game. This could prove a key moment in the match. Taylor's skidding cross is brilliantly reached by Collison but his effort fizzes over from almost under the bar.

It's a delight to see such an open game at Wembley, with both teams throwing their mothers to the wind. Even the romantic will admit the result is paramount in such games, but to win and win in style is what all fans are after for their team.

A gap in the Blackpool defence now opens up for Cole who fires in well, looking for his second. Gilks finger tips his shot away from the net and across the six yard box, an area now frustratingly bereft of advancing West Ham players. The game is finely balanced. The sun emerges at the end Blackpool are attacking. It is almost impossible to predict where this game is going. No sooner have I typed those words, than the ball sits up for Dobbie on the six yard box, only for him to scuff it wide.

Blackpool push forward, Dobbie's effort spinning away for a corner after clipping Reid's heel. A deflected shot from the set play is kicked off the line by Noble. Kevin Phillips will not be scoring the winner for Blackpool today. He has been subbed after 70 minutes. Ludovic Sylvestre is on to replace him. George McCartney's defensive talents are highlighted as he takes the ball off Dobbie and steers it to safety. As we approach the 76th minute, it's all Blackpool. Dobbie hits a long low shot through a packed area and Green just gets down in time to turn it away. West Ham are camped in their own half.

Neil Eardley towers above Cole as he heads Faubert's cross clear. Collison then finds a yard of space and a little pace but his over-hit shot looks tired. The best move of the match for West Ham now arrives as Vaz Te drives in a dipping cross to Nolan who leans back and hits the ball with venom only to see it crash back into play off the crossbar. What a goal that would have been. A goal to grace this crazy stadium that won't be paid for for another fifty years.

The game seems to be swinging back West Ham's way, the ebb and flow like a flyweight boxing match. Green's giant goal kick almost finds Vaz Te, but Eardley chases back to concede the corner. Into the last five minutes. Can West Ham find an act of ingenuity to steal the game in normal time? Yes, they can. The ball is hit into the area again by Taylor wide on the left, and squeezed away by Cole out of the keeper's grasp into the path of the grateful Vaz Te. Instead of finding the side netting, he now smashes it up high, high into the roof of the net, just under the right hand angle! 87 minutes gone... Now that is a late goal. As late as his first at Upton Park, against Watford, sparing West Ham from the ignominy of an unwanted home defeat. And his first in West Ham colours was... at Blackpool, two weeks' earlier. And now?

Four minutes injury time are indicated by Howard Webb's fourth official. I understand how Alex Ferguson feels. Much of the two hundred and forty seconds are spent raising cheers from the fans for possession passes, but it's a heart in mouth final minute as the loose ball breaks to Bednar is it... is it!! But no dramatic ending. Mr Webb blows his whistle for the final time this afternoon. West Ham are back in the Premier League, and the team that finished third have won the Championship play off final.

As it says on the Sky broadcast...

West Ham Are Promoted
Two minutes later and Sky are showing promotional material for Chelsea's

Champions League final this evening. Like anything else is more important than the football here and now. I have finally, in the flesh, in my own lifetime, seen West Ham United win a game at Wembley. At the ripe old age of 54.

WEST HAM ARE PROMOTED!

The first crowd shot at the final whistle is of the same West Ham Ladies' players I photographed before the game. Kevin Nolan declares it one of the best days of his life. Vaz Te says, 'It's tremendous in front of these amazing fans'. Kevin Nolan sporting a shirt that declares, 'Premier League 2012/13 - Nothing Beats Being Back!' goes up the steps to collect the trophy in a haze of freshly blown bubbles. Carlton Cole's last words on the event sum up the day perfectly, 'Great atmosphere! Great day! Great fans! Great team!'

David Powter, editor of 'WINGER' magazine, and I make our way to the small theatre that Wembley have built for post match media conferences. Ian Holloway looks genuinely saddened, and speaks for just a few minutes before hurrying off. Allardyce looks exhausted, but his team's achievement is clearly sinking in.

'We kept going right to the very end and fittingly for me and fittingly for Vaz Te, what a signing,' he says. 'The goals he has scored is probably the reason why I'm sat here now and we're back in the Premier League because buying him in January is arguably one of my best signings ever and I've signed some good players in my time.

'It's right up there with the best for me. It's probably better than the Millennium victory with Bolton against Preston, because it's West Ham United. One with the size of the football club and the pressure you're under, two, it's at Wembley. What a fantastic arena. It's the first time I've won here.'

Sam has a job in London next year, and I've finally written a book with a happy ending. It is a happy ending, isn't it?

West Ham: 1 Green, 2 Reid, 4 Nolan, 5 Tomkins, 9 Cole, 10 Collison, 12 Vaz Te, 14 Taylor, 16 Noble, 20 Demel (18 Faubert 57), 32 O'Neil (3 McCartney 53)
Subs not used: 13 Henderson, 22 Lansbury, 8 Maynard

As I wander back down Olympic Way towards Wembley Park, I can still hear the excited singing of those West Ham fans, thrilled to be at the home of football and determined to enjoy the hours ahead…

Nonce with a handbag!
You're just a nonce with a handbag!
Nonce with a hand-bag!
You're just a nonce with a hand-bag!